Introduction to MATERIALS AND STRUCTURE OF MUSIC

Introduction to MATERIALS AND STRUCTURE OF MUSIC

William Christ
Richard DeLone
Indiana University

PRENTICE-HALL, INC., Englewood Cliffs, New Jersey

Library of Congress Cataloging in Publication Data

CHRIST, WILLIAM.
Introduction to materials and structure of music.

1. Music–Theory, Elementary. I. DeLone, Richard Peter, joint author. II. Title.
MT7.C54516 781 74-23644
ISBN 0-13-485532-9

Printed in the United States of America

10 9 8 7 6 5 4 3 2 1

PRENTICE-HALL INTERNATIONAL, INC., London
PRENTICE-HALL OF AUSTRALIA, PTY. LTD., Sydney
PRENTICE-HALL OF CANADA, LTD., Toronto
PRENTICE-HALL OF INDIA PRIVATE LIMITED, New Delhi
PRENTICE-HALL OF JAPAN, INC., Tokyo

To our mothers, Maude and Helena

CONTENTS

PREFACE

A number of colleagues at various universities, colleges, conservatories, and community colleges have suggested that we write a volume dedicated essentially to the same goals as *Materials and Structure of Music,* Volume I, by Christ et al., yet which would provide more extensive preparatory materials than are provided in the aforementioned. This volume has been developed as a consequence, paralleling to some extent *Materials and Structure of Music,* but treating music rudiments in greater depth. This has been done by confining the coverage of basic melody to that explicitly related to tonality and harmonic outline, particularly triads I and V; by confining the study of two-voice counterpoint to tonal harmonic materials; and, of course, by limiting the range of illustrative musical examples. Nevertheless, within these limitations the authors have included a wide variety of tonal music of various types while emphasizing that music which still predominates the repertoire of most performers and listeners.

The student is guided in a logical progression from basic properties of musical sounds and their notation through concepts and techniques of musical organization including tonal harmony—triads, seventh chords, secondary dominant, and change of mode and key. Too, the structural elements of melody, rhythm, harmony, texture, timbre, and form are treated as interrelated rather than discrete elements in the organization of musical sounds. Further, units are provided to acquaint the beginning student with the relation of musical analysis to performance (thus making theory study more than a sterile academic exercise) and to give a basic perspective of the styles of traditional music of the Western world as they have evolved in the past three centuries. Lastly, problems in ear training, music reading, analysis, and invention are coordinated with various units for thorough reinforcement of the materials, techniques, and concepts presented. However, in the event some drill materials may prove insufficient, similar ones should be invented modelled after those appearing in the text.

It is intended that this text form the basis of a beginning theory course for students having demonstrable performance skills but who are in need of complementing these with rudimentary theoretical knowledge and competency necessary for greater musical perceptivity as either performing or listening musicians. By its very nature, therefore, this volume is limited in scope, and the dedicated student of music will wish to progress beyond its bounds once its contents are mastered to study in greater depth and detail a broader spectrum of the materials and structure of music.

THE AUTHORS

Music is one of the many ways God has of beating in on man—his life, his ideals, his hope in everything—an inner something, a spiritual storm, a something else that stirs the man in all of his parts, consciousness and "all at once"—we roughly call these parts (as a kind of entity) "soul."

Charles Ives
June, 1924

unit

1

MUSIC RUDIMENTS

First there was music—and then there was the word about music. At best, what man has been able to say about this expressive form of human behavior has never adequately conveyed its variety of meanings, whether intellectual, emotional, or aesthetic. Most musicians would agree that mere discussion of music and its qualities is not enough to give one a full insight into what music conveys or accomplishes. Active experience in music as a listener-performer is needed before musical understanding can be achieved. On the other hand, since music is nonverbal—containing no signs or symbols having other than musical meaning—if it is to be discussed and not just experienced, a vocabulary of descriptive words must be employed. A further complication to musical discussion exists. Music in its evolution progressed from a purely oral tradition to one in which its phenomena are represented by signs and symbols. Therefore, to explore fully the depths of music requires a knowledge (rudimentary, at least) of the special symbology used to represent or *notate* its sound processes, and a knowledge of the terminology required for its description.

Though every person may formulate, or may have formulated, his own definition of music—any or all of which may be "correct"—for the purposes of our study the following definition is submitted:

> Music is a succession of expressive sounds ordered so as to evoke human response. The reader should realize that "expressive sounds" as used here connotes a broad spectrum of possibilities: tones and combinations thereof, however produced, and noise, as well as the absence of sounds (silence). Further, the degree or nature of their "expressiveness" is that assigned by the individual and is something to which he responds individually. "Ordering" is meant to suggest that this expressive form of human behavior is not accidental but is planned, both as to the selection and sequence of sounds.

Let us then turn our attention to terminology and concepts that will prove useful in discussing, hearing, and performing music, realizing fully that such so-called "intellectualization" of music cannot substitute for the *stuff* of music, because full appreciation of music's materials and structure, as well as performing or listening to music, requires thorough understanding. For full appreciation of a musical experience involves intellectual, physical, and emotional response, each of which complements the others; no one of these can be neglected for another if the aesthetic effect of music is to be completely and effectively realized.

PITCH

To begin, let us concern ourselves with the basic elements of most musical sounds, namely, *pitch, duration, volume,* and *timbre.* Pitch denotes the "high-low" quality of a sound, a quality that, as may be seen in Example 1, is represented by the placement of notes in vertical relation to one another. (Conventional notation will be used at the moment for illustrative purposes. If it is unfamiliar, concern yourself with the general concept of highness and lowness of sound, leaving clarification of notation to subsequent pages.)

Ex. 1.

After hearing the melody in Example 1 and observing its notation, it is apparent that the last note (3) is the lowest note, and the first note (1) lies about midway in the pitch range between the highest note (2) and the last note.

One may generalize that sounds of fixed pitch can be described as being higher than, lower than, or the same as those appearing before or after any given pitch. As we refine our analytic vocabulary and skills, we will assign more exact terms to describe pitch relations (the distance between pitches), relations referred to as *intervals.* The concept of highness and lowness will become an important consideration as we proceed, for this relation between pitches is one of the primary organizational factors in music. Further, perhaps because of physical and psychological reasons, levels of pitch become important in relation to tonal movement, as music moves through tension to repose. That is, high notes require more effort to produce by voice or with most instruments, and, therefore, they are generally less "relaxed" than those that are lower. Realize that here and in subsequent brief discussions of the elements of sound, there are gradations between the extremes of high and low—that is, high, higher, low, lower, etc. You will also discover that much music contains sounds of indeterminate (unfixed) pitch: various noises, cymbal crashes, electronic sounds, and others, all of which contribute to the unfolding of that sequence of events called music.

DURATION

In the continuum of unfolding musical events, each such event has a duration—a comparative length in time in terms of the events that precede or follow. One sound may be said to be of the same duration, or of longer or shorter duration, than any other to which it is compared. The element of duration, too, becomes an important organizational factor in terms of the rhythmic motion (long-short durational relation) of the sequence of sounds. In a sense, it is the "time" counterpart of the pitch element of sound.

Ex. 2.

In example 2, each of the first three notes is shorter than notes (2) or (3); these three notes—sound (1)—are of the same duration as those marked (4); and the silence (5) is of equal duration to any of the numbered sound events preceding it. Durational relations between sounds are indicated through music notation, a subject for later discussion.

VOLUME

The third element of sound is volume or *intensity* (commonly referred to as *dynamics*), the relative loudness or softness of a sound. Those who have experienced a performance by a currently popular "rock" group and in contrast, a mother's lullaby need not dwell for long on the concept of relative dynamic levels or the effects of changes thereof. Needless to say, change of dynamic level plays an important role in the organization of music. Degrees of loudness (volume) are indicated in the musical score by special symbols that will be presented later.

TIMBRE

One other basic element of sound is that of *"tone color,"* generally referred to as timbre. Just as an auto horn sounds different from a foghorn, so do (or may) various musical events sound different from one another. Through the use of voices, instruments, and other sound-producing sources, singly and in combination, various "tone-colors" are produced in a process called *orchestration,* to be treated later. Moreover, sounds of equal or different pitch, duration, and/or intensity may be created which are of the same or varied timbre. Thus, the creator of music has at this basic level a variety of possible combinations of elements that covers the gamut of high-low, long-short, and loud-soft relations, and includes the wide range of timbres produced by various sound sources.

PROBLEMS

Analyze each of the following examples as it is performed, focusing your attention on the element(s) noted, and answer as indicated.

Ex. 3.

1. The highest pitch occurs at number ____; the lowest at ____; the approximate mid-range pitch at ____.

Ex. 4.

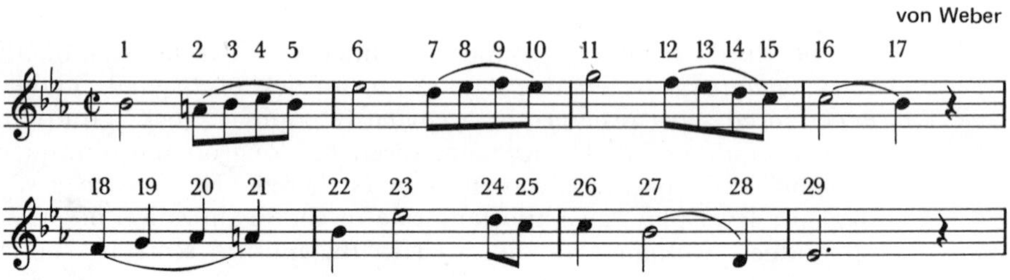

2. (a) The pitch range is encompassed by pitch numbers ____ and ____.

   (b) The first pitch is (higher/lower) than the last.

   (c) The pitch range of Example 4 is (smaller/larger) than that of Example 3.

Ex. 5.

3. (a) The sound of longest duration is indicated by number ____.

(b) The first pitch is of (longer/shorter) duration than the last.

Ex. 6.

Haydn

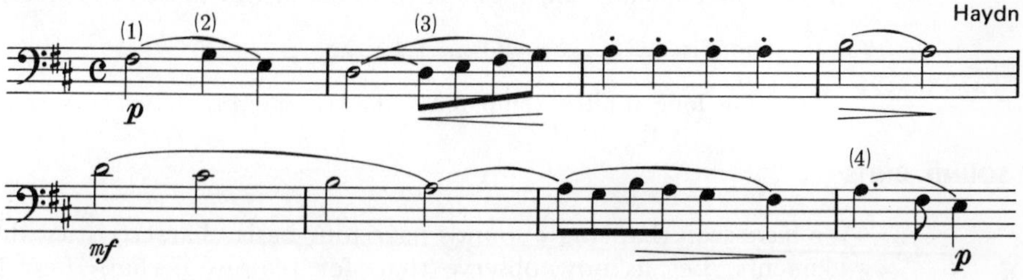

4. (a) The durations most used are those indicated by numbers ____ and ____.

(b) The ratio of the shortest to the longest duration is ____ to ____.

Ex. 7.

Haydn

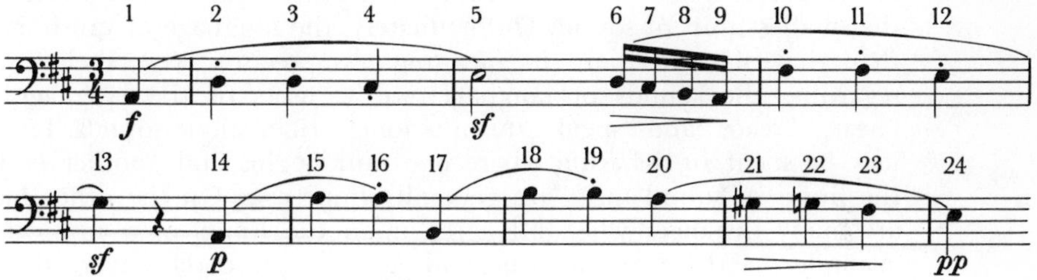

5. (a) The softest sound occurs at number ____.

(b) The sound event between the two dynamic extremes begins at number ____.

(Formal problems regarding timbre will be delayed momentarily.)

Ex. 8.

Portugal

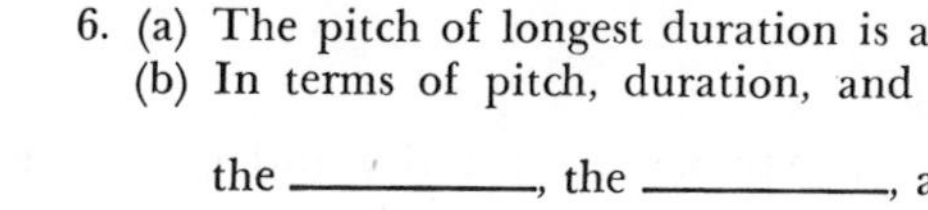

6. (a) The pitch of longest duration is also the (highest/lowest) pitch.
(b) In terms of pitch, duration, and loudness, the last pitch is, respectively,

the ________, the ________, and the ________.

Ex. 9.

Spain

7. (a) The mid-range pitch, compared to the first in terms of loudness and duration, is ________ and ________.

   (b) The longest pitch, compared to the last in terms of dynamics, is ________.

SOUND UNITS

We have seen that single sounds have four basic characteristics, dimensions, or elements. Let us now observe that, for reasons perhaps best known to psychologists, we have an innate tendency to group small events into larger units, or to do the reverse—to break large units into smaller ones—depending on our capacities to understand and assimilate. In learning to read, we all labored with our "a, b, c's," which we combined to form larger units: words. As skilled readers, we now perceive letter groupings as familiar words, and indeed as phrases, sentences, and the like. We no longer need, generally speaking, to deal with perceptual units as small as the individual letters of the alphabet. Music, too, has its a, b, c's: the individual pitches, any one of which represents the smallest unit of sound. Unfortunately, the language of music is less fixed than that of words (and its meaning less precise). Nevertheless, as is true regarding the sounds of language, we as users of the language of music "hear," "read," and "speak" in units longer than single sounds. Endless hours may be spent in debating where one unit begins and another ends because the limits of sound units are generally imprecise. On the other hand, there are many instances when all agree upon the limits of a musical unit—for example, at the beginning or ending of a piece. However, those of you acquainted with more *avant-garde* developments in music (and prose, for that matter) have found that even these limits are often indefinite. Be that as it may, in order to verbalize about this imprecise phenomenon, it is necessary that we establish certain terms and concepts having fairly precise descriptive meanings.

Therefore, let us assume as the smallest musical entity *a single sound unit.* This unit may consist of a single pitch, a noise of undetermined pitch, or combinations thereof, or it may consist of silence. Such single sound units may be strung together to form larger units or sound patterns, to which we will ultimately attach such labels as *motive, figure, scale, mode,* and the like. To go even further, we may group such sound patterns into even more extended ones—*phrase, period, melody,* or *song, sonata-allegro form, symphony, opera,* or whatever.

COMPOSITIONAL TECHNIQUES

The twin tyrants of musical expression are unity and variety. Every composer-performer must plan his presentation to serve each adequately, for to follow one or the other to excess will lead to boredom and the loss of audiences. Therefore, musicians are committed to explore sounds of varying pitch, duration, loudness and timbre that will relate to the listener. The composer, in simplest terms, has four compositional techniques he can utilize in the creation of his music: he may state a musical unit, and then repeat it, vary it, or introduce a new one; that is, he may follow an idea with one that is the same, varied, or entirely different.

In the nursery tune *Three Blind Mice,* the first pattern is repeated: "three blind mice, three blind mice"; the subsequent pattern is different but also repeated: "see how they run, see how they run"; the third (twice repeated) is different from either of the preceding two: "they all ran after the farmer's wife. She cut off their tails with a carver's knife. Did ever you see such a sight in your life"; and the last echoes the first: "as three blind mice." This simple tune (Ex. 10) illustrates the use of repetition—in this instance of three different patterns that combine to form an extended melody. In a modest way, both unity and variety have been achieved.

Ex. 10.

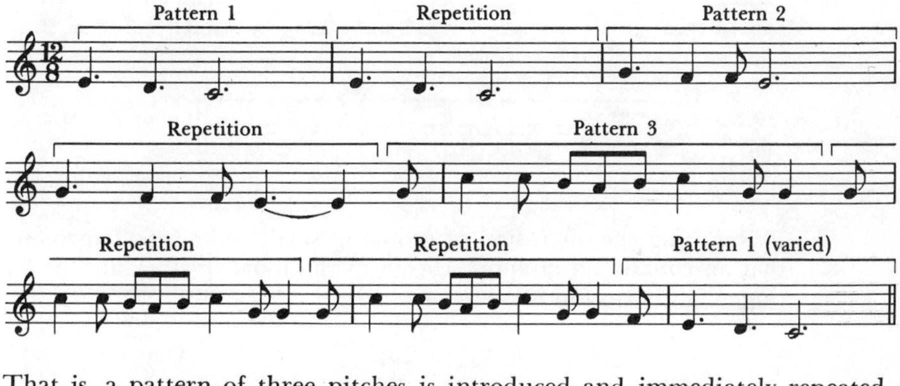

That is, a pattern of three pitches is introduced and immediately repeated, followed by another pattern that is treated in the same manner; this leads to yet another, which is twice repeated, following which a slightly varied form of the first pattern (one more pitch added) closes the song. Here, we see the employment of statement, repetition, change, and restatement (in this case, slightly varied). These techniques or processes are fundamental to the art of music—albeit they are often employed in less obvious form—and they become very malleable tools of the composer.

Let us employ a set of alphabetical symbols to represent, in gross terms, the organizational techniques employed in *Three Blind Mice.* We will assign the letter *a* to the first pattern, *b* to the second different one, and *c* to the third. We may symbolize the organization of the tune prior to the close as

Ex. 11a.

aa bb ccc. To designate the closing pattern, a variation of the first pattern, we will use the symbol *a′*. (The letter indicates the pattern from which the variation derives and the "prime" letter, that it is a varied version.)

Ex. 11b.

The whole may then be indicated as follows: *aa bb ccc a′*.

Ex. 12.

Recalling the discussion of grouping small units into larger ones, observe that an equally meaningful schema of the tonal organization or *form* of this tune might be as follows:

A	B	C	A′
(*aa*)	(*bb*)	(*ccc*)	*a′*

In this instance, uppercase letters indicate the larger perceptual units resulting from grouping related smaller patterns.

Three Blind Mice embodies some of the most practiced techniques of musical composition: statement, repetition, change, and restatement—in this case, restatement of a varied form of the first pattern.

Examples 13-17 illustrate simple formal schemes. Listen to each and describe it in terms of statement, repetition, variation, and restatement.

Ex. 13.

TWINKLE, TWINKLE, LITTLE STAR

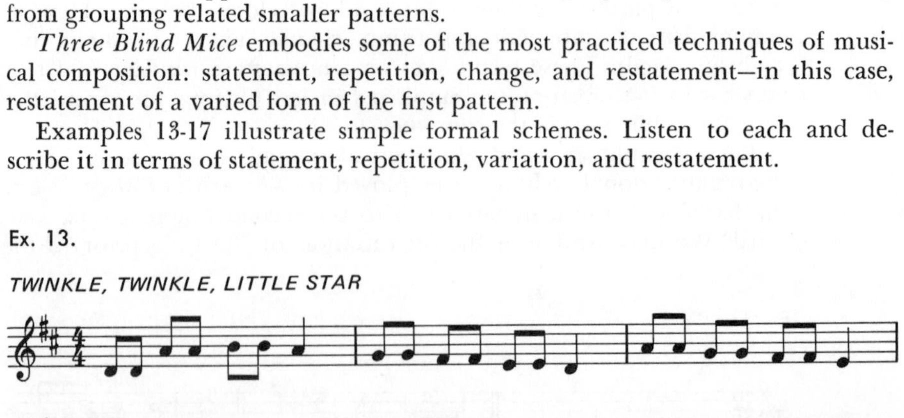

Ex. 14.

Ex. 15.

Beethoven

Vivace

(Note the similarity between this melody by Beethoven and that of Dylan entitled "Blowin' in the Wind.")

Ex. 16.

Mozart

Lively

Ex. 17.

Bach

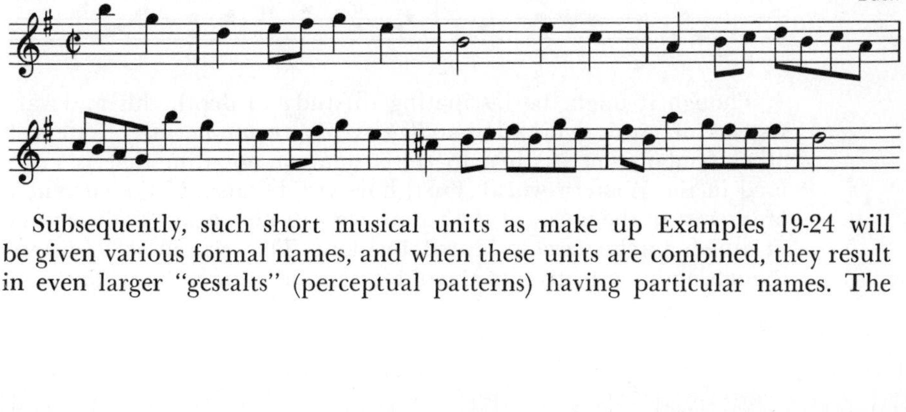

Subsequently, such short musical units as make up Examples 19-24 will be given various formal names, and when these units are combined, they result in even larger "gestalts" (perceptual patterns) having particular names. The reader is reminded of the analogous organization of language, where letters form words that in turn form sentences, paragraphs, verses, poems, or stories; but though we may readily discern such perceptual units because of our familiarity with the basic structures and uses of our language and because these larger units are set off by punctuation, we do not discern analogous units in music quite as easily. True, as we will discover, there are musical commas, periods, and other forms of sound "punctuation," but these are not always as discernible as those of language. Most of us have not used the language of music to the degree to which we have used our spoken tongue, and, therefore, the exact demarcations of musical materials, thoughts, questions, and answers are not as readily apparent.

PITCH NOTATION

As was mentioned earlier, music evolved from a purely oral tradition in which tunes were passed from one generation to another "by ear"; that is, they were not written down, and if the chain of succession was broken they were lost forever. During the course of time, various signs were developed and written down, and at first they served as cues—signs indicating the general movements from highs to lows, or the reverse, and so forth. These signs derived from the motion of the hand of the leader. For example,

. They were not arranged on a *musical staff* (see Ex. 25) and, thus, indicated no precise pitches or pitch relations. Such signs were called *neumes,* and they existed as early as the ninth century in medieval church manuscripts of a body of liturgical music called Gregorian chant. Subsequently, neumes were arranged on a staff of from one to four lines with alternating spaces, in a manner so as to clearly indicate pitches and their interrelationships—as well as durations. The result was a system of square-shaped symbols. (See Ex.18.)

Ex. 18.

MISSA IN DOMINICA RESURRECTIONIS, INTROIT

Though it might be fascinating to study in depth this and various other systems of musical notation—*syllables* (*do re mi fa,* etc.), letters, figures, or other symbols—let us turn to the system of notation that is now generally used in the Western world. First, however, because of the current resurgence of interest in the music of the guitar, we will note a sixteenth-century holdover in which pitches are indicated by dots. This system is a distant relative, though not a derivative, of the old system called *tablatures.* Each combination of pitches is indicated by dots placed on any or all of six vertical lines representing the six strings of the guitar; the dots indicate the placement of the fingers in relation to the frets (narrow metal strips placed across the finger board).

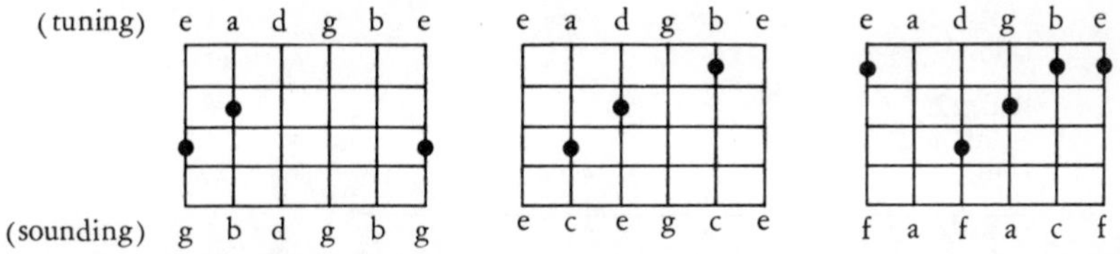

Most music today is notated on a *staff* of five lines or on a series of *staves* (usually two), a system used as early as the thirteenth century. The five lines of the staff are horizontal and parallel; pitches are notated upon and between them in a manner indicating their relative highness or lowness. (See Ex.19.)

Ex. 19.

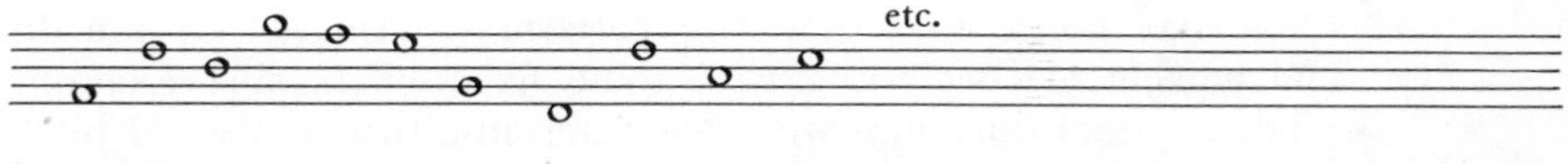

By adding another symbol called a *clef sign,* specific pitches are assigned. There are a number of clef signs, of which the two most commonly used are the *treble clef* (or G clef) and the *bass clef* (or F clef). (See Ex. 20.)

Ex. 20.

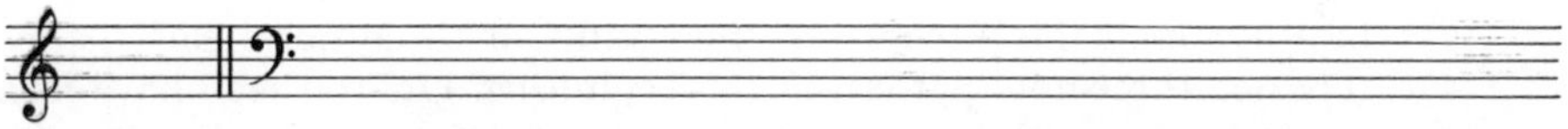

The staff to which the treble clef is affixed is called the *treble staff,* and that to which the bass clef is affixed, the *bass staff*. The treble clef indicates that the pitch g^1 is located on the second line up from the bottom of the staff. Similarly, the bass clef establishes the pitch *F* on the fourth line up. (The significance of the symbols g^1 and *F* will be explained in connection with Example 42.

Practice drawing each of these, as illustrated in Example 27, taking care to encircle the second line with the lower portion of the treble clef, and to place the dots of the bass clef above and below the fourth line. (Other clef signs are used, and some of the more common ones will be discussed at the close of Unit 2.)

Ex. 21.

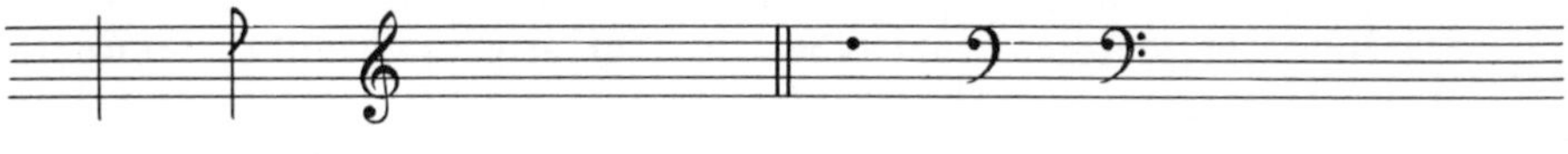

In the simplest form of musical notation a line might be used to represent the location of a particular pitch, and pitches placed above or below the line would indicate relative highness or lowness in relation to it. Obviously, there are but three directions in which subsequent pitches could move: up, down, or along the line. (See Ex. 22.)

Ex. 22.

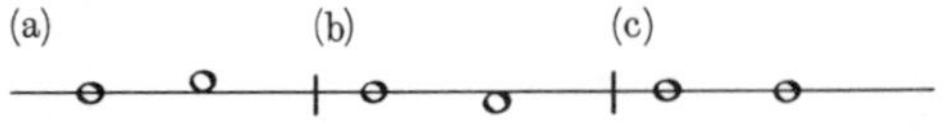

In (a), the pitch movement is upward (ascending); in (b), it is downward (descending); and in (c) it is neither ascending nor descending—rather, the second pitch is a reiteration (repetition) of the first. Furthermore, since neither the first or the second sound is of a designated pitch, we cannot ascertain the distance, or *interval,* between them. Therefore, while simple music might be so represented, we can at best merely approximate sound relations, patterns, and shapes in such a primitive notational system as suggested by Example 22.

You may notice that there are patterns determined by the direction of tonal movement. Beginning with some fixed pitch, sing Example 23 with sounds of equal duration, and then determine the number of pitch patterns.

Ex. 23.

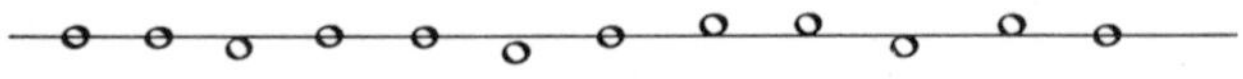

Do you hear one, two, three, or four patterns? Why? Most likely, you will have grouped the pitches into four units of three notes each because of the repeated three-note pattern at the beginning. Or, you may have heard it as a single unit, or with two divisions, or less likely, three. (See Ex. 24.)

Ex. 24.

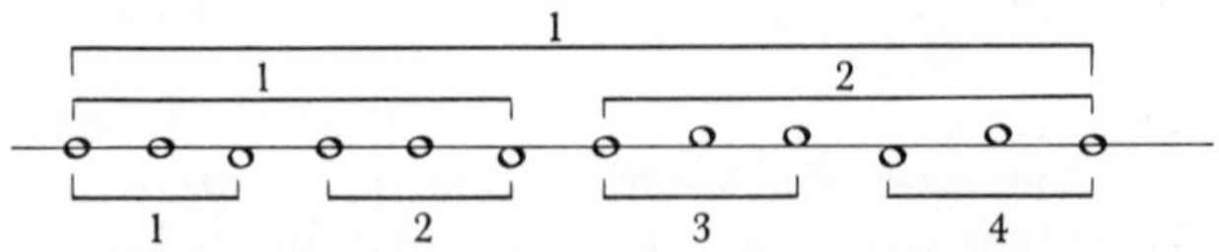

We could explore seemingly limitless possibilities of arranging such sound sets into groups of three, four, or more, but to do so would be of little value because music is rarely made of such simple, imprecise materials.

Instead, let us momentarily leave our discussion of notation to consider certain descriptive, abstract terms that relate to the design or shape of sound patterns of larger scope—that is, to the general overall contour of a melodic line. The contours of melodies are of great variety, and therefore defy simple, precise classification. However, certain general types occur with enough frequency to warrant illustration. (See Ex. 25.) It should be noted in these illustrations that although not all the pitches in any one line move in the same direction, the attendant term is generally indicative of the overall shape.

Ex. 25.

(a)

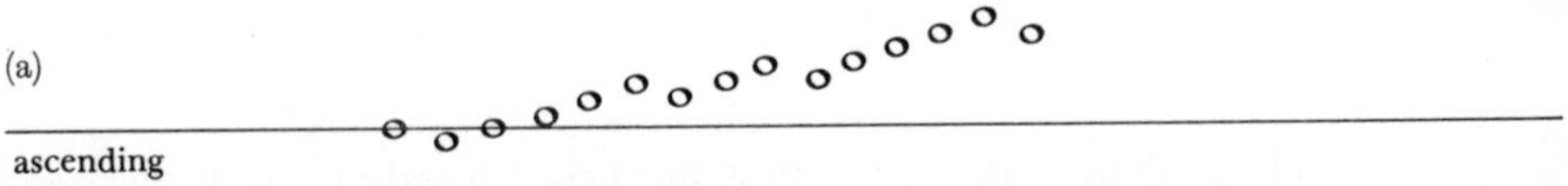

ascending

(b)

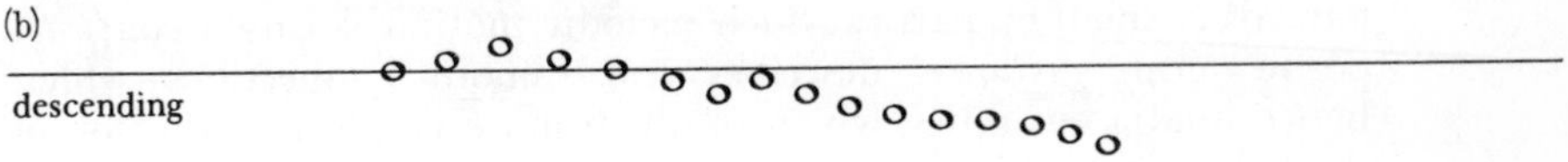

descending

(c)

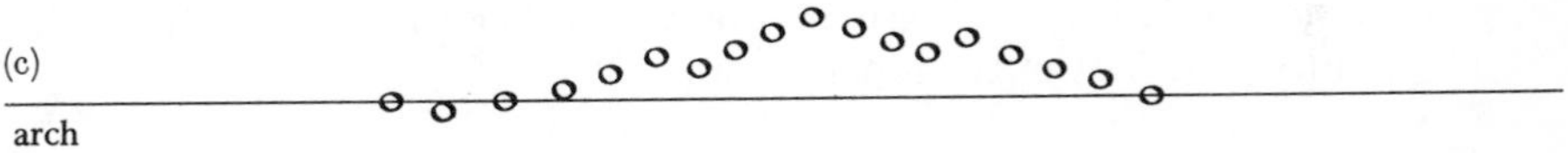

arch

(d)

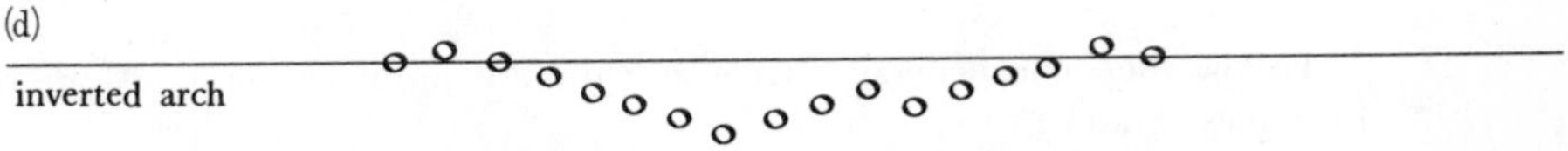

inverted arch

These terms (ascending line, *arch form,* etc.) are general descriptions of melodic movement, and need not, and indeed cannot, be applied to all melodic contours. Add them to your vocabulary for future use, and spend more time concerning yourself with more significant matters such as hearing the relation between important structural points, for example, first and last notes, the highest pitch (the point of climax) and the lowest pitch.

PROBLEMS

While the teacher performs Examples 26 and 27, first cover the example and answer as requested, then compare your answers with the notation.

Ex. 26.

(1)

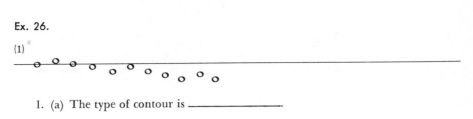

1. (a) The type of contour is ________________.

   (b) The lowest tone occurs at the ________________.

   (c) In terms of relative pitch between the first and last tones, the latter is ________________.

Ex. 27.

(2)

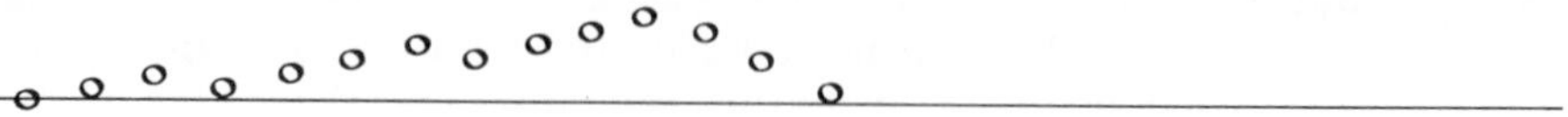

2. (a) The type of contour is ______________.

   (b) The climax occurs near the ______________ of the line.

   (c) In terms of relative pitch, the first tone is ______________ than the last.

The melodies illustrated thus far have moved generally by small or close intervals; that is, the vertical distance between adjacent sounds has been comparatively small or narrow. Such melodic motion is called *conjunct*. The opposite term, *disjunct,* describes less smooth connections—wider intervals between adjacent tones, which result in more jagged melodic contours. As we shall see, most melodies consist of various combinations of conjunct and disjunct motion; thus, linear motion is another variable that contributes to the unity or variety of the tonal stream.

PROBLEMS

Follow the same general scheme as with the problems on p. 13 in considering Examples 28 and 29.

Ex. 28.

(1)

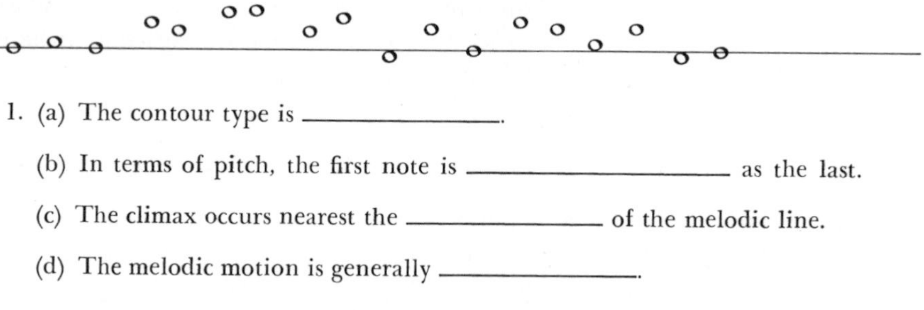

1. (a) The contour type is ______________.

   (b) In terms of pitch, the first note is ______________ as the last.

   (c) The climax occurs nearest the ______________ of the melodic line.

   (d) The melodic motion is generally ______________.

Ex. 29.

(2)

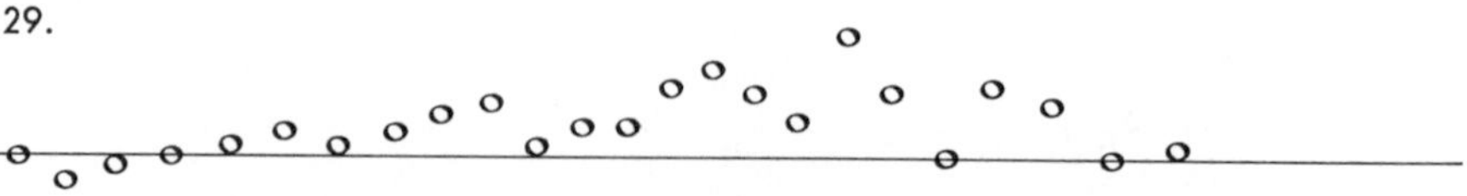

2. (a) The contour type is ______________.

   (b) In terms of pitch, the last note is ______________ than the first.

   (c) The climax occurs nearest the ______________ of the line.

   (d) The melodic motion is ______________.

MUSICAL SOUND CHARACTERISTICS

Let us consider a few generalizations about sound and the perception thereof. The normal human ear is capable of hearing a wide range of pitches (or sounds) and making extremely fine discriminations among them. All of us have noticed, for example, "out-of-tune" playing or singing. Most music does not exploit the entire range of audible sounds but, rather, is confined to a comparatively small range of tones (generally, to the range of the eighty-eight notes of the piano). *Avant-garde* music (electronic and otherwise) often exceeds this range, but before considering such extremes, it is perhaps best to consider the norm of common practice. Musical sound results from the periodic (regular) vibration of an elastic body—a string, an enclosed column of air, a membrane, an electronic generator, or an instrument itself. Such vibrations (or vibrational cycles) occur at a particular rate or frequency per interval of time (that is, per second), and are scientific measures of pitch. For example, when an orchestra tunes up, the oboist sounds , 440 cycles per second (cps); that is, if the orchestra is American and if the oboist is correct, with his double reed he will set in vibration an elastic column of air that vibrates at the frequency of 440 cps. Our ears then vibrate sympathetically at the same frequency, and we perceive the pitch produced. Moreover, when the rate of vibrational cycles per second increases, the ear perceives a higher pitch; for example, , 660 cps. Conversely, pitches that are lower have fewer cps: 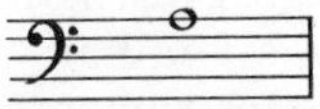, 220 cps. The human ear normally hears a range of pitches roughly between 16 and 20,000 cps, assuming they are sufficiently loud; to give an idea of the extent of this range, the approximate range of the piano is between 30 and 4,000 cps, and that of the violin, between 200 and 3,000 cps.

Much more might be said about *acoustics,* the science of sound; however, it is a broad subject, one that we may only allude to, for our concern is less with *how* we hear than with *what* we hear.

SOUND SOURCES

Sources of musical sounds may be divided into four general groups, according to the initial source of vibration as previously mentioned. These groups are elaborated in the following table:

Group	*Vibrational Source*
1. strings (piano, cello, harp, voice)	string (vocal chord)
2. woodwinds and brasses (piccolo, bassoon, French horn, tuba)	air column
3. percussion: (a) woodblocks, triangle, cymbals;	(a) elastic material (wood or metal)
(b) bass drum, timpani	(b) membrane
4. electronic instruments (synket, electronic organ)	electronic oscillators

Obviously, this list does not include all the various instrumental types. However, for our purposes, suffice it to say that Groups 1–3 encompass the instruments of usual orchestras—namely, *woodwinds:* piccolo, flute, oboe, English horn, clarinet, bassoon, and contrabassoon; *brasses:* French horn, trumpet, trombone, and tuba; *percussion:* timpani, drums, cymbals, and triangles; *other instruments:* piano, voice, organ, and harpsichord; the *strings* (the virtual foundation of the orchestra): violin, viola, cello, and bass; and the *harp*. These instruments are used in varied groupings and proportions sometimes in combination with electronic instruments) in order to realize the particular timbre (orchestral sound) the composer may desire.

A relatively new group of electronic instruments has been introduced in this century as composers have searched for sounds not produced by more usual means. They are divided into two general groups: conventional instruments that are amplified (the electric guitar, for example); and electronic tone generators, whose pure sounds may be used as is, or may be mixed (synthesized) or modified by the use of electronic filters and echo chambers. Though the sounds thus produced may pose problems for the auditor, electronic sound occupies the attention of many composers of today who seek to relate to contemporary audiences.

Tones produced on all instruments except the electronic oscillator are not single tones (pure tones) but are *composite tones,* a complex combination of many tones. Though we are conscious of but a single pitch (the *fundamental tone*), the relative strengths of additional tones sounding above (called *partials* or *harmonics*) account for the tone color or timbre of a particular instrument. (This subject will be more thoroughly discussed in pp. 61–62.)

It is important that you become familiar with the timbres (tone qualities) of all instruments and of various instrumental combinations, for it is within this parameter (timbre) that the composer "colors" the sounds he evokes, thus adding another dimension to the sonorous web he weaves. Through *orchestration,* he varies the sequence of tone qualities in much the same way, and for the same reasons, that he alters the other parameters that we have discussed. This additional dimension of sound permits almost unlimited variety and complexity, a factor that must be considered, of course, in the eternal quest for unity and variety and in the evocation of our responses thereto.

Each sound on each instrument may be produced in many different ways, and may occur with other equally varied sounds in virtually limitless combinations. Some of the most obvious but also the subtlest effects are evoked through orchestration, and the listener-performer can profit greatly from listening to a great deal of music while concentrating primarily on the varying timbres of sound.

SCORING

Those of you familiar with the problems of reading a single line of music will be sympathetic with the problems of a conductor faced with the task of reading a musical score of some twenty-four or more staves. A typical score indicates the individual part of each instrument within each family—ranging downward from highest to lowest—designating pitch, duration, and loudness, as well as the appropriate clef and key. Starting from the top of a musical score for a small orchestra, for example, the notation proceeds from the individual parts for first and second flutes (the higher of the two flute parts is called "first," and the lower, "second"; this system also obtains with the other instruments), oboes, clarinets, and bassoons; to those for first and second horn, trumpets, trombones, and a tuba; timpani and/or other percussion; special instrument(s); and first and second violins, violas, cellos, and basses. (See Ex. 30a.)

Ex. 30a.

SYMPHONY NO.5, I

Ex. 30a continued.

Fortunately, many parts are duplicated (doubled) by various instruments and, thus, the score may be reduced to a lesser number of different parts than might first seem apparent, thus reducing the task of comprehension. However, the problem is complicated by the fact that certain instruments appear to be playing different pitches when indeed they sound the same. For instance, in the section marked (a) in Example 36a, the clarinet and violins are sounding the same pitches. Though it is not within the scope of this brief introduction to dwell on the subject in great detail, it should be understood that not all instruments *sound* the pitches suggested by the notation, for they are what are called *transposing instruments*—that is, instruments whose actual sounds are different from those notated. For example, the clarinet indicated in this instance is a B♭ clarinet, which sounds a pitch lower than indicated in the score. In actuality, the clarinet and violins play the same pitches:

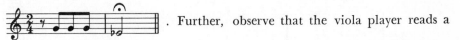

. Further, observe that the viola player reads a different clef (discussed at the end of Unit 2), the result of which, in comparison to the clarinet and violin, is a replication of their sounds eight notes lower; represented on the bass clef, with which we are familiar, the viola part in section (a) sounds as follows:

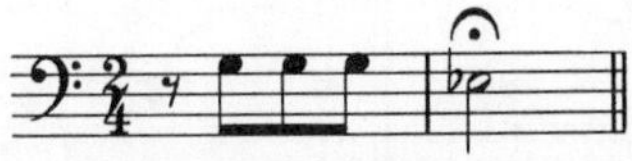

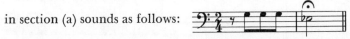

(While it is not pertinent to this discussion, it is opportune to observe that the famous pattern cited immediately above is called a *motive,* a motive being a short, distinctive musical unit which recurs in a work or section as a unifying feature.) Finally, observe that in section (a) the string bass actually sounds the same pitches that are played by the cellos. Look further to the section marked (b), where the E♭ horns and first trumpet sound the same pitches:

Some instruments are *C instruments*—that is, they sound the pitch indicated—and others are *transposing instruments,* whose pitches are different from those notated. Some examples of instruments pitched in C are piano, flute, oboe, bassoon, trombone, and orchestral strings, except for the string bass as previously mentioned. Some instruments that are generally considered transposing are English horn, clarinet, and French horn. Much more might be said about this subject, but let us instead consider one other "complication" to the life of the conductor or performer.

Composers are not always content to use conventional instrumental transpositions, and may write what is commonly known as a *C score.* Note in Example 30b that Beethoven elects to write for clarinets, French horns, and trumpets in *C.* (See p. 20.)

Ex. 30b.

SYMPHONY NO.5, IV

Beethoven

In the section marked (a), the clarinet, horn, and trumpet players must make the proper transposition in order to sound the pitches the composer desires. In this instance the B♭ clarinets and trumpets duplicate the oboes, though visualizing the following:

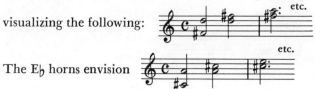

The E♭ horns envision

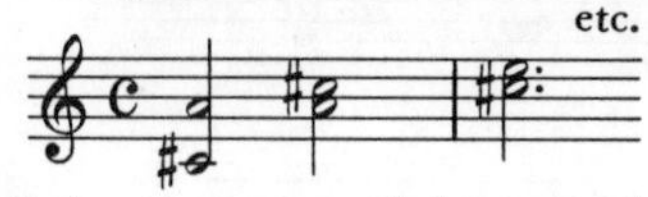

but double the pitches of the trumpets, eight notes lower:

In scoring, human voices are arranged in much the same way as are the families of instruments—that is, downward from highest to lowest. Thus, female voices appear above male voices as follows:

Female—soprano
alto

Male—tenor
bass

Each of the above voice categories may be further subdivided: for example, first soprano and second soprano, or first bass and second bass. Other terms are used to describe particular voice types: dramatic soprano, lyric tenor, mezzo-soprano (middle soprano), contralto, baritone (a male voice whose range falls between tenor and bass). Four-part vocal settings (with which you will soon become familiar) are generally arranged for soprano, alto, tenor, and bass—in that order from top to bottom—and are often designated as SATB. Such settings occur either in open score with each voice assigned a separate staff (Ex. 31a),

Ex. 31a.

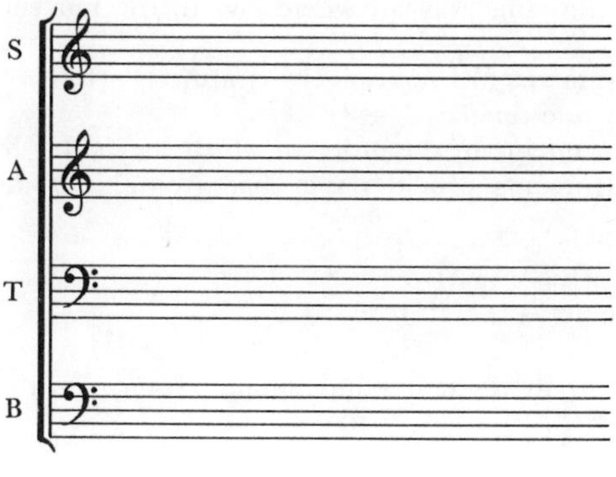

or in closed score (Ex. 31b).

Ex. 31b.

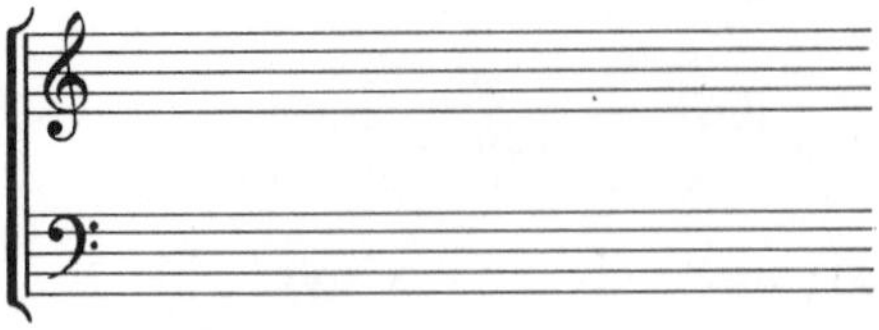

The choice between the two depends on the relative complexity of the individual parts; lines that are complex and that overlap others create problems of music-reading that can be avoided by the clear separation of the individual parts. Just as it is important to recognize the difference between the sound of the oboe and that of the violin, so it is important to realize the difference between the sound of the soprano and bass, or soprano and mezzo-soprano for that matter; each voice has a color, a timbre, that plays an important expressive role in the presentation of musical sounds.

PROBLEMS

For recognizing various instruments and voices:

1. Listen to the Britten *Young Person's Guide to the Orchestra.* Note how the particular instruments sound, singly and in combination. Note the overall division into instrumental families (woodwinds, brasses, strings, percussion).

2. Listen to the second movement of Bartók's Concerto for Orchestra. This movement is in three large sections. The first and last sections are very similar; the second section is different (most notably in the use of a longer, more sustained melodic line, and in its concentration on only one family of instruments).

   In the first section:
   (a) What type of instrument is used for the short "introduction"? Does this instrument recur in the same way anywhere else in the movement? If so, where?
   (b) Small groups of instruments are successively "featured." How many instruments are featured at one time?
   (c) List the featured instruments in the order in which they enter the piece.
   (d) What family of instruments provides the "background" to the featured instruments?

   In the second section:
   (a) What family of instruments is featured?

3. Listen to the quartet "Un dì, se ben rammentomi" from Verdi's *Rigoletto,*

which occurs shortly after the beginning of Act III. (The piece is in two large sections, fast (*allegro*) and slower (*andante*).

In the first section, listen to the differences in range and timbre of the four voices (soprano, alto, tenor, and bass).

In the second section:
(a) Make a list of the different voices that enter (soprano, alto, tenor, or bass), up to and including the first entry of the bass.
(b) In the remainder of the quartet, listen to the timbre that is achieved by the blend of the four solo voices.

LOUDNESS

We have chosen to speak of the basic elements of pitch and timbre before concerning ourselves with volume and duration. The loudness or softness of a tone depends on the amplitude of the vibrational cycle, mentioned earlier in the section on musical sound characteristics. In regard to the oboist's *a* 440 cps, the stronger the wind pressure, the greater the amplitude of the reed vibration and the louder the sound, and vice versa.

When a harp string is plucked strongly, the back-and-forth motion of the string is greater than when it is plucked gently and the sounds heard are correspondingly louder. The sound decays (fades away) after the pluck, as the string returns to a position of rest. It should be noted at this point that pitch and volume are mutually exclusive aspects of sound, acoustically speaking, and that frequency of vibration and amplitude of vibration relate to two different sound characteristics. They are independent of each other. As musicians know, the aforementioned *a* 440 may be sounded softly or loudly; moreover, the pitch remains constant (when properly performed) in both instances—even, for that matter, if the sound increases or decreases in volume.

In acoustical terms, loudness is measured in *decibels,* a decibel (db) denoting approximately the smallest degree of loudness perceptible by the human ear. For example, musical sounds may range from the softest tone of the violin, about 25 db (*pianissimo*), to the *fortissimo* of the full orchestra, about 120 db. Degrees of loudness are indicated by various words and symbols appearing in the musical score. The words (or abbreviations thereof) are generally in one of four languages—Italian, English, French, or German—the former being more commonly used than the others. There is no easy way to learn these words or symbols except to memorize them. As we shall see, they are imprecise and relative in their meanings, and at best they indicate but comparative levels of intensity. Some of those most frequently used appear in the table below, and if they are not now familiar they should be committed to memory—obviously, one cannot realize the subtleties of dynamic interplay from the inspection of a musical score if one is unfamiliar with the basic indications thereof. Imprecise though they may be, they indicate the range of dynamics from softest to loudest. However, when extremes are indicated, they are frequently indicated by the use of superlatives compounded of the basic terminology. This becomes apparent from studying the table.

English	*Italian*	*Italian Abbreviation*	*French*	*German*
soft	piano	p	doux	leise
loud	forte	f	fort	laut
very soft	pianissimo	pp	très doux	sehr leise
very loud	fortissimo	ff	très fort	sehr laut
moderately soft	mezzo-piano	mp	modéré	mässig leise
moderately loud	mezzo-forte	mf	modéré	mässig laut

Infrequently, greater extremes are called for, and are represented by combinations such as *ppp* or *ffff;* this is an indication that in the evolution of musical practice, the dimension of dynamics is becoming increasingly important as an expressive parameter of musical sound.

Transitions between degrees of loudness are indicated by words and symbols such as the following:

Symbol	*English*	*Italian*	*Italian Abbreviation*	*French*	*German*
<	becoming louder	crescendo	cres.	augmenter	lauter werden
>	becoming softer	decrescendo	decres.	diminuer	leiser werden

Familiarize yourself with the meaning of the words and symbols in the two tables above, and then complete the following problem.

Symbol	*German*	*English*	*French*	*Italian*
f	________	________	________	________
pp	________	________	________	________
<	________	________	________	________
mf	________	________	________	________
p	________	________	________	________
ff	________	________	________	________
>	________	________	________	________
mp	________	________	________	________

PITCH NOTATION

Before considering the element of duration, let us return once more to pitch and the way it is generally notated. We interrupted the presentation of this important aspect of sound to dwell on other matters. Recall, if you will, that two staves—treble and bass—are most frequently used to designate pitches.

When both of these appear together in a score, the treble is placed above the bass staff (except in orchestral scores, where instruments are grouped according to families—winds, brasses, strings, etc.). Further, the pitches placed on the staves are assigned *pitch names,* the first seven letters of the alphabet (a–g) in ascending order; the letters of this basic set appear in small and capital forms and with appropriate subscripts or superscripts (numbers placed above or below, and to the right of, the letters) and with "accidentals." The relative pitch of each to the other is designated in a spectrum of pitches ranging from lowest to highest. *Accidentals* are symbols placed immediately before a note to denote its relation to the basic seven. Those notes falling between the basic seven notes are indicated by the use of sharp (♯) or flat (♭) signs, and the natural sign (♮) is used to cancel the effect of either of the others. Example 32 illustrates the use of sharps and flats.

Ex. 32.

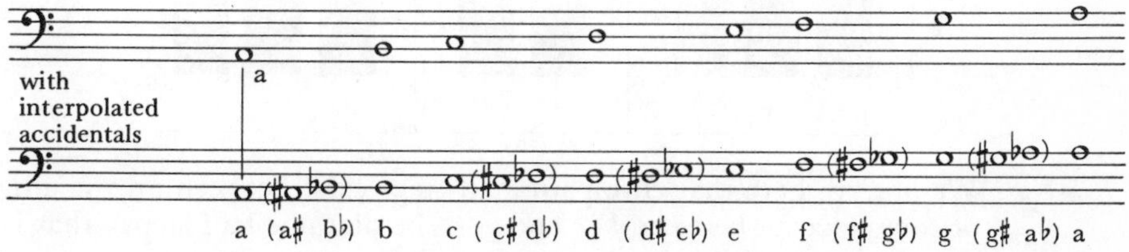

As you have no doubt observed, there are pitches (pitch names) between which no accidentals occur. This pinpoints one of the major weaknesses of our notational system—the failure to portray accurately the true distance (*interval*) between pitches. For instance, to the eye, adjacent pitches on the upper staff in Example 32 appear equally spaced (space-line-space-line, etc.), suggesting that the intervals between them are of the same size. Yet, this is obviously not true as exemplified in the lower staff, where some notes are immediately adjacent while others are separated by an intermediate tone. Therefore, the musician is faced with the real problem of differentiating one interval size from the other in order to realize the notation properly, for, as we can see, intervals that appear equal from a visual standpoint are not necessarily so.

HALF STEP; WHOLE STEP

Let us begin interval discrimination by discussing the smallest interval (at least in conventional music), the *half step,* or *semitone.* To this end, consider Example 33: a segment of the piano keyboard with the octave *a–a* indicated.

Ex. 33.

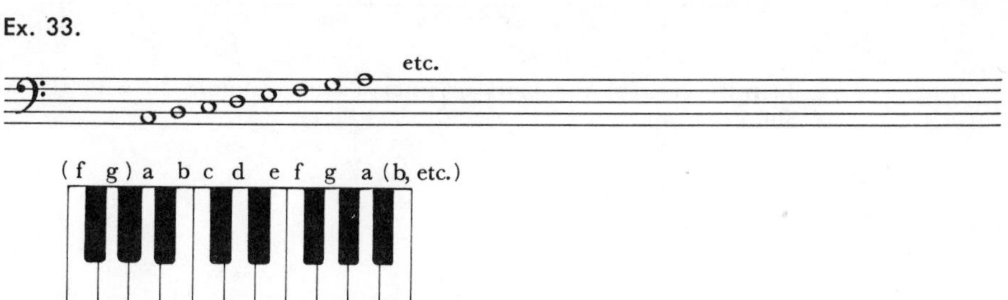

You can see that there are two half steps (that is, adjacent tones) in this pitch series, *b–c* and *e–f*. Semitones such as these—having *consecutive* letter names —are called *diatonic half steps.*

The *chromatic half step* designates the smallest interval existing between adjacent pitches having *the same letter names,* one of which is altered by an accidental; for example, *a–a♯*. For further clarification, see Example 34 (a more elaborate version of Example 39), in which the other half steps encompassed in the gamut of *a–a* are indicated.

Ex. 34.

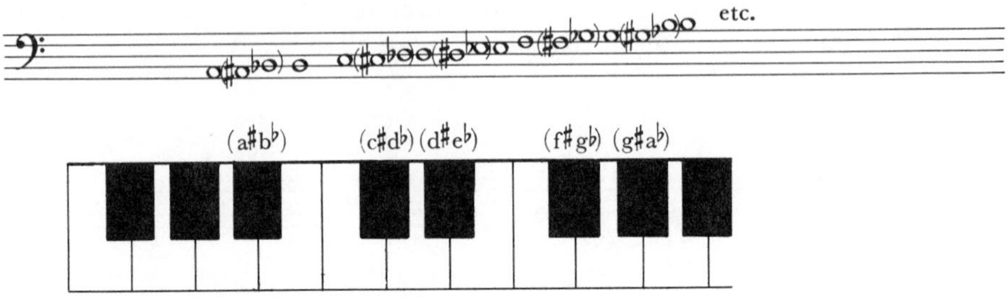

We observe here that chromatic half steps exist between all the adjacent keys or tones (except between *b–c* and *e–f,* the diatonic half steps), that is, between *a–a♯, b–b♭, d♭–d, d♯–d♮,* etc.

An interval spanning two half steps, or semitones, is called a *whole step* or *whole tone.* Such intervals occur in the basic pitch set between *a–b, c–d, d–e, f–g,* and *g–a;* or, for that matter, between *b♭–c, c♯–d♯, e–f♯,* etc. Though most whole steps exist between pitches with consecutive letter designations (*b–c♯, e♭–f, g♭–a♭,* etc.), those between pitches of the same letter name are possible (*b♭–b♯,* for example), but are rarely used.

PROBLEMS

1. Using the treble clef on the staff in Example 35, notate and identify all the intervals possible in the *f–f* octave. (Use the abbreviations dhs, chs, and ws for diatonic half step, chromatic half step, and whole step.)

Ex. 35.

2. Identify each of the pairs of intervals in Example 36 with the appropriate abbreviation.

Ex. 36.

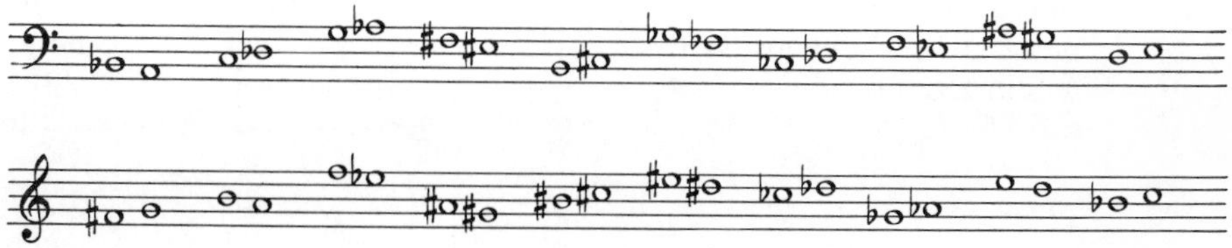

PITCH NOTATION (cont.)

To this point, we have limited our presentation of pitch notation to the octaves *a–a* and *f–f,* which were chosen for illustrative purposes because they lie within the confines of the bass and treble staves. Let us consider now the notation of pitches that exceed the range of either of these. To do so, we must use *ledger lines,* short lines placed above or below either staff to extend the range of the staff in either direction (up or down). (See Ex. 37.)

Ex. 37.

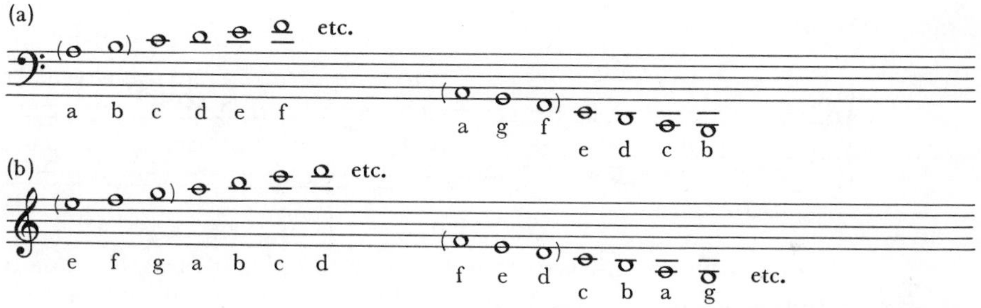

Another familiar method for extending staff range is the use of octave signs (*8ve*- - - - -), by which one may avoid excessive use of ledger lines. Either of the staves in Example 37 may be further extended. Take the latter, for instance, and extend the first half of it upward (Ex. 38).

Ex. 38.

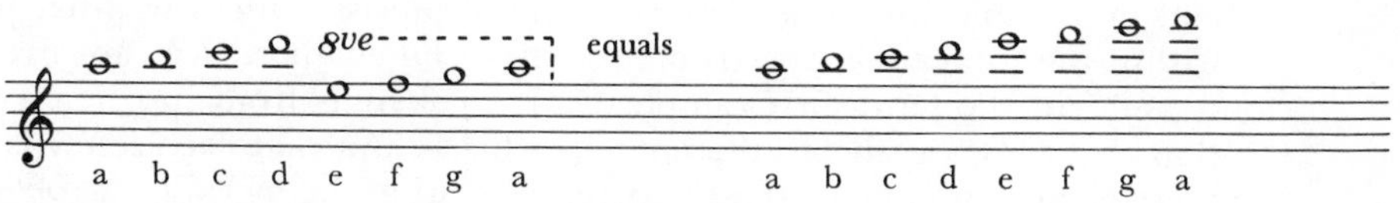

Likewise, extend the second half downward (Ex. 39).

Ex. 39.

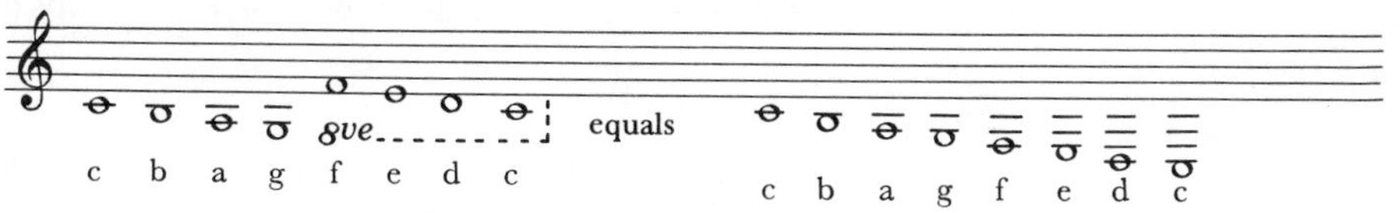

The gap between the bass and treble staves is bridged by the use of a ledger line, and we would well appreciate the value of its use and of others in terms of visual comprehension if, instead, we were forced to use the notational system in Example 40.

Ex. 40.

Compare this system to the more conventional notation of the same pitch series—the combined treble and bass staves (called the *great staff*), with added ledger lines (Ex. 41). (It should be noted that the great staff is used for much music—piano and choral, for example.)

Ex. 41.

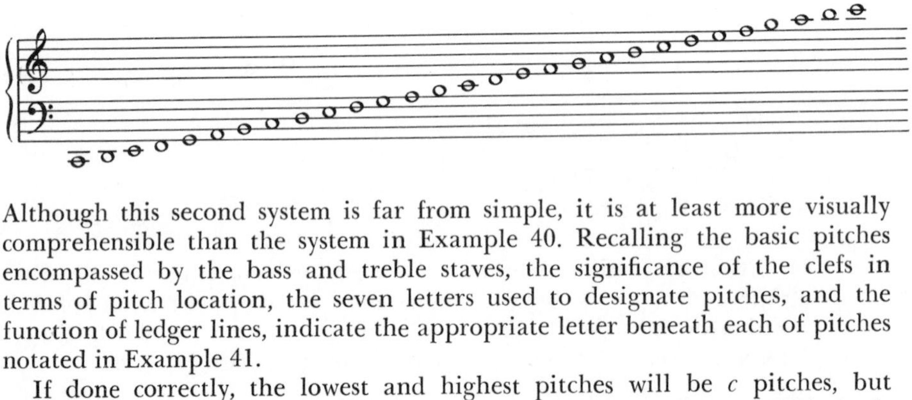

Although this second system is far from simple, it is at least more visually comprehensible than the system in Example 40. Recalling the basic pitches encompassed by the bass and treble staves, the significance of the clefs in terms of pitch location, the seven letters used to designate pitches, and the function of ledger lines, indicate the appropriate letter beneath each of pitches notated in Example 41.

If done correctly, the lowest and highest pitches will be *c* pitches, but pitches obviously much different in terms of cps or *actual* pitch. This leads then to the use of another type of symbol—superscript and subscript numbers, and upper- and lower-case letters—to more precisely identify pitch placement within the total tonal spectrum. You have noted that there are five *c*'s, four *d*'s, etc., in the series in Example 47. It is obvious from inspecting the notation that they are all of different pitch levels and that each letter is repeated every eight notes, the interval between repetitions being called an *octave*.

Let us again consider the same pitch series now appearing in Example 42 and note the symbols used to differentiate between the various levels of pitch and the various octaves. Observe that the symbol sets change at each *c*. And though the vast array may at first cause dismay, through practice the terminology can be easily mastered—and in fact must be—for even though it serves no real purpose in reading notation, it proves most useful and necessary in the discussion thereof.

Ex. 42.

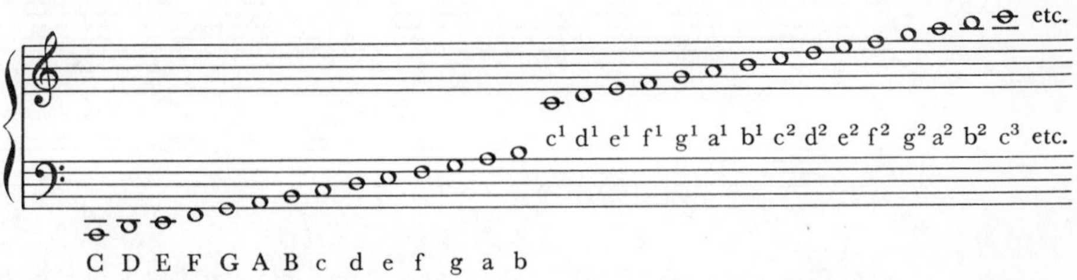

Though not completely illustrated in Example 42 this system may be continued in either direction by adding numbers in proper sequence. The method of extension upward is suggested by the last pitch in Example 42. As the superscript for that *c* is 3, the pitch being designated c^3, the next pitch above would be d^3; the next octave up would begin with c^4, etc. On the other hand, to extend Example 42 downward from the first note (C) would result in the designation shown in Example 43.

Ex. 43

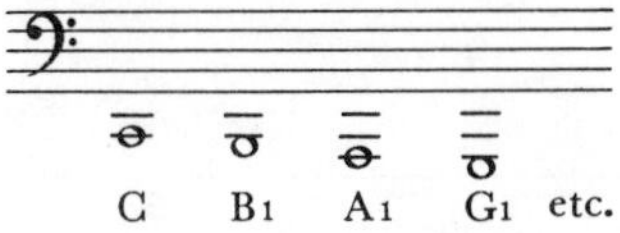

PROBLEMS

1. Assign appropriate pitch-octave designations below the staff for each pitch notated in Example 44.

Ex. 44.

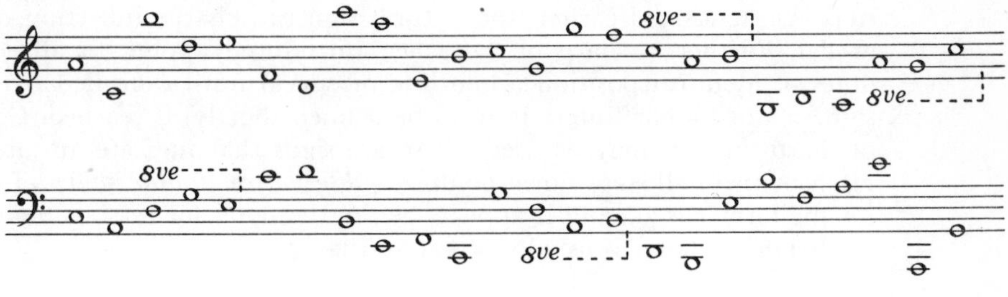

2. Notate the pitches indicated in Example 45.

Ex. 45.

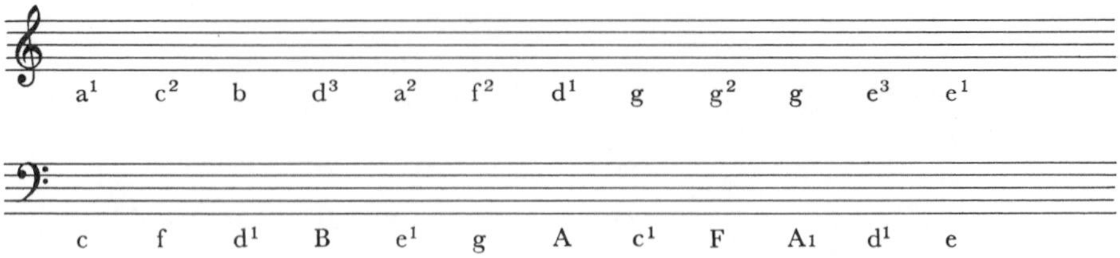

3. Play problems 1 and 2 at the piano. Then, locate and play in the same manner notes suggested by others.

ACCIDENTALS

Our set of symbols becomes even more complex when we add the so-called accidentals; however, the basic system operates the same. For instance, consider Example 46, in which all the pitches of the octave c^1–c^2 are notated. From studying this brief example you can see the basic procedure, which may be applied to other octaves in the same manner.

Ex. 46.

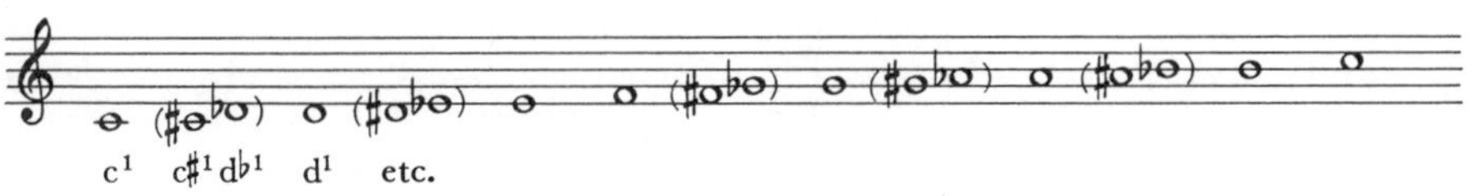

Accidentals may be used in two ways: as an integral part of the notation of fundamental pitches within a particular pitch series, or to alter (inflect) pitches. In the latter sense, one may generalize that a sharp is added before a note to indicate that the basic pitch is to be raised one half step; flats are placed before notes to indicate that the basic pitch is to be lowered one half step. As mentioned earlier, the natural sign cancels the inflection of a sharp or flat. Further, a sharp or flat when introduced applies to all subsequent notes of identical position (same line or space) until cancelled by a natural sign, or until a bar line (a term to be defined shortly) is reached. Compounds of sharps or flats may be used: these are signs that indicate an alteration of pitch by two half steps down or up: *double flat* or *double sharp.* The symbol for the former is ♭♭, and it appears before the note; for reasons unknown, the symbol of the latter is usually 𝄪 rather than ♯♯.

DURATION

The element of pitch has been the focus of our attention for some time, for we believe that the realization of pitch events poses the greatest challenge to the student of music. In a way, this is a nonsensical approach to the study of music because we all know that pitch and duration are not separate entities. Rather, in music they are wedded, for any sound event, no matter how short or long, has a measurable duration—that is, it exists for a particular time within a particular time frame. Further, sound events are comparable in terms of duration; that is, one sound event may span the same unit of time as another, or one smaller or larger. Such durations may be related one to another and, indeed, may be measured in terms of various time units. Fortunately for the student, the vocabulary required to discuss time units, events, and the like is not extensive. But even so, the system of notation we will examine itself reveals certain idiosyncrasies and challenges to most students.

Simple sequences of sound events may consist of relatively few different types of durations, and in such sequences, one is able to differentiate short and long or shorter or longer sounds within a short time. For example, the durations of the tones of the following Stephen Foster tune might be indicated as follows:

— — — —— — — — — ——
Beautiful dream - er, wake un - to me

Obviously, this set of symbols is imprecise, to say the least, since the durations are only approximated and the durational unit is undefined. But although the notational system now in common use (except in *avant-garde* experiments) indicates time units, their relative frequency within a time frame, the relational durations of sounds, and groups of time units measured according to various organizational schemes, it too is imprecise: the durational symbols are proportional and not absolute in value. Despite this fact, no better system has yet been devised and universally adopted for measuring and relating the durations of single or simultaneous sound events. Some composers employ timing devices to measure durations in seconds or even smaller units, but such methods are still experimental and have not been used in the realization of most notated music. The notation of sound durations has a history of development similar to that of pitch (the one being closely related to the other), following the same progression from approximate to more exact notation.

Let us first consider the basic concept of *time unit, pulse,* or *beat*—that real or imagined regularly-recurring short stimulus that we sense and perhaps react to by tapping our foot or clapping our hands. One who is sensitive to the sound of his own heart knows that it normally pulses or beats at a regular rate. It beats faster in moments of intense excitement or after strenuous exercise, and then slower after a return to normal. That is, it beats at a faster *rate, frequency,* or *tempo* at one time than it does at another. In general, the heartbeat fluctuates within a range of frequencies from 60–100 beats per minute, 80 being somewhere near the norm. The pulses of music cover a wider range of frequencies, or tempos, perhaps from as few as 30 to as many as 200 beats per minute. To determine precise tempos, musicians use clock-like (mechanical or electronic) devices called metronomes, which sound a designated number of pulses per minute. More often, though, they rely on such imprecise terms as *fast, slow, moderate,* etc., for general tempo indications. Further, though much music moves to a regular continuous pulse, the tempo may change (increase or lessen), either at a regular rate or more abruptly, for the sake of variety or other expressive effects.

There is a measurable time span between pulses or beats—and between sound events encompassing more than one beat, for that matter. To illustrate this point, tap your finger as you sing the phrase of *Beautiful Dreamer* shown below, letting the vertical lines indicate the pulse (one tap for each), and the arched lines, the duration of each sound.

Beau - ti - ful dream - er, wake un - to me

Thus, we can see that each sound persists to the beginning of the next, that the three syllables of the first word have a duration of one beat-span each, that the two syllables of the second word have three beat-spans each, and so forth. In addition, it is important to observe that each sound event has both a point of beginning and a point of ending; this should be clear from the symbolization of the duration of the final word "me," a sound that encompasses *three* beat-spans but must be represented by four pulses in order to clarify the precise point of sound termination.

Just as we tend to group pitches into patterns, so do we with durations, common groupings being patterns of two or three pulses. Moreover, in so doing we sense (or imagine) a dynamic difference between pulses so grouped, generally hearing patterns of two as strong-weak, and of three as strong-weak-weak. (The patterned grouping of beats recurring within a composition is called *meter;* patterns of two are designated *duple meter,* and patterns of three, *triple meter.*) Recall your favorite march or Viennese waltz and the differences between these two groupings become readily apparent. If none come to mind, sing aloud the "Marine's Hymn" ("From the Halls of Montezuma," etc.) while tapping or clapping the basic beat. Compare its pulse pattern with that of "The Band Played On" ("Casey would waltz with a strawberry blonde," etc.).

We will not spend further time developing a set of abstract symbols for representing durations; rather, let us turn to musical notation itself. Before doing so, however, we should note that the differentiation of strong and weak pulses is basic to performance and listening. In fact, the very patterns a conductor employs to co-ordinate his musical forces make use of this observable difference. His *downbeat* (deriving from the downward motion of his hand) indicates a strong pulse in relation to which the others are generally of lesser intensity (whether real or imagined). (The opposite term is *upbeat,* an upward sweep of the conductor's hand signalling the last pulse of a beat group.)

DURATION NOTATION

The duration of a sound is indicated by the symbol that designates the pitch—that is, the note type itself. This is an oversimplified generalization, but accept it for the moment and we will amend it as subsequent developments require. The most-used basic note types (note values or durational symbols, if you like) are six: whole note 𝅝 , half note 𝅗𝅥 , quarter note 𝅘𝅥 , eighth note 𝅘𝅥𝅮 , sixteenth note 𝅘𝅥𝅯 , and thirty-second note 𝅘𝅥𝅰 . Others less frequently used are the breve 𝅜 , and the sixty-fourth note 𝅘𝅥𝅱 . All contain noteheads: 𝅗 or ● ; all save the whole note have a note stem (a vertical line) attached; and, eighth through sixty-fourth notes have stems with flag(s) attached:

As you can deduce, the head and/or the stem with flag indicate(s) the duration of one note relative to another; it does not indicate a particular absolute duration. In other words, the descriptive titles quarter, eighth, sixteenth, etc., indicate the proportional relation between the individual note values. Indeed, this is a notational system based on mathematical ratios: two half notes equal a whole, or four quarters, or eight eighths, etc.; a whole note is twice the duration of a half note, sixteen times that of a sixteenth note, etc. (See Ex. 47a.)

Ex. 47a.

Each symbol of sound duration is complemented by a symbol called a rest, which designates silence. These differ from pitch symbols to a degree, but are identical in terms of mathematical ratios. They are: whole rest 𝄻 , half rest 𝄼 , quarter rest 𝄽 , eighth rest 𝄾 , sixteenth rest 𝄿 , and thirty-second rest 𝅀 . Less common are the breve rest 𝄻𝄻, and the sixty-fourth rest 𝅁 . (See Ex. 47b.)

Ex. 47b.

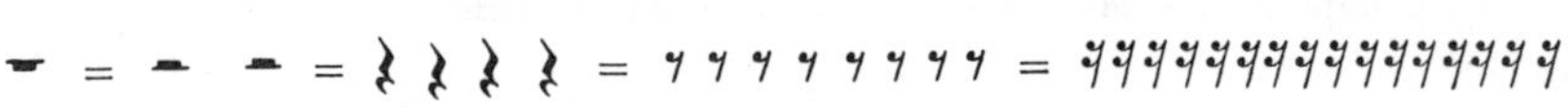

In writing these symbols, pay particular attention to the following hints: Noteheads are oval (not round). Note stems should be vertically attached to the heads; if up, they are appended to the right extremity, and if down, to the left. Stems of notes appearing on the mid-line of a staff may be up or down; generally, stems of notes below the mid-line are up, and down if above. Attach flags to the right side of the note-stem, regardless of its vertical direction. Whole rests generally hang from the fourth line up; half rests sit atop the third line up; and the others generally center above the mid-line, with the flags always attached to the left side.

PROBLEMS IN NOTATION OF DURATIONS

Practice notating the durational values indicated below the staves in Example 47c, and when appropriate, locate them at various pitch levels.

Ex. 47c.

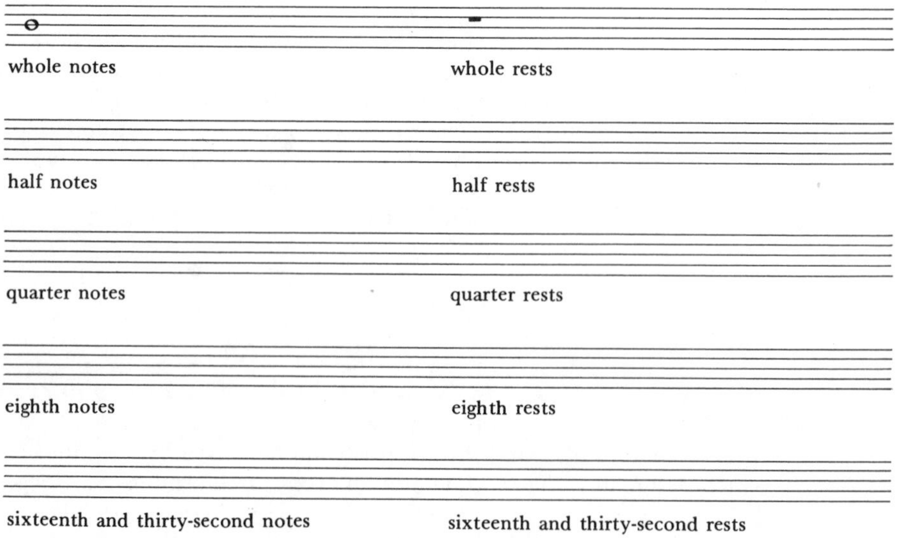

You will develop notational skills through practice. Also, you will no doubt develop both your own "shorthand" for rapid sketching and a more conventional notation for finished manuscript. Extreme care should be exercised in regard to the latter, for, obviously, the development of a "good hand" for precise, neat scoring is necessary if the sound events you have conceived are to be realized according to your intentions.

PROBLEMS IN DURATIONAL RELATIONSHIPS

Complete the following exercises in relative duration:

1. One ♩ = ____ 𝄾 or ____ 𝅘𝅥𝅯 or ____ 𝅘𝅥𝅰.

2. Four 𝅘𝅥𝅮 = ____ 𝅗𝅥 or ____ 𝄾 or ____ 𝅘𝅥 .

3. Two 𝄾 = ____ 𝅘𝅥𝅮. or ____ 𝄿 or ____ 𝅘𝅥𝅯 .

4. Eight 𝅘𝅥𝅮 = ____ 𝄼 or ____ 𝄽 or ____ 𝅝 .

The basic durations presented above may be increased by placing another symbol, the dot (·), after a note or rest. Adding a dot to a note increases the basic value of the note by one-half: 𝅗𝅥. = 𝅗𝅥 + 𝅘𝅥 . Rests may be treated in the same manner: 𝄼. = 𝄼 + 𝄽 .

It is conventional practice to place vertical lines on the staff to facilitate the performance of music, though it is possible to notate an extended series of sounds without them. Such lines are called *bar lines,* and the space that two of them encloses is called a *measure.* In Example 48 you can see that each measure consists of three pulses (beats), that the measures are set off by six bar lines—none appearing at the very beginning—and that there are six measures in all. What is not apparent is that *there is no cessation of sound between notes,* either within a measure, or across a bar line—that is, between notes on either side of the vertical line.

Ex. 48.

Furthermore, in general notational practice the relative duration of sound is only suggested by the spacing of the notes: compare the space between the notes of equal duration (𝅘𝅥) with that between 𝅘𝅥. 𝅘𝅥𝅮 in the second measure. Spacing becomes quite important when staves are combined, for the relative placement of notes within a measure and their vertical relation to one another can contribute much to the ease or difficulty of execution. To illustrate this point, let us write Example 48 on two staves for soprano and bass. (See Ex. 49.)

Ex. 49.

It is quite obvious that the bass part creates perceptual confusion rather than clarity, because the vertical coincidences of sounds are obscured by the erratic placement of durations within the measure. The object in notation, then, is to show or suggest the durational relations, both vertical and horizontal, so as to aid as much as possible the performance of the sounds. Two additional notational symbols were introduced in Example 49: the bracket, at the beginning, which indicates that the two lines of music occur simultaneously; and the double bar closing the last measure (two vertical lines used to indicate the close of a work or of a major section within it). A further aid to clarity is that except for the whole rest, which is placed at the midpoint within a measure (and which is always used to denote an entire measure of silence), all rests are placed so as to indicate their coincidence with the attending sound event.

METER SIGNATURES

Our notational scheme is complete except for one other set of symbols called *meter signatures* (sometimes referred to as *time signatures*). Meter signatures are symbols consisting of *superposed numbers* ($\genfrac{}{}{0pt}{}{2}{4}$ $\genfrac{}{}{0pt}{}{3}{2}$ $\genfrac{}{}{0pt}{}{6}{8}$) appearing at the beginning of a piece and elsewhere throughout it; they indicate two important factors: the number of pulses (beats) per measure, and the durational value of each beat. The upper number indicates the former, and the lower, the latter. These symbols *do not* indicate the pulse rate—that is, the time frame in which the beats occur—and, therefore, the term meter signature is preferred to that of time signature. For example, $\genfrac{}{}{0pt}{}{2}{4}$ indicates that the ♩ (𝄽) (quarter note or quarter rest) is the unit of measurement, and that there are two such units per measure or bar. To clarify this point, "America" (cited in Example 48 without meter signature) is properly notated as in Example 50.

Ex. 50.

Note that the numerals of the signature are placed above and below the midline of the staff. You have no doubt thought of the possibility of designating the beat unit by the proper note value, as in Example 51.

Ex. 51.

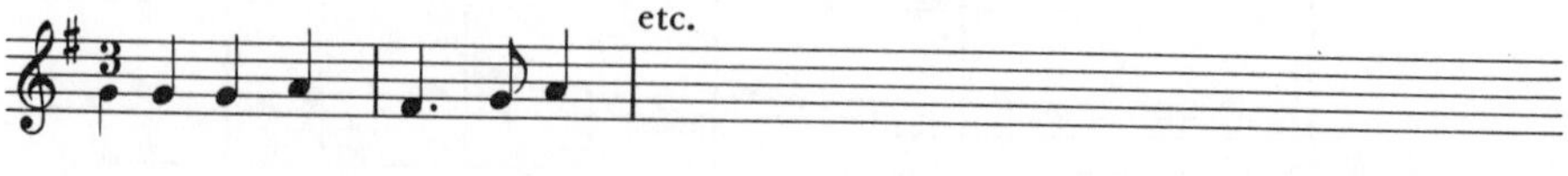

And, in fact, some music contains metric indications of this nature. However, symbols such as $\frac{2}{4}$, $\frac{3}{4}$, etc., are most commonly used.

PROBLEMS

1. Indicate the proper meter signature suggested below.

	Beat Unit	*Beats Per Measure*	*Signature*
(a)	♩	3	________
(b)	♪	4	________
(c)	𝅗𝅥	2	________
(d)	eighth note	5	________
(e)	sixteenth note	7	________

2. Place the appropriate meter signatures on the staves in Example 52.

Ex. 52.

(a)

(b)

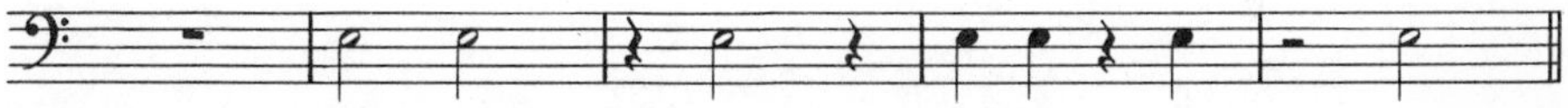

(c)

(d)

(e)

3. As you tap your finger at a moderate tempo, intone each of the passages in Example 52.

PITCH (INTERVALS)

Until now, we have limited our discussion of pitch relations to two intervals, the half step and the whole step. This, of course, is all the terminology required to denote adjacent pitches. But we know that music made of such simple relations would be monotonous indeed if no larger intervals were used for the sake of contrast or variety. True, we could describe all intervals in terms of the number of whole and/or half steps between them, but to do so would be cumbersome, to say the least. For example, we might say that the octave contains twelve half steps or, for that matter, five whole steps and two half steps, or any other such description; and we would be correct. On the other hand, a simpler system has been devised, which designates this interval and accounts for intervallic differences mandated by the imprecision of staff notation. First, we assign to an interval a numerical term, which, in simple terms, encompasses the number of different pitch names contained therein. Thus, a third contains or encompasses three different letter names; a fourth, four; a fifth, five; and so on. Consider Example 53.

Ex. 53.

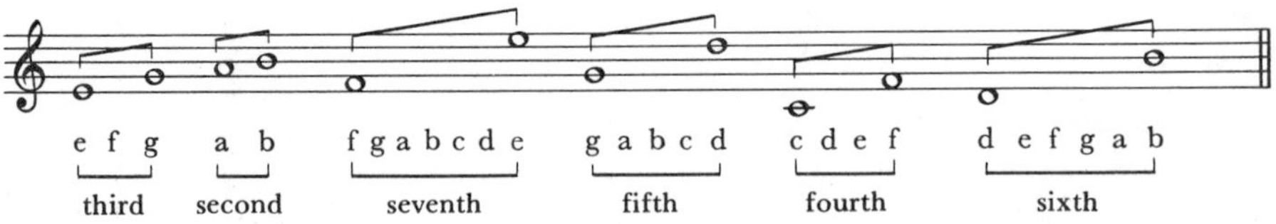

The name given two pitches of the same letter name is *prime* (or *unison,* if the pitches are identical). (See Ex. 54.)

Ex. 54.

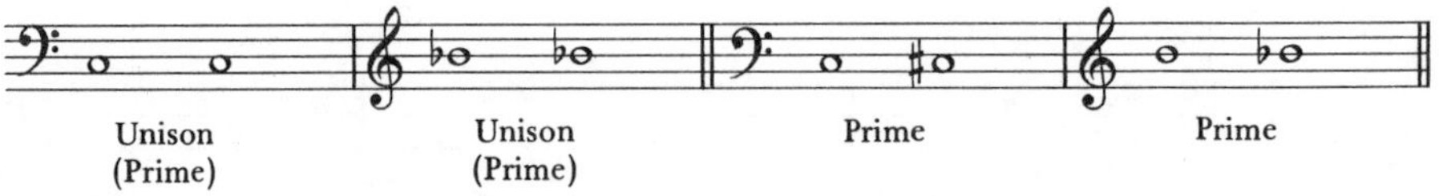

A rather easy method of determining a basic interval is to inspect the relations between notes, in terms of lines and spaces. A study of the following will help in this regard:

Primes	notes on same line or space
Seconds	line to adjacent space; space to adjacent line up or down
Fourths	line to two spaces up or down; space to two lines up or or down
Sixths	line to three spaces up or down; space to three lines up or down

Octave	line to four spaces up or down; space to four lines up or down
Thirds	line to adjacent line up or down; space to adjacent space up or down
Fifths	line to two lines up or down; space to two spaces up or down
Sevenths	line to three lines up or down; space to three spaces up or down

PROBLEM

Indicate below the staves in Example 55 the appropriate interval designation, using a numerical indication (1 = prime, 2 = second, 3 = third, etc.).

Ex. 55.

(a)

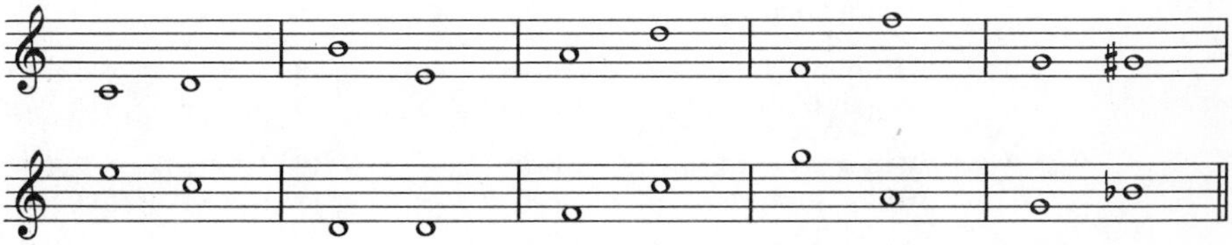

(b)

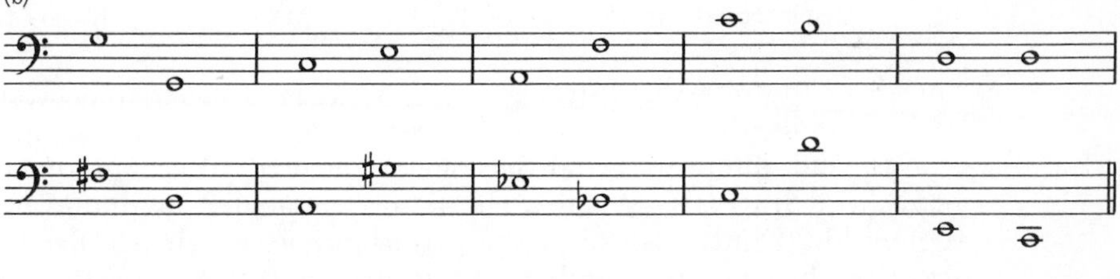

The above system has not taken into account the different sizes of some intervals—for example, the last interval in each part of Example 55. Note that they are both thirds; yet upon closer inspection we see that the interval g^1–$b^1\flat$ is not the same size as the interval C–E, in terms of half and whole steps. That is, g^1–$b^1\flat$ spans three half steps (or a whole step plus a half step), but C–E encompasses four half steps (or two whole steps).

To differentiate these intervallic differences, we add a set of terms that more specifically describe the interval. In the case of the two thirds just cited, the first is called a *minor third* (m3), and the second, a *major third* (M3). More precisely, the first is an interval of a m3 upward, and the second, a M3 downward. A table of frequent intervals with the appropriate descriptive term is presented below. Note that major and minor are used to describe seconds, thirds, sixths, and sevenths, major intervals being larger than their minor equivalents. Augmented and diminished describe the various sizes of primes, fourths, fifths, and eighths; they designate intervals respectively larger or smaller than their perfect equivalents.

Number	*Name*	*Example*	*Half Steps*	*Whole Steps*	*Abbreviation*
1	Perfect prime (unison)	*c–c*	0	0	P1
	Augmented prime	*c–c♯*	1 chromatic	0	A1 or +1
	Diminished prime	*c–c♭*	1 chromatic	0	D1 or °1
2	Minor second	*c–d♭*	1 diatonic	½	m2
	Major second	*c–d*	2	1	M2
3	Minor third	*c–e♭*	3	1½	m3
	Major third	*c–e*	4	2	M3
4	Perfect fourth	*c–f*	5	2½	P4
	Augmented fourth	*c–f♯*	6	3	A4 or +4
5	Diminished fifth	*c–g♭*	6	3	D5 or °5
	Perfect fifth	*c–g*	7	3½	P5
	Augmented fifth	*c–g♯*	8	4	A5 or +5
6	Minor sixth	*c–a♭*	8	4	m6
	Major sixth	*c–a*	9	4½	M6
7	Minor seventh	*c–b♭*	10	5	m7
	Major seventh	*c–b*	11	5½	M7
8	Perfect octave	*c–c*	12	6	P8
	Diminished octave	*c–c♭*	11	5½	D8 or °8
	Augmented octave	*c–c♯*	13	6½	A8 or +8

Not all of the intervals listed are used with the same frequency: major and minor seconds, thirds, sixths, and sevenths; perfect primes, fourths, fifths, and octaves; and diminished fourths and augmented fifths are the more commonly used intervals. Actually, the terms augmented or diminished may be applied to all intervals except the perfect prime, which is a fixed indivisible quantity; thus, one may find °6 (diminished sixth), +7 (augmented seventh), and the like.

The above set of designations is sufficient to describe most intervals, but the student should be prepared to apply the principles of designation outlined above in describing less common events. For example, the interval b♭–c♯ is a second (two different pitch names), yet the actual intervallic distance is larger than that of either a minor or major second, that is, an augmented second. The use of double sharps or double flats could further complicate matters, resulting in an interval of *b♭–c𝄪* (a doubly augmented second) or to be absurd, *b♭♭–c♯♯*, a triply augmented second. Composers generally avoid such remote relationships since they can be more simply indicated. For example the first interval can most readily be expressed as *b♭–d* (M3), and the second as *a–d* (P4).

It takes time to develop facility in the identification (both visual and aural) of intervals, and the student should work diligently until this is accomplished. The following exercises will suffice to begin the study, but similar ones should be devised and practiced until mastery is achieved.

PRIMES, SECONDS, THIRDS

PROBLEMS

1. Identify the intervals in Example 56, placing below them the appropriate abbreviations—M3, P1, etc.

Ex. 56.

(a)

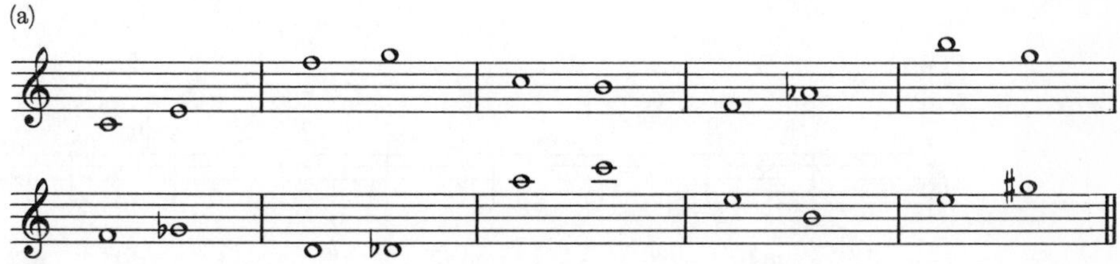

(b)

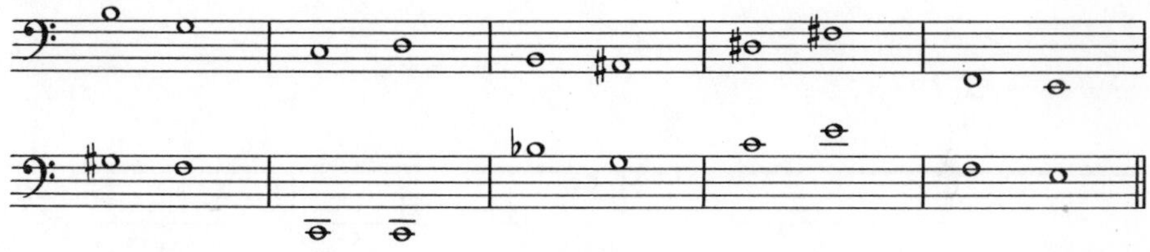

2. Following the procedure in Problem 1, identify the intervals in Example 57, placing the symbols below the staff but between the adjacent pitches of the melodies cited.

Ex. 57.

(a)

(b)

3. Cover Examples 56 and 57 as the melodies are performed slowly, and identify the intervals by ear.

(a) ___ ___ ___ ___ ___ ___ ___ ___ ___ ___

(b) ___ ___ ___ ___ ___ ___ ___ ___ ___ ___

(a) ___ ___ ___ ___ ___ ___ ___ ___ ___ ___

(b) ___ ___ ___ ___ ___ ___ ___ ___ ___ ___

4. Notate the intervals indicated:
(a) above the given pitch (see Ex. 58);

Ex. 58.

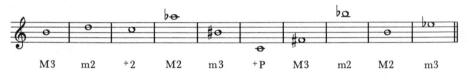

M3 m2 +2 M2 m3 +P M3 m2 M2 m3

(b) below the given pitch (see Ex. 59).

Ex. 59.

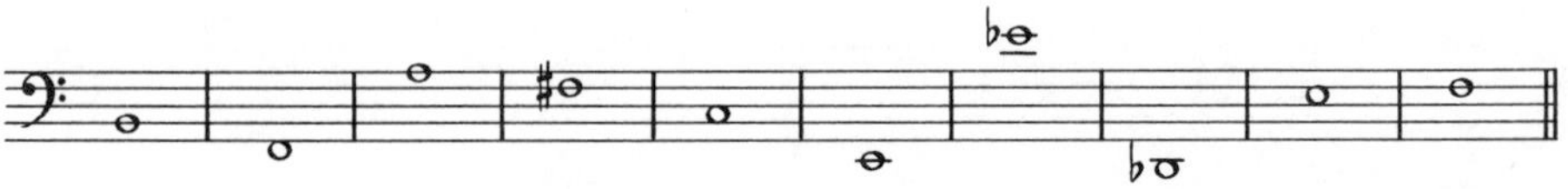

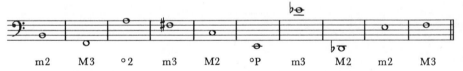

m2 M3 °2 m3 M2 °P m3 M2 m2 M3

5. Cover Examples 58 and 59 as they are performed, and identify the intervals by ear.

(a) ___ ___ ___ ___ ___ ___ ___ ___ ___ ___

(b) ___ ___ ___ ___ ___ ___ ___ ___ ___ ___

6. Find melodies for your own instrument (or voice) and analyze them as above. Generally, such melodies will necessarily be conjunct because of their limited intervallic content.

As our study of intervals progresses, we will consider other than *melodic intervals* (that is, intervals related horizontally) using the same nomenclature to describe vertical intervallic relationships called *harmonic intervals.* For the moment, however, let us consider various arrangements of seconds and thirds as melodic units or "pitch sets." Obviously, using the two types of seconds only as building blocks we may produce various pitch sets—of two, three, four, or more notes. But for now, and for the sake of simplicity, let us limit our study to sets of three pitches. By so doing, we see that there are three resulting patterns. (See Ex. 60.)

Ex. 60.

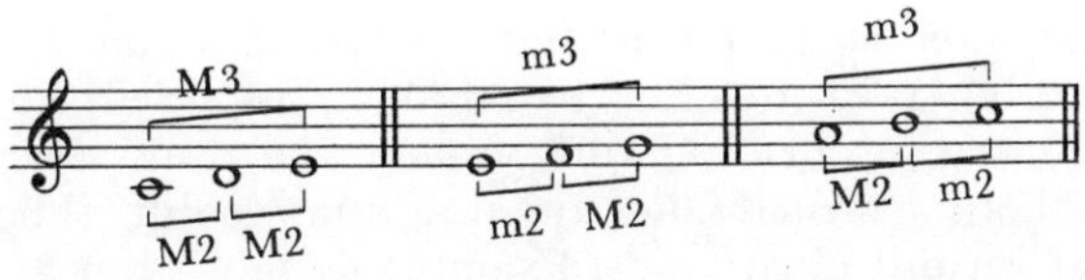

After performing them, note the intervallic structure of each. From this, we may generalize that a M3 encompasses two M2s; and that a m3 comprises a M2 and a m2, or a m2 and a M2. Further, such arrangements may be located at any pitch level and, of course, may move up or down, as illustrated in Example 61.

Ex. 61.

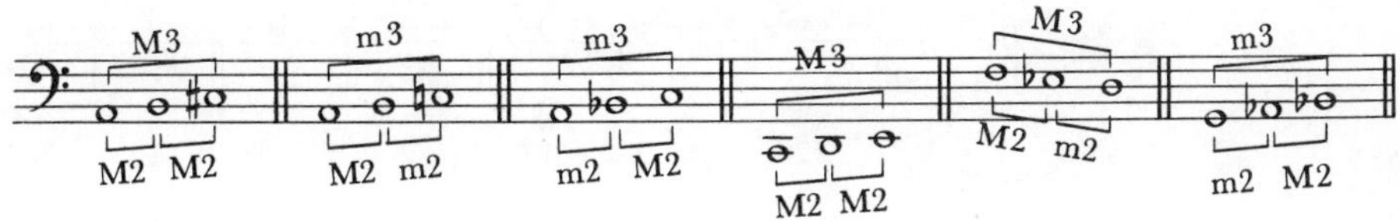

PROBLEMS

1. In Examples 62 and 63, cover the staff of each three-note pattern as it is played slowly. Listen carefully and indicate the size of the third encompassed in each, and of the constituent seconds.

Ex. 62.

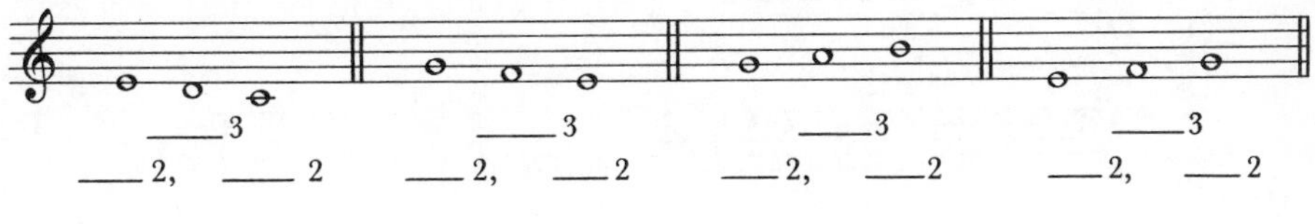

Ex. 63.

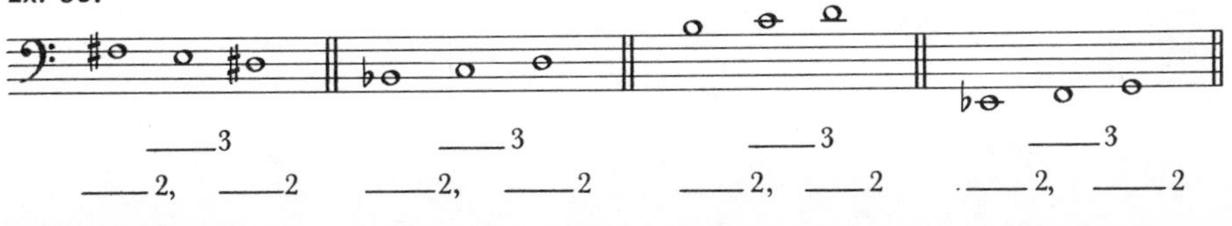

2. Construct similar exercises of your own and practice hearing them with the aid of a partner-performer. You will see that the simple building blocks of seconds and thirds constitute much of the tonal materials of more extended pitch sets and melodies of a large body of music, both simple and complex.

Space does not permit the addition of further drill materials at this juncture, so devise and practice other exercises that involve the performance and hearing of seconds and thirds until these intervals become readily familiar and recognizable.

We have said that intervals may exist both horizontally (melodically) and vertically (harmonically). With this fact in mind, let us briefly consider the latter in order to familiarize ourselves with seconds and thirds that are vertically related, from both a visual and an aural standpoint. Though such intervals can exist at various pitch levels, Example 64 shows but a few. Study them carefully as they are performed.

Ex. 64.

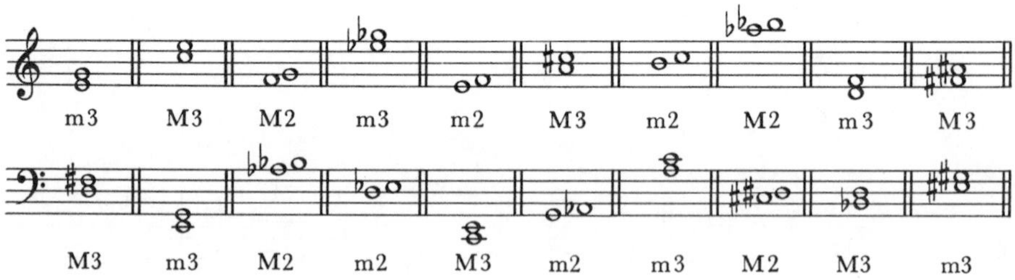

PROBLEMS

1. Cover the staff of Example 65 as the harmonic intervals are performed slowly, and designate the appropriate abbreviation of each below the staff.

Ex. 65.

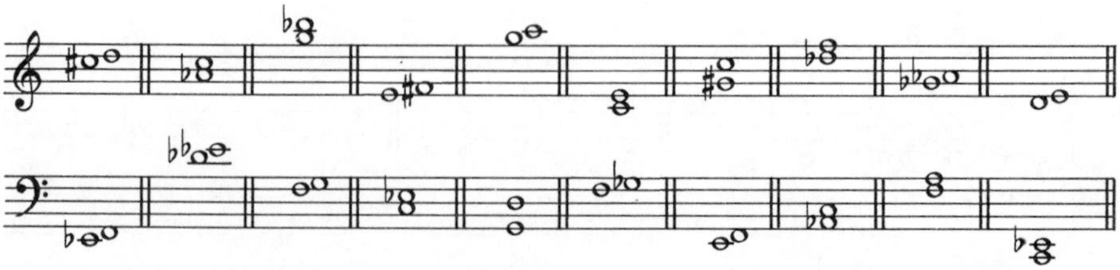

2. Complete the intervals in Example 66 above the note given.

Ex. 66.

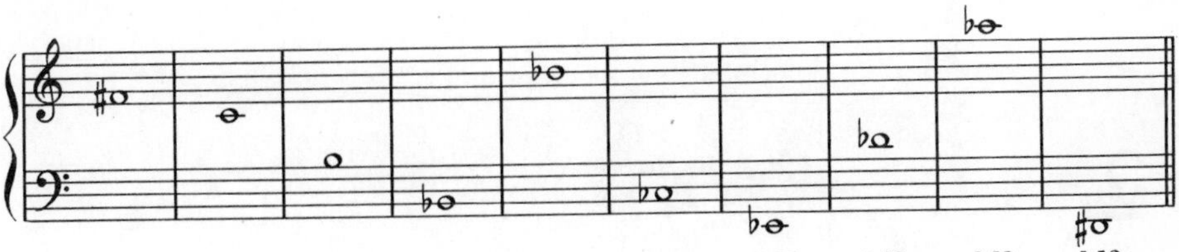

m2 m2 M3 M2 m3 m3 M3 M2 M2 M3

3. Complete the intervals in Example 67 below the note given.

Ex. 67.

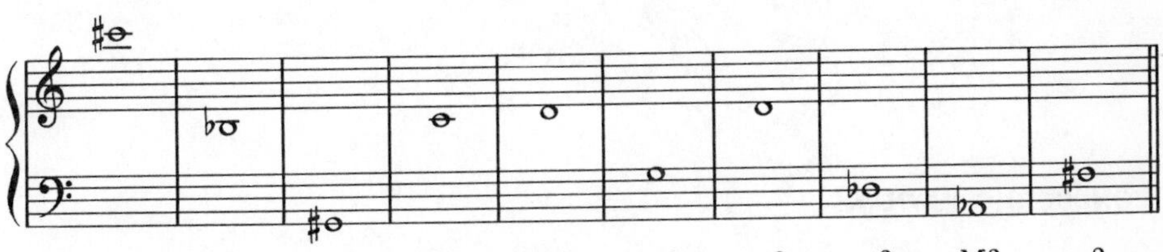

M3 M2 M2 M3 m3 m2 m3 m2 M3 m2

4. Cover both the staff and the interval designations in Examples 66 and 67 as they are performed, and identify each interval aurally. Then check your answers against the result of your visual analysis.

unit

2

MUSIC RUDIMENTS (continued)

CONDUCTING PATTERNS

Recalling our previous discussion of meter and meter signature, let us now further elaborate this concept, and consider additional symbols used in the notation of sound duration, and other related matters. First, it will be helpful to concentrate on certain conducting patterns commonly used to indicate various beat patterns of two, three, and four. Though we do not anticipate that practicing such patterns will lead you to a professional conducting career, they will help in the performance and perception of pulse pattern and rhythmic flow. As indicated earlier, the *downbeat* (derived from the downward motion of the conductor's hand) is the strong beat of a measure, the first beat compared to which the other beats of the measure are of somewhat lesser weight. (The *upbeat* must be as distinguishable as the downbeat, for it signals the close of one measure and prepares for the next to be indicated by the ensuing downward motion of the hand.) Each conductor, or student for that matter, evolves his own "style" of indicating pulse patterns, which can be better demonstrated than illustrated by visual representation. Nevertheless, the four drawings that follow are abstract representations of the patterns for two, three, and four beats, and they should be demonstrated by the instructor. Practice each of them over and over so that they become second nature; then you can concentrate on more urgent matters. The size of the pattern generally varies according to dynamics. That is, soft passages call for restrained beats, and loud passages, broader ones. For our purposes, let us assume that the downbeat should be aimed at a point about at the waistline, and the upbeat (that preceding the next downbeat), at about eye level. With this in mind, conduct a two-beat pattern at a moderate pace with the right arm, copying the general outline of the following diagram. Note that the downbeat "glances" off to the right and up slightly, thus clearly separating the movement of down ↓ and up ↺ :

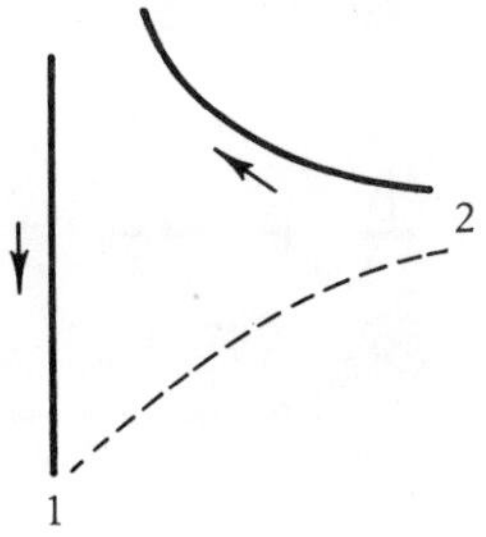

The "glance" is reversed when done by the left hand:

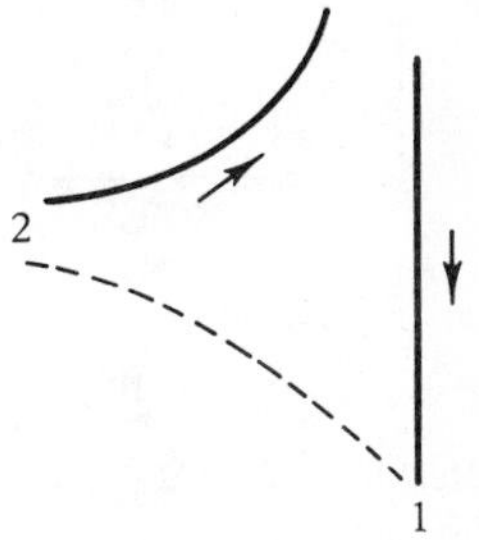

For our purposes, we will concentrate on conducting with the right hand. Now that you are familiar with the two-beat pattern, let us apply it to the performance of some patterns in duple meter. It is customary to begin a conducting pattern with a preparatory "beat," thus suggesting the tempo and permitting the performers an opportunity to prepare themselves for the execution. Therefore, begin conducting with a preparatory beat, which at the moment we will restrict to the upbeat.

PROBLEM

Conduct Example 1 while intoning the durations indicated. Note that metronomic markings are given to establish the beat rate or tempo. Let the teacher establish the tempo; or when practicing alone, use a metronome and concentrate on maintaining a constant pulse and, of course, accurate execution of the rhythms and conducting pattern as well.

Ex. 1.

♩.= 80 (80 notes per minute)

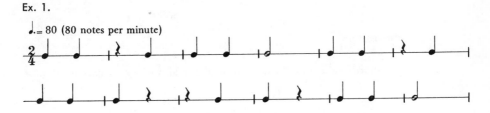

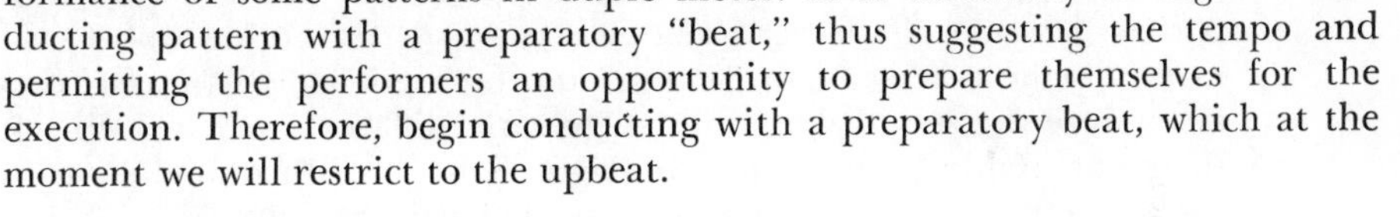

Ex. 1 continued.

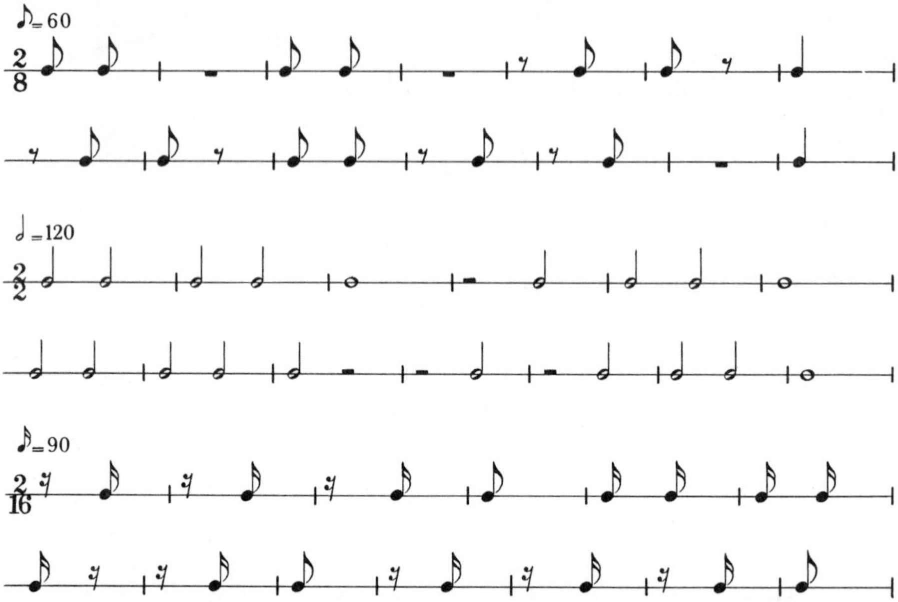

The three-beat pattern has certain similarities in shape to the two-beat pattern because of the vertical downbeat and converging upbeat. Therefore, care must be taken not to "glance" too far right at the impact of the downbeat, since the second beat must be clearly differentiated by being further to the right. (Only patterns for the right hand are illustrated hereafter; those for the left hand are "opposites," as shown in the drawing of the two-beat pattern immediately above.)

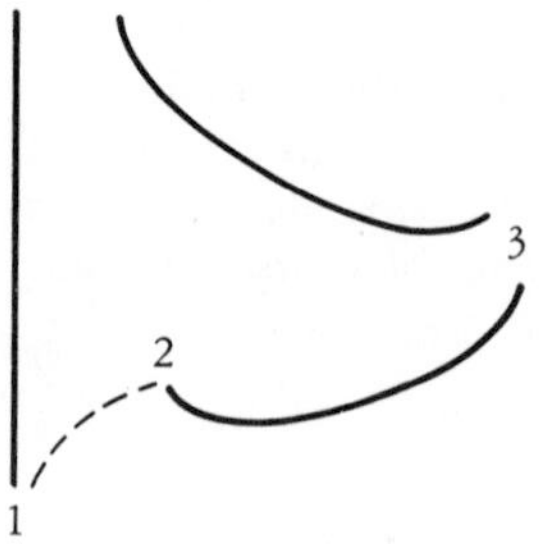

PROBLEMS

1. Practice the three-beat pattern above at various tempos until it is relatively easy to perform.

2. Then intone Example 2 while conducting as indicated.

Ex. 2.

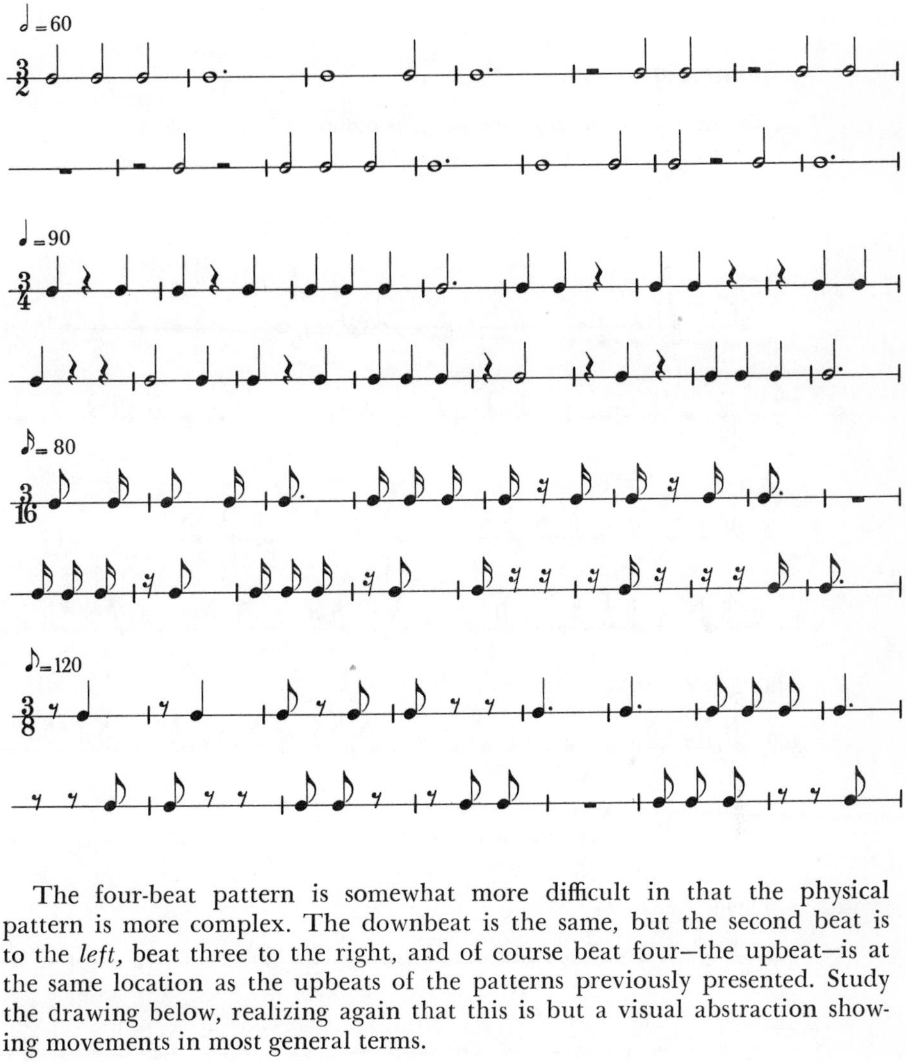

The four-beat pattern is somewhat more difficult in that the physical pattern is more complex. The downbeat is the same, but the second beat is to the *left,* beat three to the right, and of course beat four—the upbeat—is at the same location as the upbeats of the patterns previously presented. Study the drawing below, realizing again that this is but a visual abstraction showing movements in most general terms.

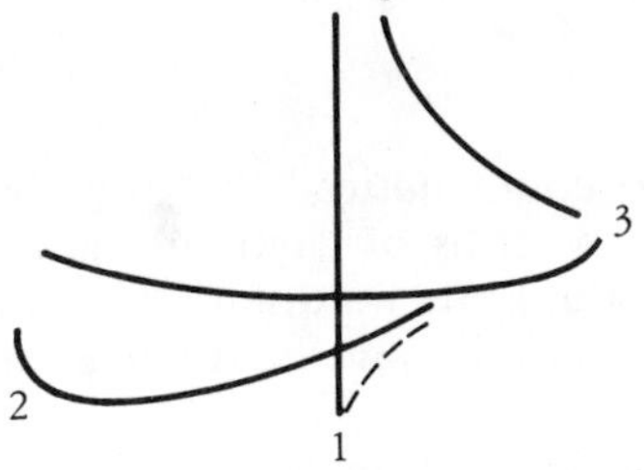

When this pattern is familiar enough to be executed in a consistent, steady manner, proceed to the following.

PROBLEM

Conduct while intoning the patterns indicated in Example 3.

Ex. 3.

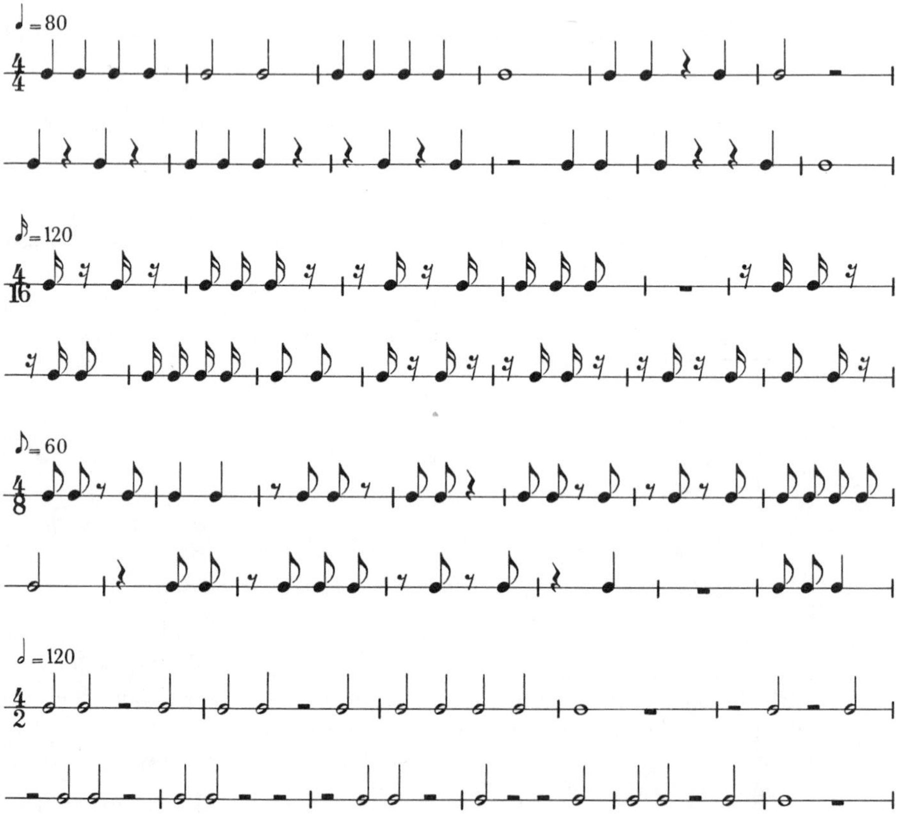

BEAT SUBDIVISIONS

You have no doubt noticed that the above problems have been relatively uncomplicated in terms of rhythmic notation. That is, there have been no subdivisions of the beat: no durational value less than that of the basic beat was used. Furthermore, no particular pitches were assigned the various durations.

Before going further, let us try some similar problems (durations only), subdividing the basic beat into patterns of two and four (the usual beat divisions of the so-called *simple meters*). Before doing so, however, let us consider a notational symbol that simplifies the perception of subdivision groupings: the *beam*. The beam is used in instrumental notation primarily to show clearly the groupings of notes within a basic beat. For example, rather than writing the following:  , we can beam the notes together in groups of two, thus clearly demarcating the two beats:  . Moreover, such beams may be used for groups of four sixteenth notes as follows:  or  , and for other note values as well, representing subdivisions of basic beats. It is general practice not to beam together notes beyond one beat or beyond one measure, though this occurs in some rhythmically complex music.

PROBLEM

Intone Example 4 while conducting the appropriate pattern at the tempo indicated.

Ex. 4.

TIES AND DOTS

Recall that dots are used to indicate an elongation of the duration to which they are appended. A *tie,* a curved line connecting two or more notes of the same pitch, may be used to achieve the same result. For instance, consider the pairs of notes in Example 5; they express identical durational values.

Ex. 5.

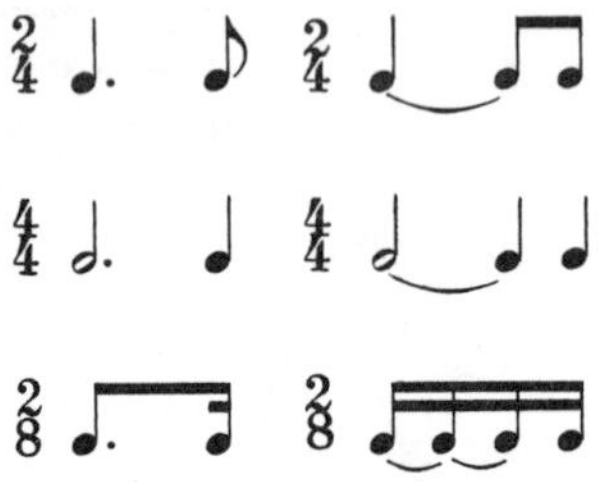

The same holds true for Example 6, the notes of which are in triple meter.

Ex. 6.

When to use a dot or a tie depends on a number of factors. Of primary importance is that the notation reveal the underlying metric scheme and beat subdivisions as simply and clearly as possible.

Ties are used in other ways—to indicate duration that extend past bar lines:  or  ; or for durations for which there are no visual single symbols:  . (Although the latter might be notated thus: 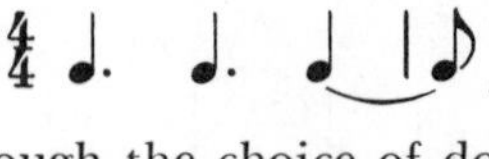, to do so would obscure the basic four-beat pattern). Though the choice of dots or ties is not bound by hard and fast rules that apply in all instances, the notation of musical sounds must always have as its ultimate goal the representation of sound events in as clear and concise a manner as possible. Study the music for your instrument and try to confirm for yourself these general notational structures. In your own notation, strive to show clearly the basic beat by beaming the subdivision thereof, and consider carefully your choice of dot or tie in view of the foregoing general principles. Avoid such unclear nota-

tion as  or , which confuse both the mind and the eye. These might have been written as follows:

 and 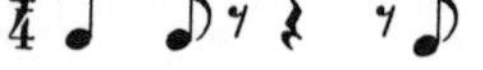; they would thus have clearly indicated the beat patterns (three and four) and the subdivisions thereof.

PROBLEM

Intone the rhythms in Example 7 while conducting.

Ex. 7.

SYNCOPATION

In performing Example 7 you may have observed that through the use of rests and/or ties, the basic patterns of strong-weak beats are temporarily obscured, that is, unreinforced. For instance, the downbeat of measure 3 in Example 7, line (a) is not accentuated because of the tie, and in measure 8 a rest occurs on the downbeat. Such contradiction of the "natural" beat accents is called *syncopation*. One other device used to produce this effect is the *dynamic accent,* an accent sign placed above or below the head of the note to indicate that the note should receive additional stress. (See Ex. 8.)

Ex. 8.

Syncopation may also be achieved within the notation itself by rearranging an established order of beat subdivisions. Note in Example 9 that beats 3 and 4 of measures 1 and 3; beats 1, 2, and 3 of measure 2; and beats 3 and 4 of the penultimate (next to last) measure are examples of *syncopes* (irregularly stressed patterns) that create the effect of syncopation.

Ex. 9.

PROBLEM

Intone Example 10 while conducting.

Ex. 10.

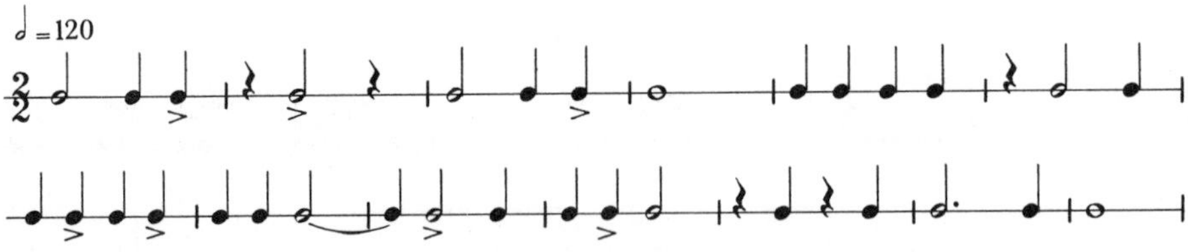

PITCH ACCENT

We have seen that emphasis on particular notes may be achieved by sounding these notes louder than others through the use of dynamic accents. A pitch may be emphasized (accented) not only by dynamic stress, but also by relative tonal placement or relatively longer duration. That is, the notes at the extremes of a pitch gamut have a particular prominence or accent (high being more prominent than low) because of their positions in relation to these notes between. This type of tonal emphasis is called *pitch accent.*

Pitches stressed because of their relative longer duration within a tonal context are said to have an *agogic accent.* (See Ex. 11.) These two terms are used less than *dynamic accent,* but they will prove useful in our subsequent determination of what we shall call for the moment *pitch focus.*

Ex. 11.

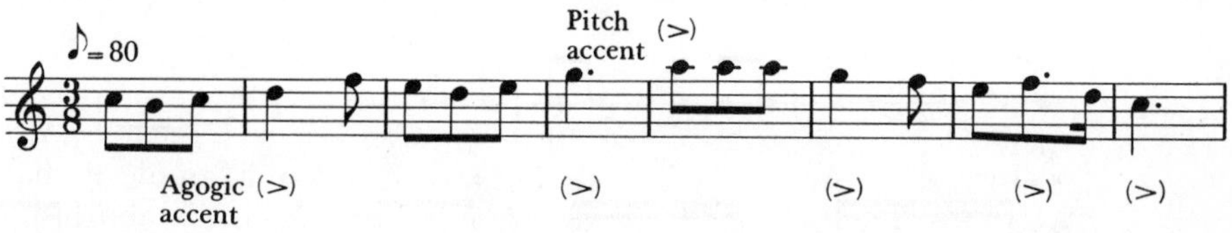

PROBLEMS

1. Conduct and intone the patterns in Example 12.

Ex. 12.

Ex. 12 continued.

2. Once you are able to perform the patterns of Example 12 listen to someone else intone each and notate it without referring to the score.

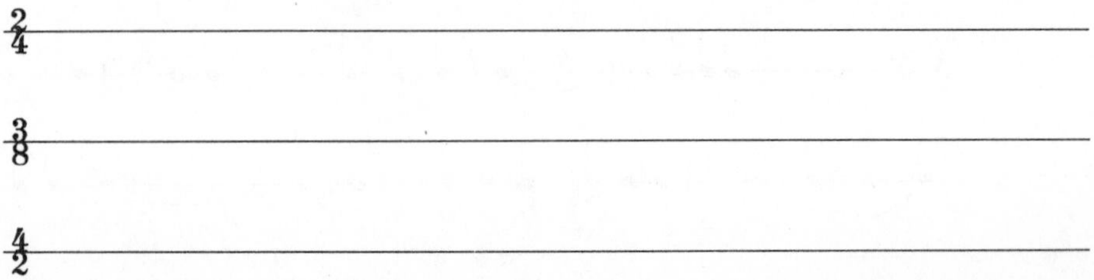

$\frac{3}{4}$ ____

$\frac{2}{8}$ ____

$\frac{3}{2}$ ____

$\frac{4}{8}$ ____

Check your results against the rhythms notated above, and repeat the patterns you were unable to perceive and notate correctly until you have mastered them.

3. Perform the following, given the beginning pitch of each.

Ex. 13a.

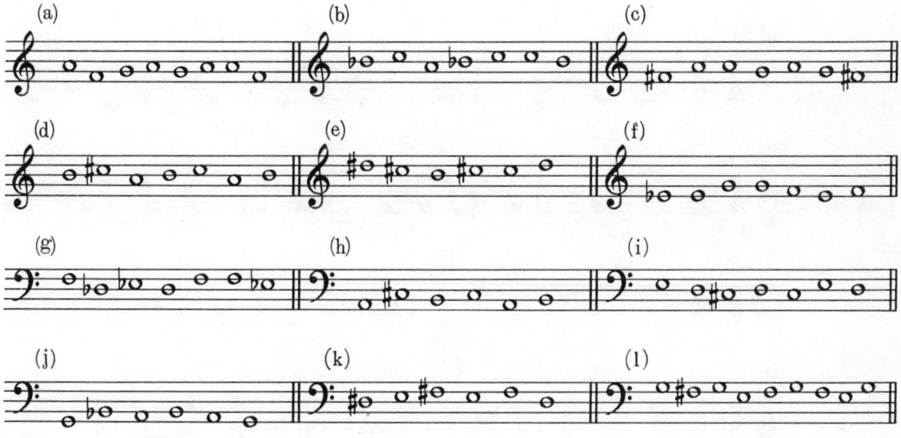

(Notate the above as they are performed.)

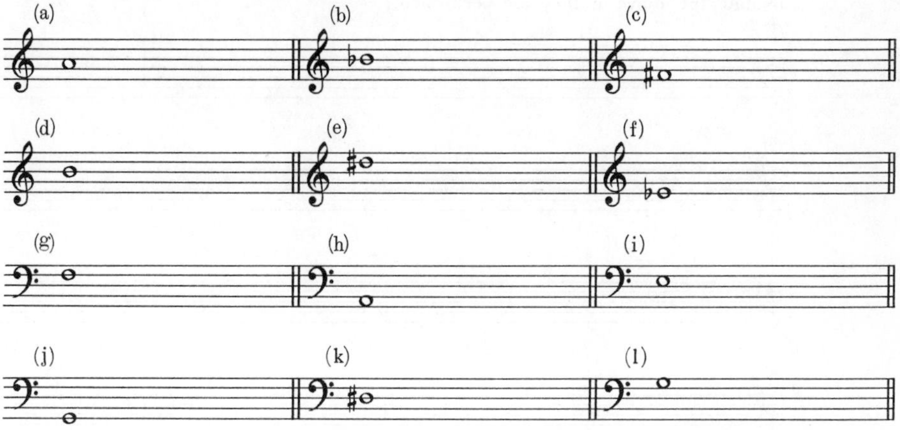

4. Cover the passages in Example 13a and notate each as it is performed.

5. Apply the procedures of Problems 3 and 4 to Example 13b.

Ex. 13b.

①

②

③

④

⑤

⑥

⑦
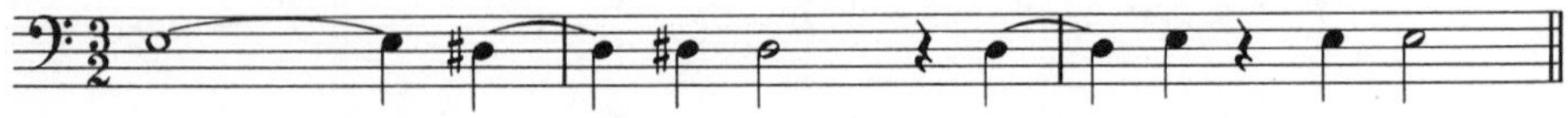

⑧

(Notate the above as they are performed.)

①
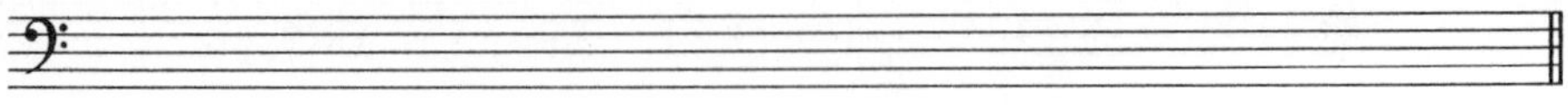

②
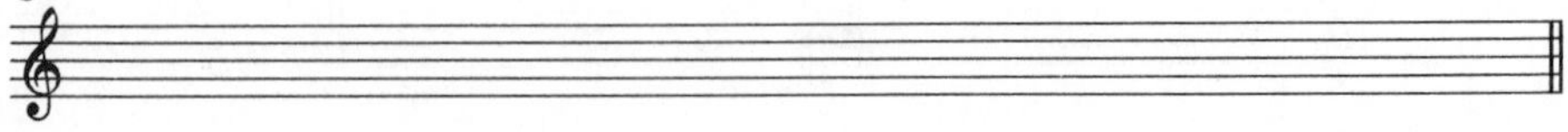

③
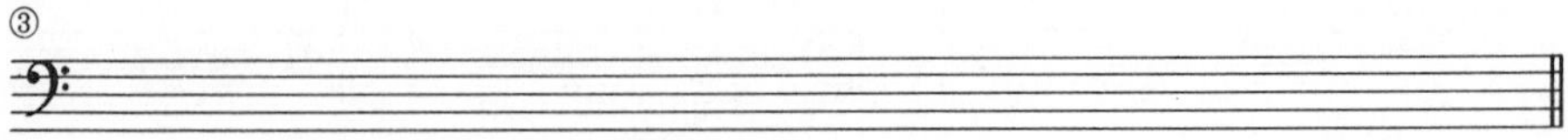

④
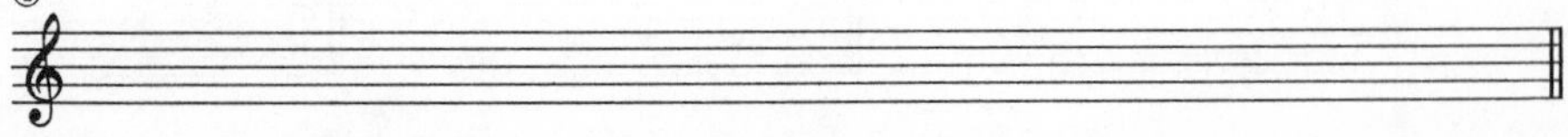

⑤

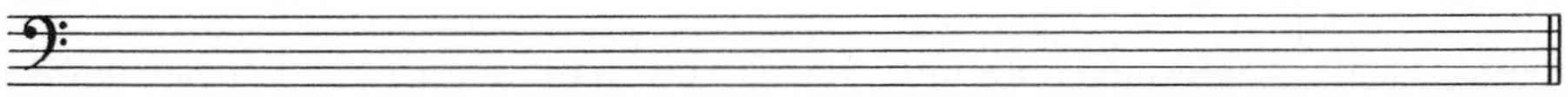

⑥

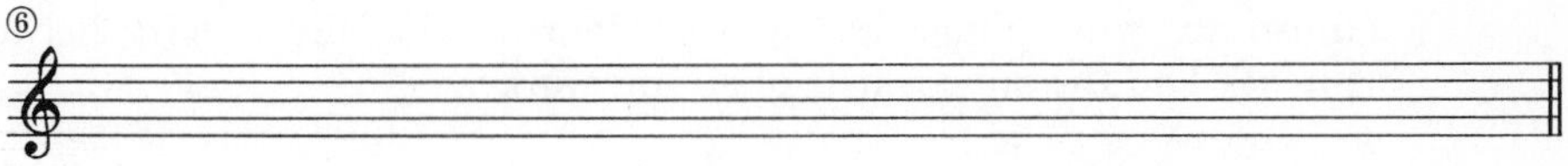

⑦

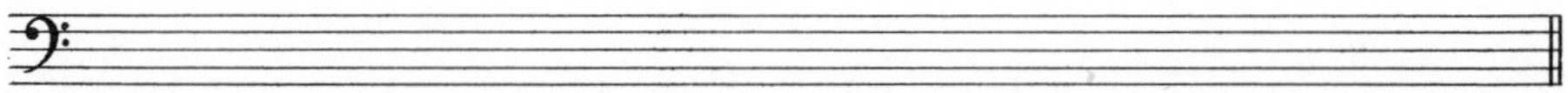

⑧

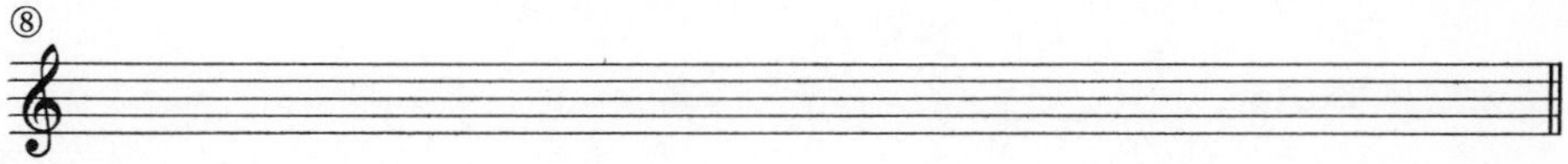

6. Invent patterns similar to those above and perform them. Then, have someone else perform each, after which you sing it back and notate it. (Repeat such drills until you have mastered seconds and thirds combined with the rhythmic vocabulary developed thus far.)

FOURTHS AND FIFTHS

Let us now extend our pitch series to include fourths and fifths, make certain observations about them, and place them in various contexts in order to learn to perform and hear them. Recall that there are two general types of fourths—perfect and augmented—and three types of fifths—perfect, augmented, and diminished. We will concern ourselves first with the perfect intervals and then proceed to the others. As mentioned earlier, fourths appear either as line-to-space or space-to-line relationships, and fifths, space-to-space or line-to-line. Though the visual recognition of fifths or fourths is relatively easy, it is somewhat more difficult to determine the particular type—perfect, augmented, or diminished. This results from the aforementioned failure of our notational system to visually differentiate between whole steps and half steps. To clarify this point, consider Example 14 and note that all intervals except those involving the pitch *b* are perfect. That is, f^1–b^1 is an augmented fourth, and b–f a diminished fifth.

Ex. 14.

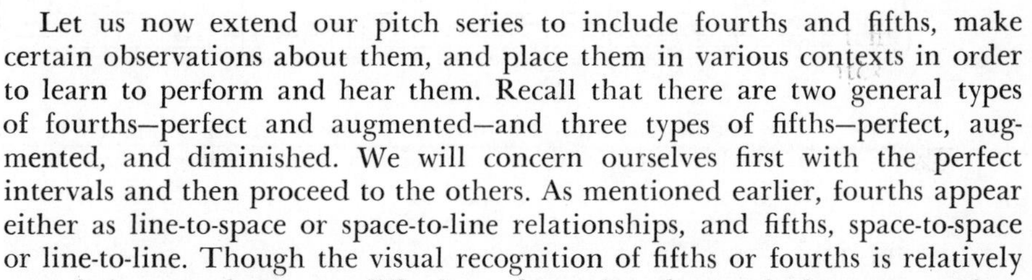

To alter an A4 to a P4 requires either that the upper note be lowered a half step or that the lower note raised the same interval. The reverse applies to the d5: the upper note must be raised a half step or the bottom one lowered the same degree. Though we have used the "white notes" of the c-octave to illustrate, you should realize that fourths and fifths exist between other pitches, and the same is true of all intervals.

PROBLEMS

1. Identify the intervals in Example 15, using abbreviations below the staff.

Ex. 15a.

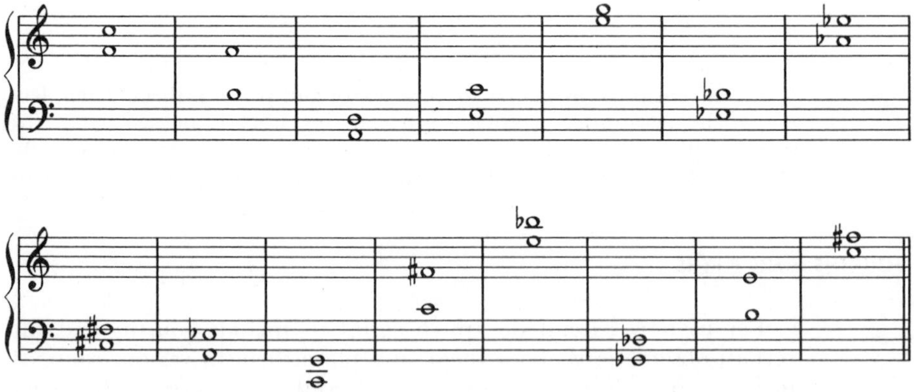

The augmented fifth (A5) does not appear in this example, but is prevalent in much music. Consider it as being a half step larger than the P5. (See Ex. 15b.)

Ex. 15b.

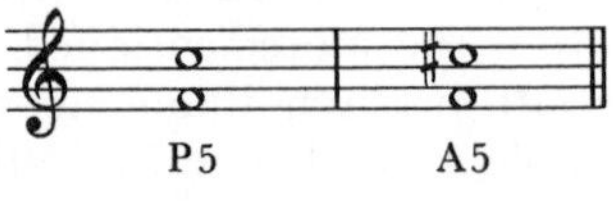

2. Follow the same procedure in Example 15c, and look for the augmented fifth as well as other intervals thus far introduced.

Ex. 15c.

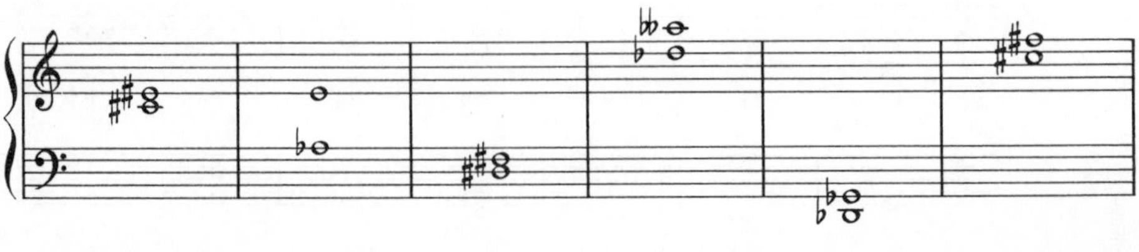

OVERTONE SERIES

Now that we have developed our interval vocabulary to this point, let us briefly consider a natural phenomenon basic to musical tone production resulting from the vibration of an elastic body, air column, or string. As mentioned earlier, most musical tones are not pure tones consisting of a single pitch but, rather, complex tones containing a large number of simultaneously sounding pitches. The pitch one hears predominantly is called the *fundamental,* and the softer ones sounding "above," *overtones, partials,* or *harmonics.* These pitches are related to one another in a set order called a *harmonic series* or an *overtone series.* Before visually illustrating this phenomenon, test it aurally with a simple experiment. With your right hand, silently depress the piano keys representing the pitches c^1, e^1, and g^1, and hold them while vigorously striking C with the left hand and immediately releasing it. You will hear the pitches c^1, e^1, and g^1 (and others) softly sounding above. Were you to experiment further under more scientific conditions, you would determine a harmonic or overtone series within a four-octave range above the fundamental note (sometimes called *first partial*) C, which is shown in Example 16.

Ex. 16.

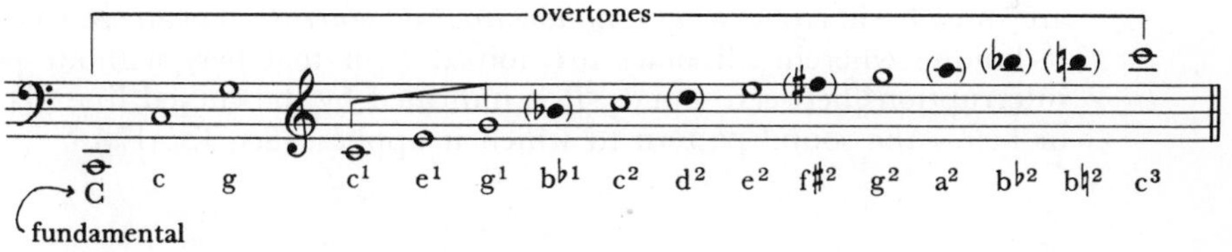

In simple terms, the complex of tones contained in the overtone series results from the vibration of the elastic body both as a whole, and in parts. The whole produces the fundamental, and the proportionate parts, which vibrate faster, produce the higher, less prominent pitches.

Let us digress momentarily to observe that pitches indicated by the black notes in Example 15 are not exactly "in tune" with the piano (or other instruments currently used), which is tuned according to a *tempered* system in which the octave is divided into twelve equal semi-tones. That is, such instruments are tuned in *equal temperament.* The subject of temperament is a complex, extensive one that we can only touch upon here. Later study will reveal that all pitches within the octave are acoustically "out of tune" in terms of natural or pure tones—except the octave itself—but through the introduction of the "pitch adjustments" of the equal temperament system, which our ears now accept, the composer was free to move from one gamut of pitches to another without creating tonal relationships that are unacceptably "out of tune." (For further information regarding temperament, the student may wish to consult the *Harvard Dictionary of Music* or a similar source.)

In closing this discussion of the harmonic series, it is important to realize that harmonics play a predominant role in the determination of instrumental color or *timbre.* Acoustical studies have revealed that the sound peculiar to a particular instrument is determined to a large extent by the relative degrees of loudness and softness of the overtones it produces. For example, the flute produces an almost "pure" tone because of its general lack of high harmonics, while the nasality of the oboe, in contrast, results largely from the relative prominence of almost all harmonics. Timbre, too, is a fascinating subject which the student may wish to pursue further in various reference sources.

(As will become apparent, when *chords* are discussed, the pitches c^1, e^1, and g^1 in Example 16 above form an important harmonic structure called the *major triad,* whose prominence in the natural overtone series suggests to many that this "chord of nature" is the veritable basis of all music.)

ARTICULATION

To this point we have not concerned ourselves with the various ways in which sound durations may be performed or *articulated;* until now, we have proceeded as if all sounds are performed in the same manner. The character of a sound set can be subtly varied by means of articulation, of which there are three basic types: *legato, nonlegato,* and *staccato.* Legato is a performance technique wherein all notes are joined (run together) without perceptible interruptions between sounds; it is indicated by the curved line placed above or below the sound pattern to which it applies. (See Ex. 17.)

Ex. 17.

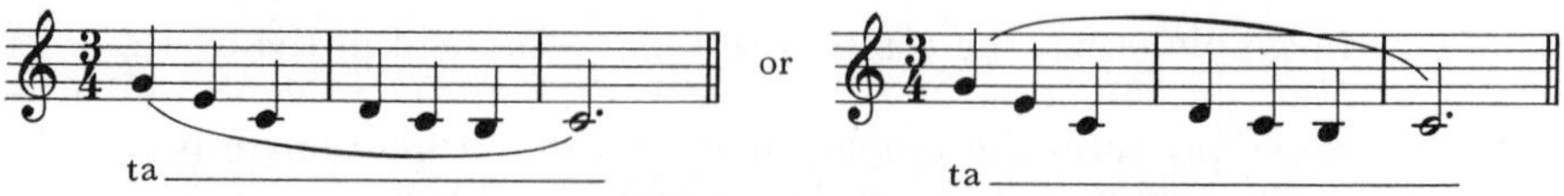

Nonlegato is indicated in one of two ways: with no added symbols (Ex. 18a) or—if the composer wishes to emphasize that there be no pause between articulation and that each note be slightly stressed—with the use of a portato sign (a short line) above or below the notehead (Ex. 18b).

Ex. 18a.

Ex. 18b.

Staccato represents the opposite extreme from legato. In this type of articulation the sounds are shortened by approximately one-half, thus leaving pauses between them; the symbol used to indicate staccato is a dot placed above or below the notehead (See Ex. 19).

Ex. 19.

(a)

(written)

(b)

(performed)

There are various other types of articulations, most of which represent variants of one of these three basic types.

TEMPO INDICATIONS

Earlier we mentioned the term tempo, which applies to frequency of beat per minute, and we have practiced problems having metronomic markings. Let us consider other tempo indications called *tempo marks,* which, though imprecise in nature, are widely used in the performance of music. This impreciseness has led to much argument among performers and conductors as to the *precise* tempo of a particular work, but until the invention of the metronome (ca. 1816), such terms and phrases sufficed to suggest the general wishes of the composer in this regard. In the broadest sense, there are three basic tempos—*slow, moderate,* and *fast*—and these may be modified one way or another by the addition of the modifiers *very, somewhat, more, less,* etc. The list is virtually endless, so let us concern ourselves for the moment with but a few of the more common ones. These are arranged in the following table in approximate order of slowest to fastest. (The Italian terms are most widely used, and should be given particular attention.)

English	*Italian*	*German*	*French*
very broad (slow)	larghissimo	sehr breit	très large
broad	largo	breit	large
slow	lento	langsam	lent
slow	adagio	getragen	lent
moderate	andante (walking)	gehend	allant
moderate	moderato	mässig	modéré
rather fast	allegretto	nicht zu schnell	pas trop vite
fast	allegro	schnell	vite
lively	vivace	lebhaft	vite
very fast	presto	eilig	rapide
very, very fast	prestissimo	sehr eilig	très rapide

PROBLEM

Indicate the appropriate Italian term for the following:

1. slow ______________
2. moderate ______________
3. broad ______________
4. fast ______________
5. very fast ______________
6. rather fast ______________

If you have performed much music, you have already noticed that there are many additional modifications of the above terms, as well as other words and phrases used to designate tempos. A knowledge of the above will suffice for our purposes, however.

Gradual changes from one tempo to another within a work may be effected by changing the metronomic indications; some of the most common words that serve this purpose are listed in the table below. Obviously, there are but two basic ways of gradually changing a tempo—by speeding it up or slowing it down. Also, there are only two ways such changes can be accomplished in terms of time-span: gradual or abrupt, with varying degrees in between.

Increase Tempo

English	*Italian*	*German*	*French*
accelerate	accelerando	schneller werden	accélefer
faster	più mosso	bewegter	plus animé
gradually faster	accelerando poco a poco	schneller werden allmählich	accelerer peu à peu

Decrease Tempo

English	*Italian*	*German*	*French*
retard (gradually)	ritardando	langsamer werden	ralentissant
retard (immediately)	rallentando	zurück halten	ralentir
less fast	ritenuto	zurückgehalten	retenu
	meno mosso	weniger bewegt	moins vite

When the performer is allowed to alter the tempo freely, the general terms used to describe this are *freely, rubato, frei,* and *liberé.* Again, there are many variants of the above terms and others as well. Some terms apply to both tempo and dynamics: for instance, *calando* indicates that both the tempo and the volume are to be decreased. One last term that should become a part of your vocabulary cancels out such tempo changes as may have occurred and signals the return to the original one.

English	*Italian*	*German*	*French*
original tempo	a tempo tempo primo	erstes Zeitmass	premier tempo

PROBLEMS

1. Indicate the appropriate Italian term for the following:

   (a) retard ____________________

   (b) less fast ____________________

   (c) accelerate (gradually) ____________________

   (d) faster ____________________

   (e) original tempo ____________________

   (f) freely ____________________

2. Perform (intone) each section of Example 20 on the syllable "ta," conducting the proper pattern at the same time.

Ex. 20.

(a) Moderato

(b) Lento

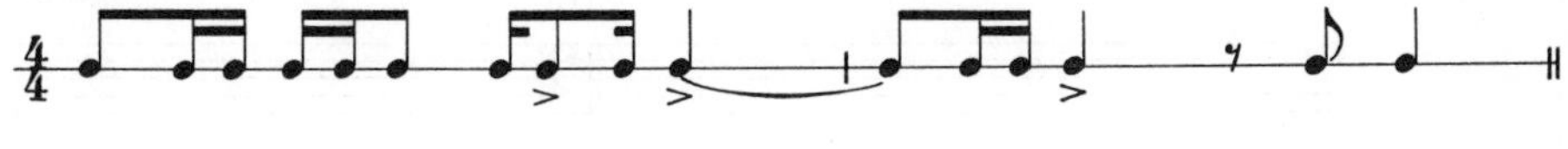

Ex. 20 continued.

(c) Allegro

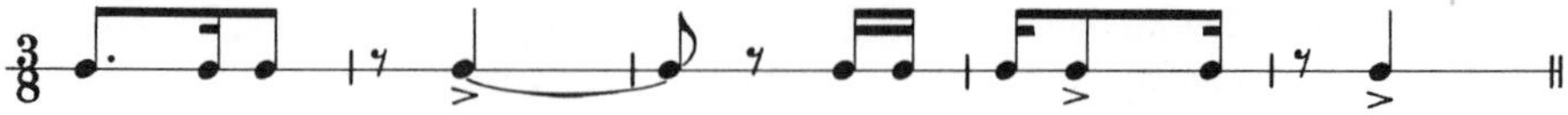

(d) Allegretto

(e) Largo

(f) Schnell

3. (a) Sound the first pitch of each of the pitch patterns in Example 21, and sing it through.

Ex. 21.

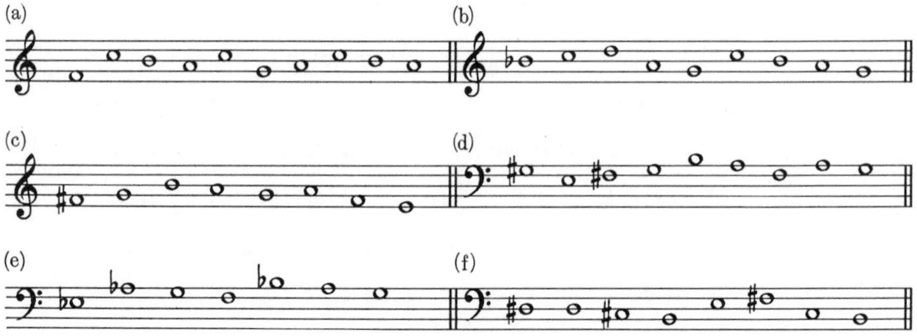

(b) Indicate beneath the staff the melodic intervals that occur.
(c) Cover the music in this example, and notate each passage as it is performed.

4. (a) Sing each of the passages in Example 22a after having sounded the first pitch.

Ex. 22a.

(1)

(2)

(3)

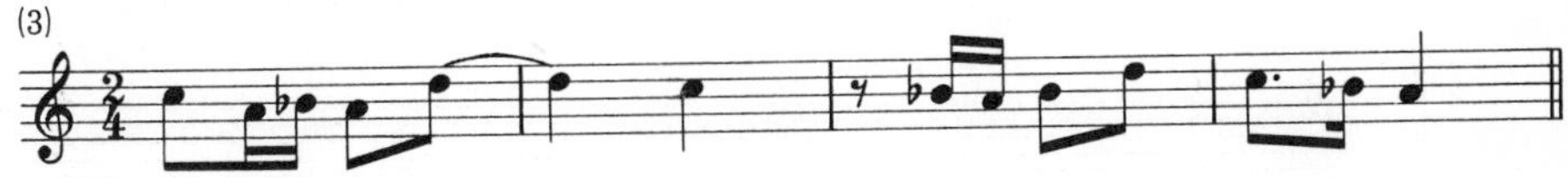

(4)

(5)

(6)

(7)

(Notate the above.)

(1)

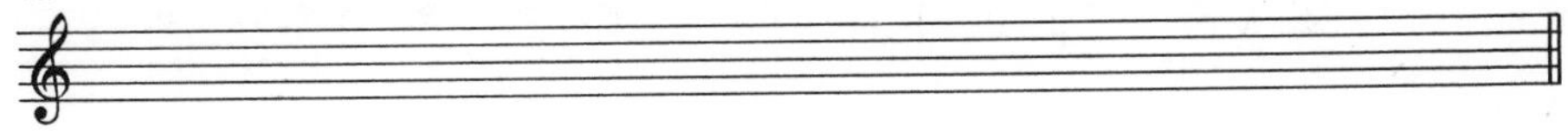

(2)

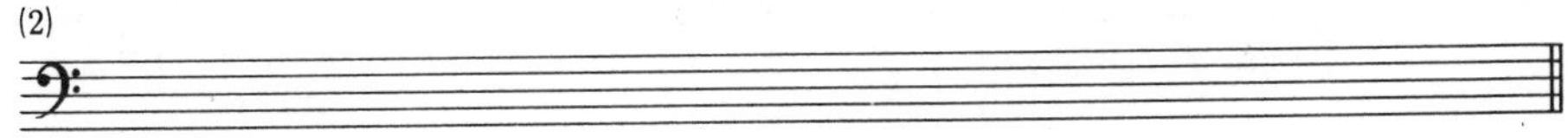

Ex. 22a continued.

(3)

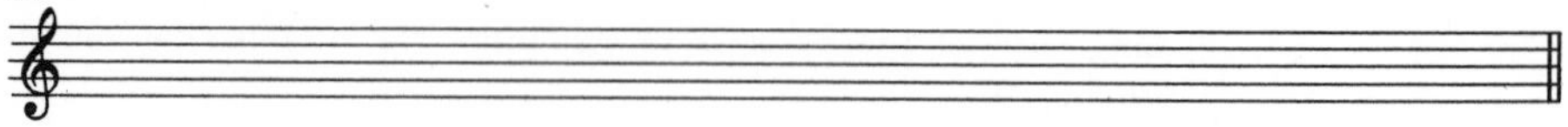

(4)

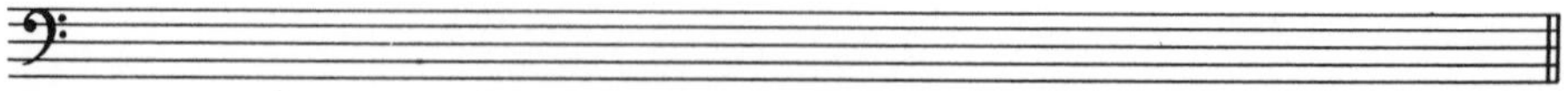

(5)

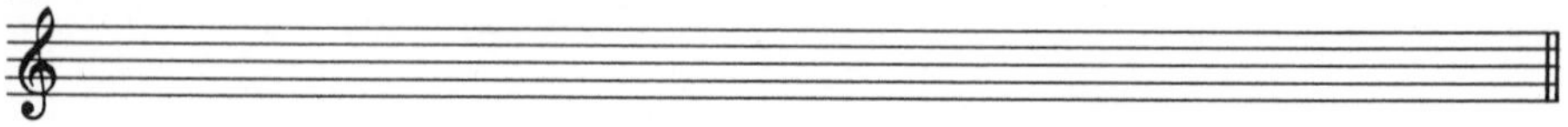

(6)

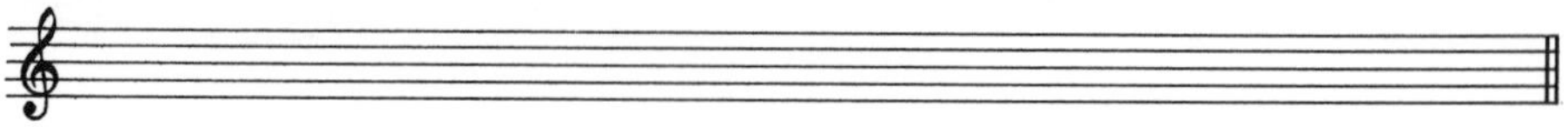

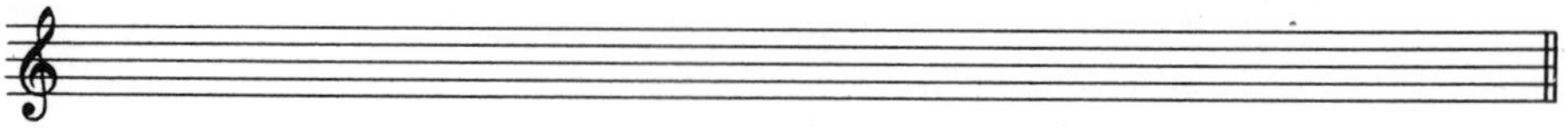

(7)

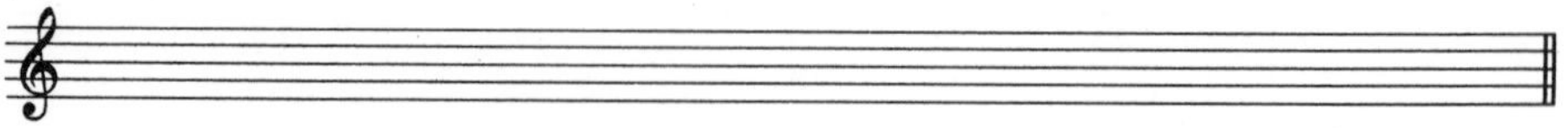

(b) Repeat the process while conducting.
(c) Cover the music, and after each pattern is repeated until it is well in mind, notate it (given the beginning pitch, clef, and meter signature). Check your results.

5. Follow the instructions given in problem 4, as you work with Example 22b.

Ex. 22b.

(1)

(2)

(3)

(4)

(5)

(6)

(7)

(8)

(Notate the above.)

(1)
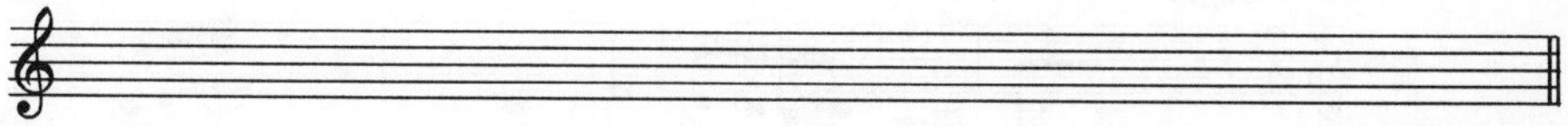

(2)
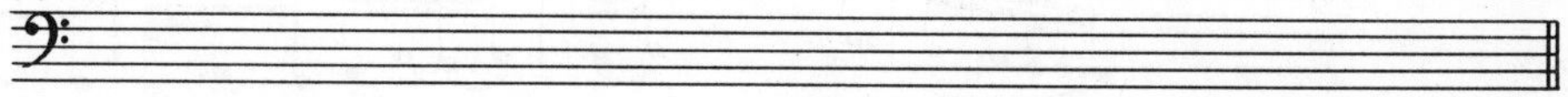

(3)
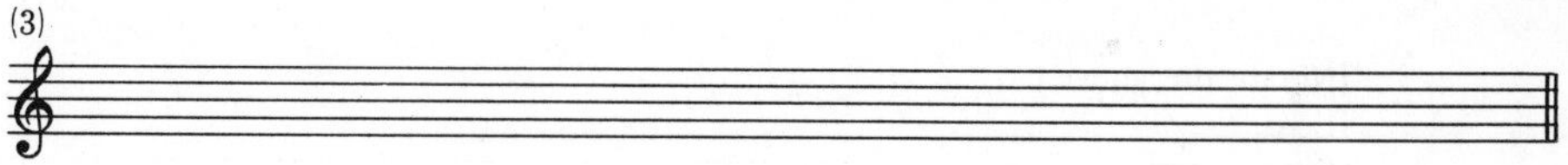

(4)
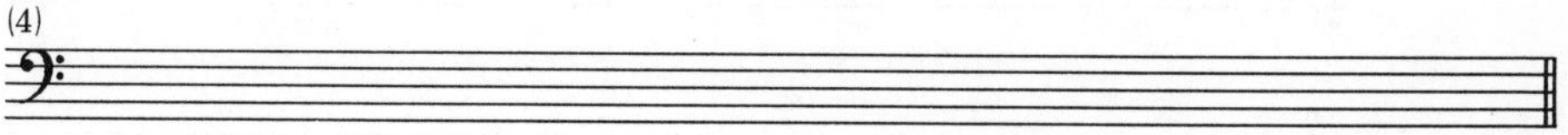

(5)
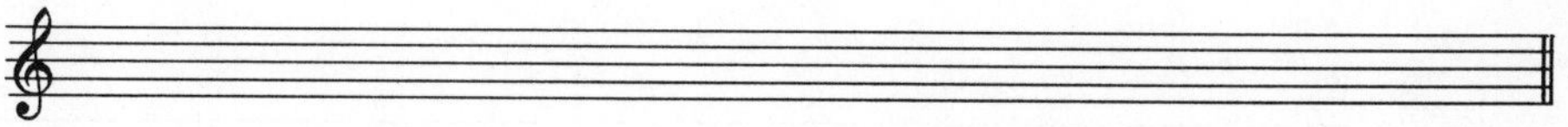

(6)
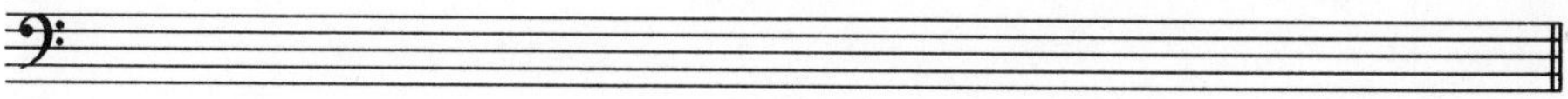

(7)
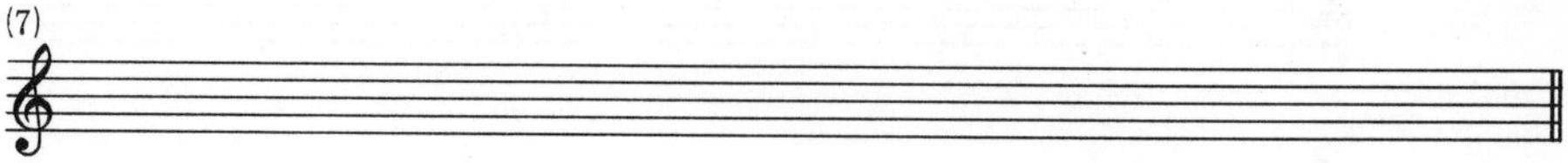

(8)
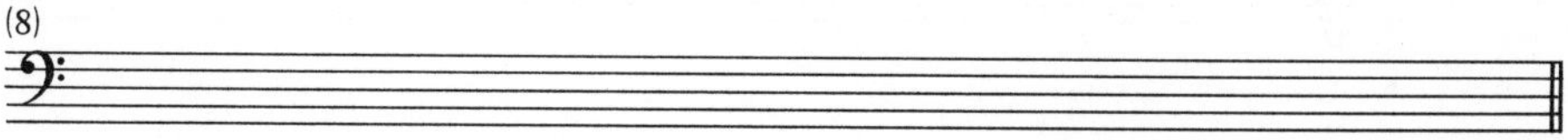

6. Do the same with the more extended melodies in Example 22c. However, when notating them, break each into four-measure segments.

Ex. 22c.

(1) **Allegro** Schumann

(2) **Andante** Beethoven

(3) **Adagio** Beethoven

(Notate the above.)

(1)

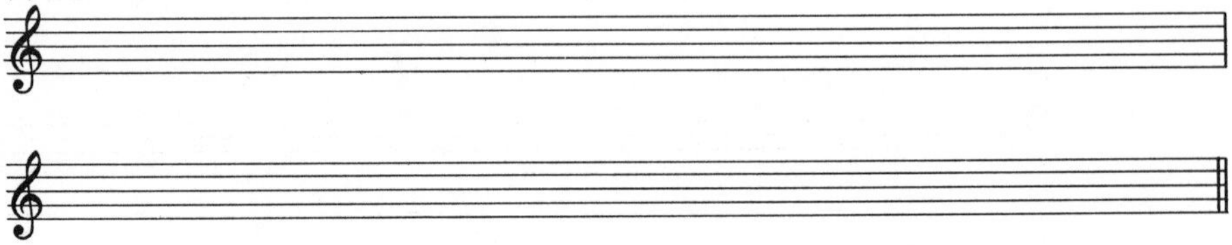

(2)

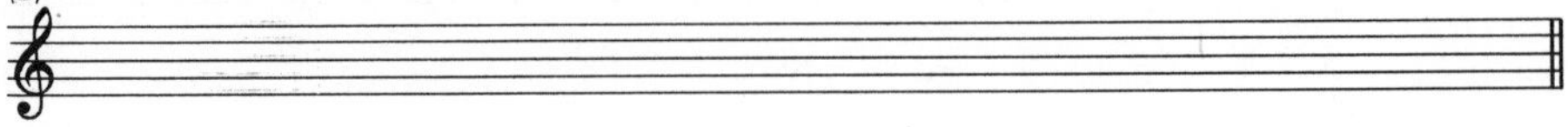

(3)

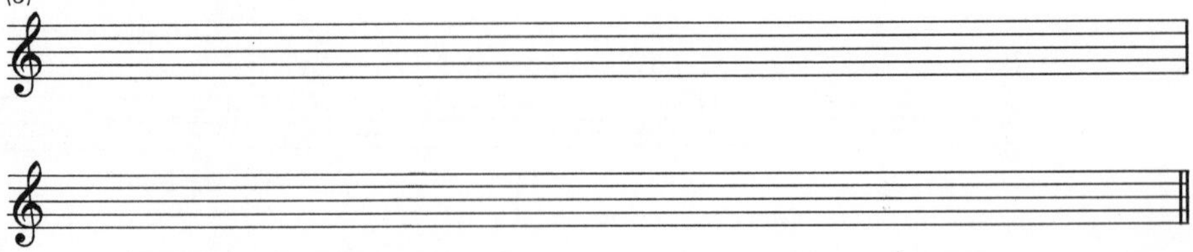

7. On the blank staves in Example 23, notate each of the patterns therein after hearing it three or four times. If it seems too long, break it into segments of five or six pitches and listen to each segment three or four times.

Ex. 23.

(1)

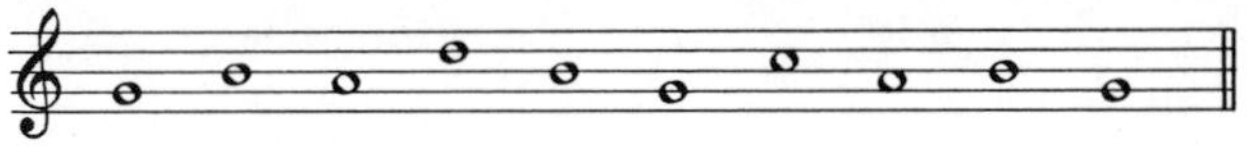

(2)

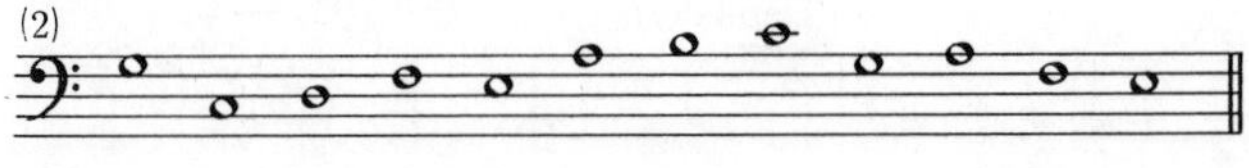

(3)

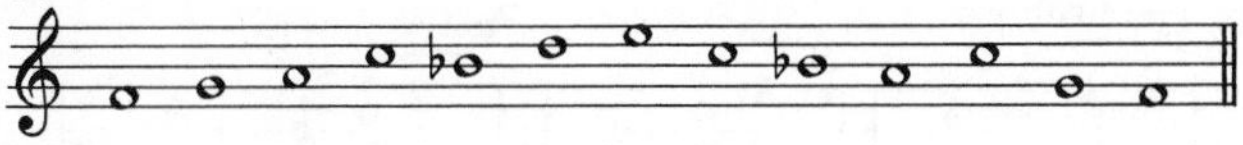

(Notate the above.)

(1)

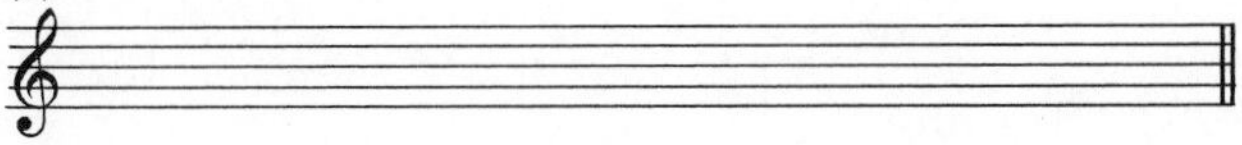

(2)

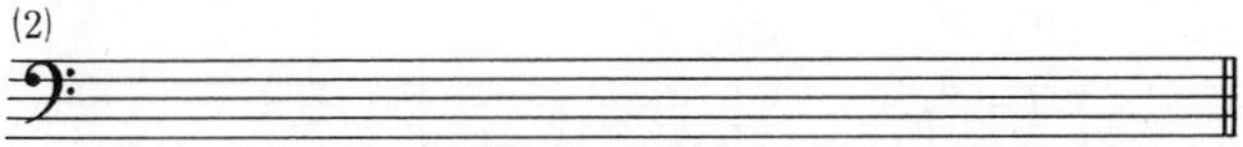

(3)

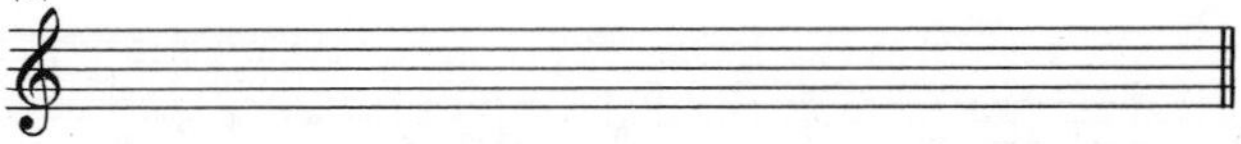

8. Name the intervals in Example 24 as they are performed.

Ex. 24.

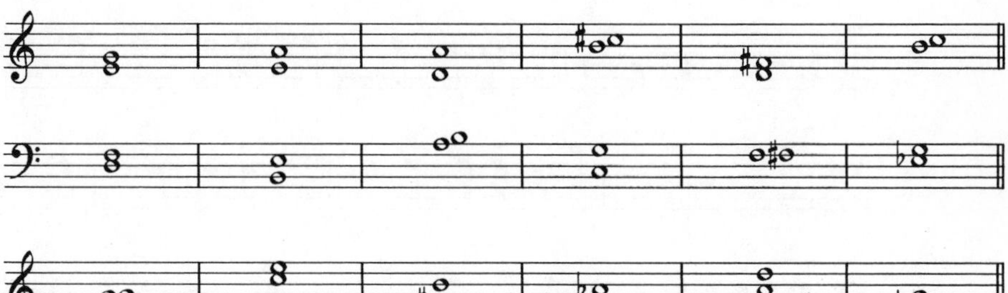

(You are encouraged to create exercises similar to problems 2–8 and to continue drilling until you have mastered the intervals and rhythm patterns presented up to this point.)

9. The tempo indications of the melody in Example 25 are given in English above the staff. Write the corresponding directions below the staff in Italian, German, and French. Sing this melody, and then play it on the piano.

Ex. 25.

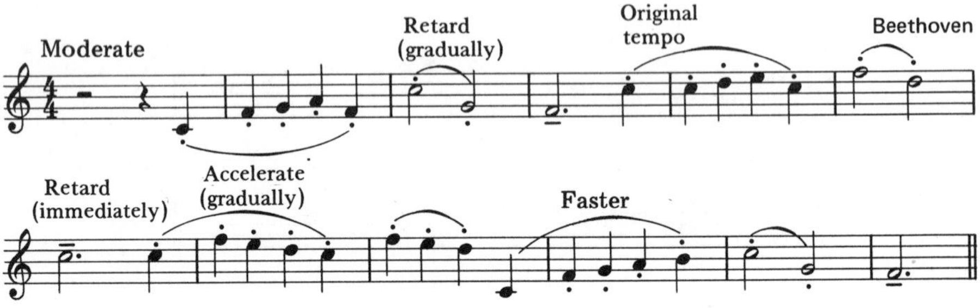

10. Determine the formal scheme (*aaba,* etc.) of the music in Example 26.

Ex. 26.

(a)

(b)

COMPOUND METER

We began our study of meter with an introduction of simple meter, that is, metric patterns in which the upper number of the attendant meter signature indicates beats per measure, and the lower, the unit beat. One may generalize that meter is the basic pattern of temporal units that measures the time frame of a piece of music. Customarily, two sets of terms are used in referring to meters: (1) *simple* and *compound,* and (2) *duple, triple,* or *quadruple.* The latter set of terms indicates beat grouping by measures—two, three, or four beats per bar—and the former, the division of the basic beat by either two or three (or multiples thereof). In other words, *simple duple meter* indicates two beats per measure with divisions of the beat by two, whereas *compound triple meter,* for example, denotes three beats per measure with beat divisions of three.

We have examined simple meters, so let us turn to compound meters, whose signatures, though similar in some respects to those of simple meters, are somewhat different in interpretation. The beat unit in compound meter is a dotted note having no equivalent whole number: 3/𝅗𝅥. = 3/? . This being the case, compound meter signatures differ from those of simple meters in that the upper numeral indicates the number of beat divisions in a measure, and the lower, the note value of the division unit rather than the number of beats and beat unit per measure. For example, the symbols cited above should read 3/𝅗𝅥. = 9/4 . The right hand signature indicates that there are nine quarter notes in the three-beat measure, patterned in three groups of three. Compound triple meter is exemplified by the commonly used meter signatures 9/4 , 9/8 , 9/16 . (See Ex. 27.)

Ex. 27.

(a) Fast Anon.

(b) Beethoven

(c) Lively Bach

From this point of departure, one may deduce that meter signatures having six as their upper number indicate duple compound meters (Ex. 28);

Ex. 28.

an upper number of twelve would indicate quadruple compound meter (Ex. 29).

Ex. 29.

One may generalize, then, about compound meters that the grouping of beat divisions is by three, and the note value of each division unit—whether thirty-two, sixteen, eight, four, or two—is indicated by the lower number. For further clarification, consider the following chart:

Ex. 30a.

= Two beats per measure; 𝅘𝅥𝅯. is the beat unit; three 𝅘𝅥𝅰 constitute one beat.

Ex. 30b.

= Three beats per measure; 𝅘𝅥𝅮. is the beat unit; three 𝅘𝅥𝅯 constitute one beat.

Ex. 30c.

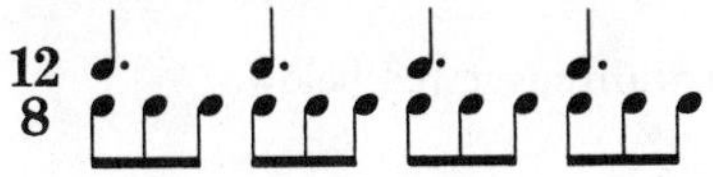

= Four beats per measure; 𝅘𝅥. is the beat unit; three 𝅘𝅥𝅮 constitute one beat.

Ex. 30d.

= Two beats per measure; 𝅗𝅥. is the beat unit; three 𝅘𝅥 constitute one beat.

Ex. 30e.

= Three beats per measure; 𝅝. is the beat unit; three 𝅗𝅥 constitute one beat.

Note also that the beat unit (dotted notes) is three times the duration of the subdivision unit (non-dotted notes).

PROBLEMS

1. As in the preceding chart, write out a measure of each compound meter indicated below, showing the beat unit and the basic subdivision thereof.

(a) $\frac{6}{2}$ (d) $\frac{12}{4}$

(b) $\frac{9}{32}$ (e) $\frac{6}{16}$

(c) $\frac{6}{8}$ (f) $\frac{9}{8}$

2. Affix the proper meter signature to each measure of Example 31a.

Ex. 31a.

(1) Beat unit and division given

(2) Beat unit given

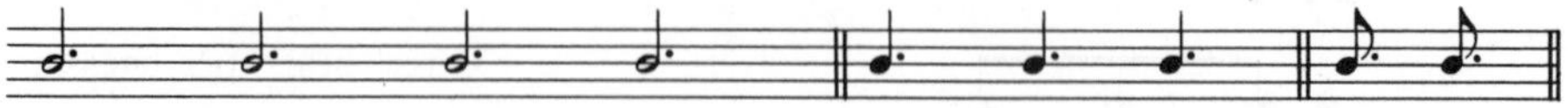

(3) Beat division given

3. Indicate the appropriate meter signature suggested below:

	Beats Per Measure	*Beat Unit*	*Signature*
(a)	3	𝅘𝅥𝅯.	
(b)	2	𝅝.	
(c)	4	𝅘𝅥.	
(d)	3	𝅘𝅥𝅮.	
(e)	2	𝅗𝅥.	

4. Conduct duple, triple and quadruple patterns at a moderate tempo while tapping three-beat subdivisions. When this can be done easily, continue to Problem 5.

5. Intone Example 31b with "ta" while conducting at a moderate tempo.

Ex. 31b.

(a)

(b)

(c)

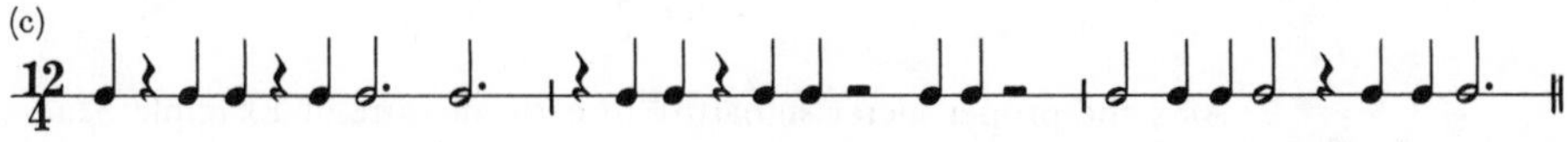

(d)

(e)

(f)

(g)

6. Once you have mastered the passages in Example 31b, listen to someone else perform them and write them down without referring to the score. Check your results against the rhythms notated, and repeat the patterns you missed until you have mastered them.

7. Perform Examples 32a and 32b given the first pitch of each passage.

Ex. 32a.

(1)

(2)

(3)

(4)

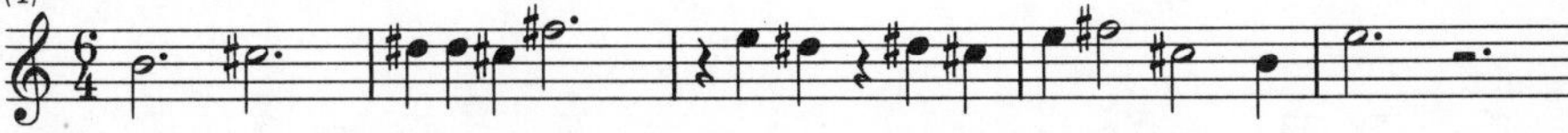

Ex. 32b.

(1)

(2)

(3)

Ex. 32b continued.

To this point we have avoided terms commonly used to designate musical patterns larger than motives, choosing to concentrate on more fundamental matters. However, now that our interval vocabulary is complete, let us consider certain basic terms that will appear hereafter. Refer to Example 32b (5) and note that rhythmic activity is punctuated by cessation of motion at two points, measures four and nine, such points being called *cadences.* The sound event from the beginning to cadence, or from cadence to cadence is called *phrase,* which in much music embraces four measures. Two phrases, generally, constitute a *period* which, in this instance, is asymmetrical since the first phrase consists of four measures and the second, of five, rather than an equal number of measures. Note that in this example the phrases are indicated by curved lines above the notes, called *phrase marks.*

SIXTHS, SEVENTHS, AND OCTAVES

Our interval vocabularly will be complete with the addition of sixths, sevenths, and octaves. Recall that sixths are generally of two types—major and minor—although diminished and augmented forms are sometimes found. Sixths and octaves are represented by line-to-space or space-to-line relations. (See Ex. 33.)

Ex. 33.

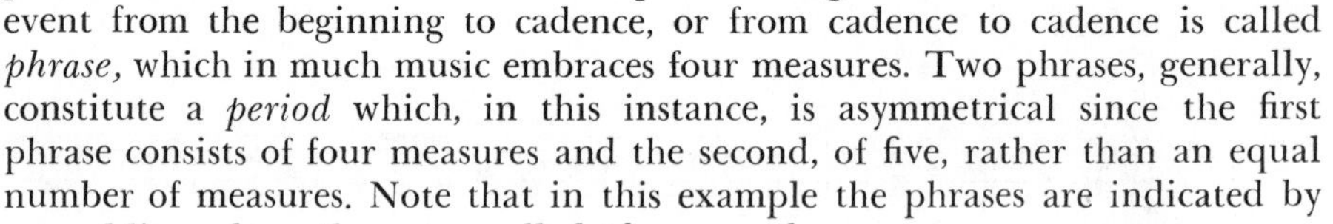

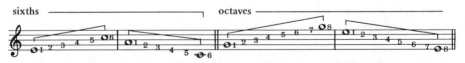

Sevenths comprise space-to-space or line-to-line relationships. (See Ex. 34.)

Ex. 34.

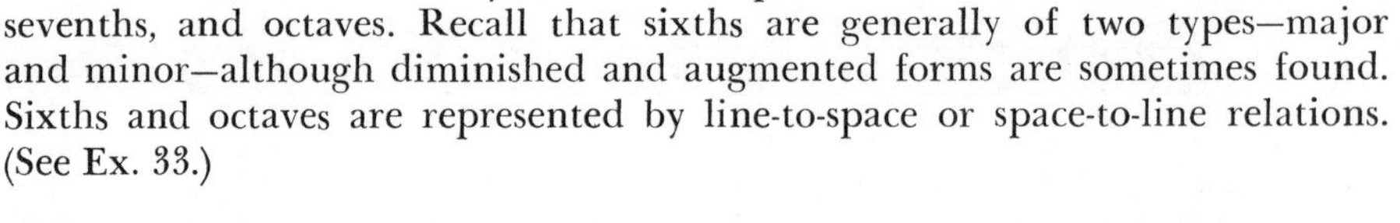

It may prove helpful to relate sixths to fifths and sevenths to octaves, at least initially, in learning to create and identify them. The interval of a minor sixth is a half step larger than a perfect fifth, and the major sixth, a whole step larger. (See Ex. 35.)

Ex. 35.

The interval of a major seventh is a half step smaller than a perfect octave, and the minor seventh, a whole step smaller. (See Ex. 36.)

Ex. 36.

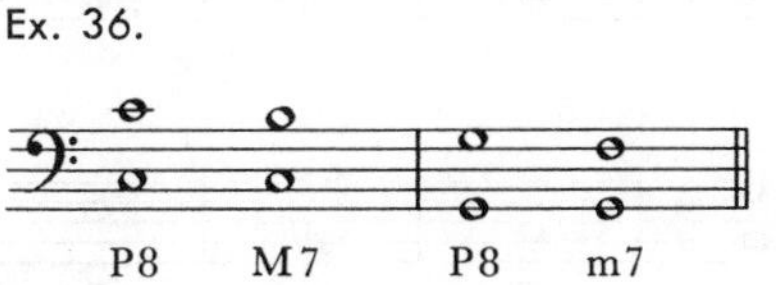

Sixths and sevenths vary between major and minor as a result of the presence of the half step introduced between patterns of whole steps. Observe the pitch gamut C–A, and note the resulting distribution of sixths (Ex. 37),

Ex. 37.

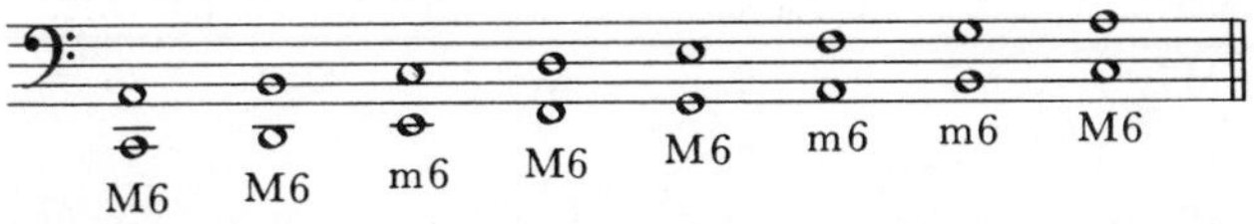

and of sevenths (Ex. 38).

Ex. 38.

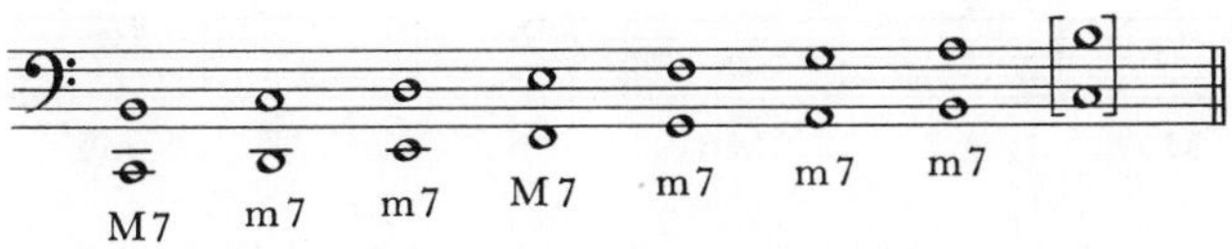

The octaves in a pitch series (say from c up to c^1), on the other hand, are all perfect.

For the sake of simplicity, diminished and augmented sixths, sevenths, and octaves may be considered derivatives of the basic set—major, minor, and perfect—for purposes of both construction and recognition. (See Ex. 39.)

Ex. 39.

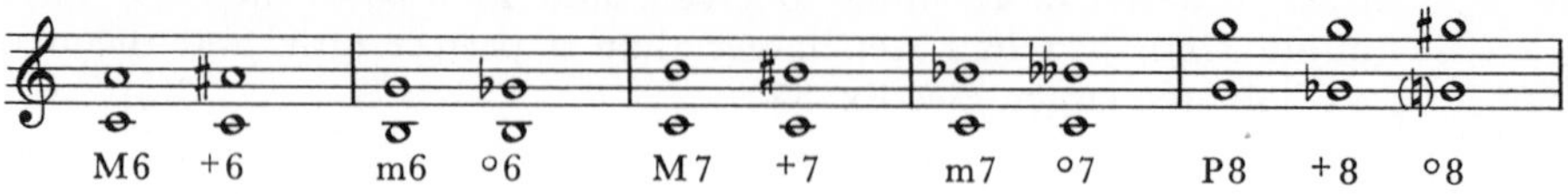

PROBLEMS

1. Designate below the staff the intervals in Example 40.

Ex. 40.

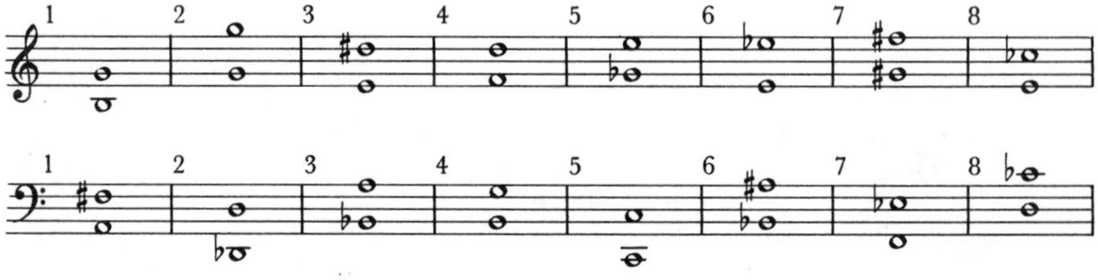

2. Complete the indicated intervals above the pitches given in Example 41.

Ex. 41.

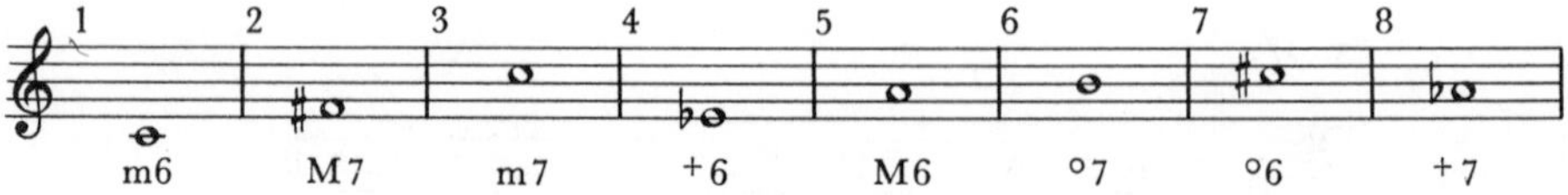

3. Complete the indicated intervals below the pitches given in Example 42.

Ex. 42.

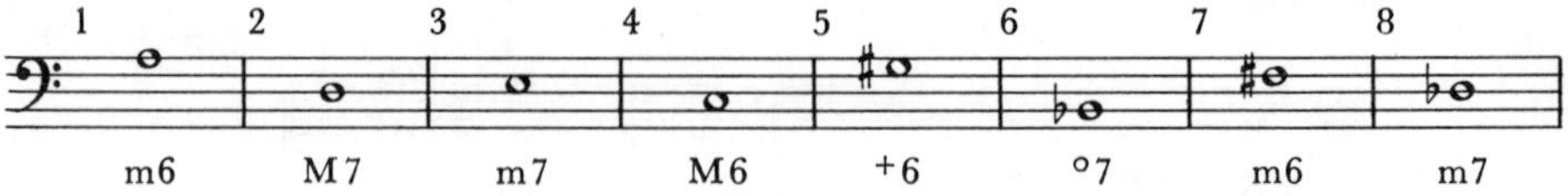

4. Cover a and b below as they are performed, and identify the intervals by ear.

	1	2	3	4	5	6	7	8
(a)	___	___	___	___	___	___	___	___
(b)	___	___	___	___	___	___	___	___

5. Seek out melodies for your own instrument (or voice), especially those having a number of major-minor sixths and sevenths and perfect octaves, and analyze them as in Problem 1.

OTHER TERMS

In addition to the many signs, markings, and terms that express dynamics, tempo, and articulation, there are others that indicate the general mood and character of a piece. Such terms are varied and numerous, and we suggest that you commit them to memory as you come across them in your studies. However, learning a few of these may prove beneficial at this time, and, hence, they are listed below for your convenience. Concentrate on the more widely used Italian terms, and keep in mind that many of these may be combined with tempo indications to express more precisely the particular spirit or mood to be evoked. For example, *andante cantabile*—flowingly in a singing style.

English	*Italian*	*German*	*French*
agitated	agitato	lebhaft bewegt	agité
animated	animato	belebt	animé
expressive	expressivo	ausdrucksvoll	espressiv
with fire	con fuoco	feurig	ardent
gracefully	grazioso	zierlich	gracieux
impassioned	appassionata	leidenschaftlich	passionńe
mysteriously	misterioso	geheimnisvoll	mysterieux
majestically	maestoso	feierlich	majestueux
with movement	con moto	bewegt	mouvementé
singing	cantabile	gesangvoll	chantant
with animation	con anima	munter	avec verve
sustained	sostenuto	getragen	soutenu
sweet	dolce	zart	doucement
vigorously	con brio	schwungvoll	avec force

FURTHER BEAT SUBDIVISIONS

Until now we have concerned ourselves with comparatively few divisions of the basic beat into two, three, or occasionally four parts. Let us now consider further subdivisions, beginning with four and progressing to six as we move from simple to compound meters, and let us spend some time learning to hear, perform, and notate patterns of such basic subdivisions.

The first division of the quarter note is into two eighths; and thereafter into four sixteenths, that is, two groups of two. While tapping the basic pulse, intone each of the eight-beat patterns in Example 43 until you have mastered it. For variety, conduct duple, triple, and quadruple meters at various tempi while practicing them. As you master them, improvise various sequences of the beat patterns—for example, 1, 3, 2, 7, 4, 7, 6, 5, 8, 1, etc.

Ex. 43.

Of course, Example 43 can be greatly varied by the use of rests. (See Ex. 44 and 45.)

Ex. 44.

Ex. 45.

Musical life would be so much simpler if rhythmic streams were made up of a series of such short patterns, or gestalts. One would only have to memorize them all and then call on them when needed. Unfortunately, the number of possible permutations is excessive, as Examples 44 and 45 may suggest, and it becomes even greater when ties are used. Therefore, though learning the basic patterns will prove very helpful, it will not solve all of your reading and hearing problems, for composers are seldom content to stick to "basics" for any length of time. Continuous practice in reading and aural identification is requisite to facility; there is no other substitute. Therefore, practice the beat patterns abstracted in Problems 1–3 below, and then proceed to the music for your instrument (or voice) to apply what you have learned.

PROBLEMS

1. Using Example 49 as a model, complete the eight basic patterns using the eighth note as the beat unit, and practice them the same way.

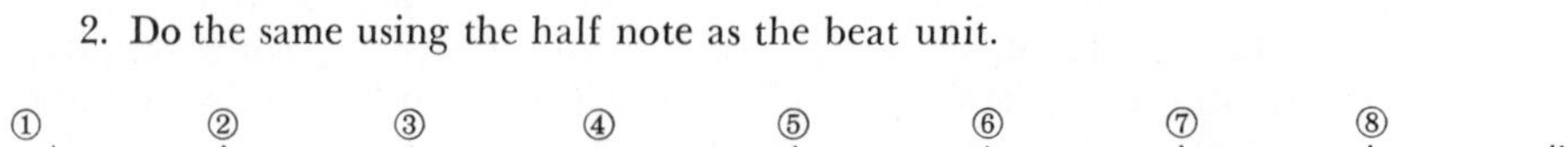

2. Do the same using the half note as the beat unit.

3. Make one variation of each of the patterns in Problems 1 and 2, using appropriate rests, and practice the patterns until you have mastered them.

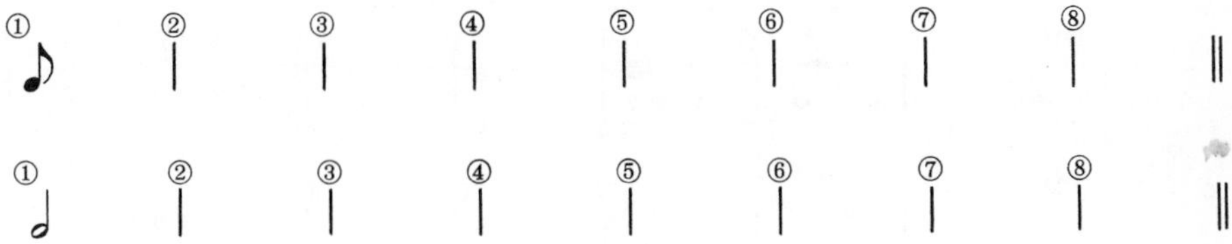

4. Listen while short sequences of variations in Problem 3 are intoned. Sing them back and then notate them. Check your results.

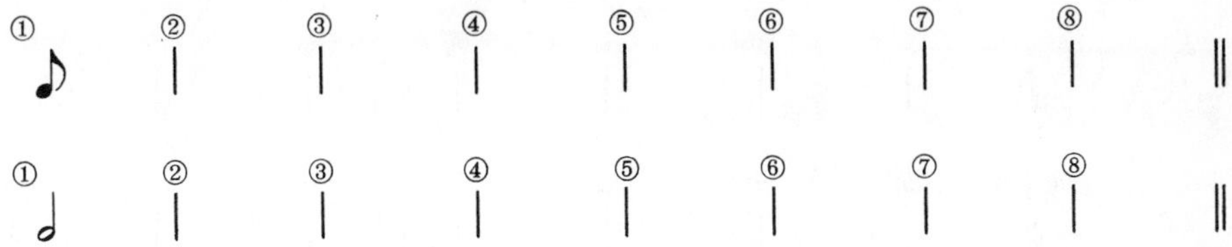

The beat of compound meters is divisible by three, and then by six—that is, three groups of two. Following the same procedures outlined above in regard to simple meters, practice some of the most prevalent patterns resulting from the subdivision of the beat into three and six parts, using ♩. as the beat unit.

PROBLEMS

1. While tapping the basic pulse, intone each of the beat patterns in Example 46 until it is mastered.

Ex. 46.

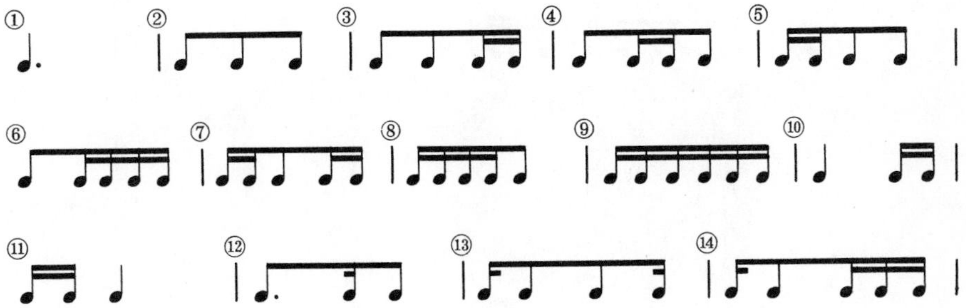

2. Conduct duple, triple, and quadruple meters at various tempi while practicing them.

3. Improvise various sequences of these patterns.

4. Make a variation of beat patterns of Example 46 by using appropriate rests, and perform it the same way.

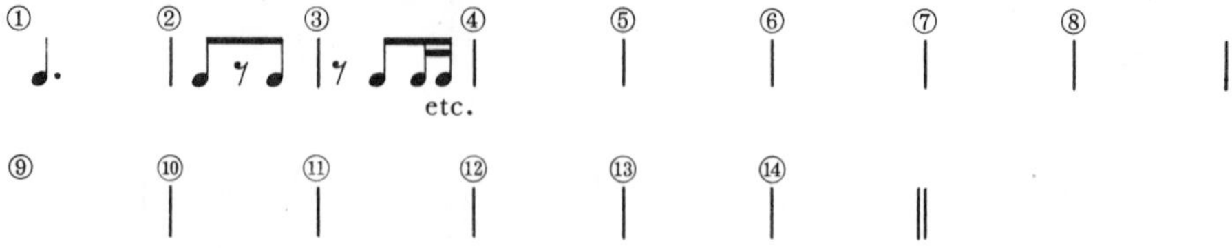

5. Using the dotted eighth note as the beat unit, notate the basic patterns below; use Example 46 as a model.

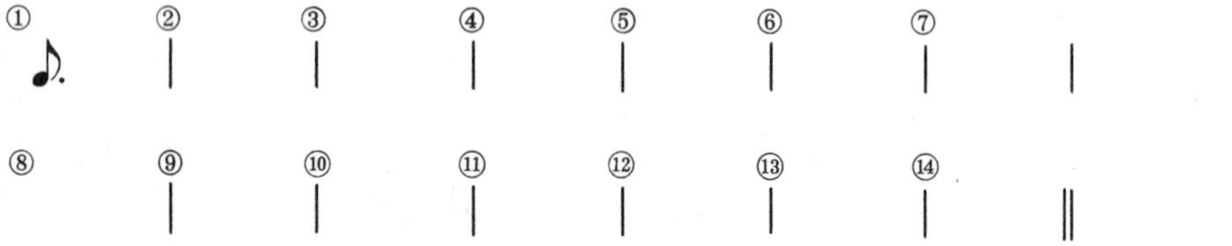

6. Drill with these patterns, as in Problems 1–4.
7. Repeat the procedure, using the dotted half note as the beat unit.

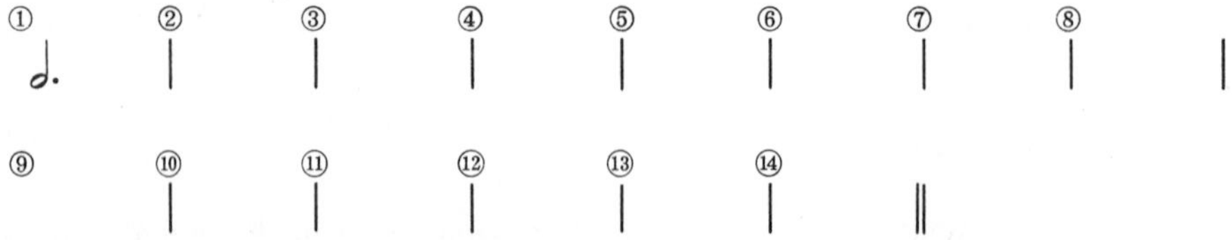

8. Make a variation of the basic beat patterns in Problems 5 and 7 using appropriate rests, and practice them until they are mastered.

(a)

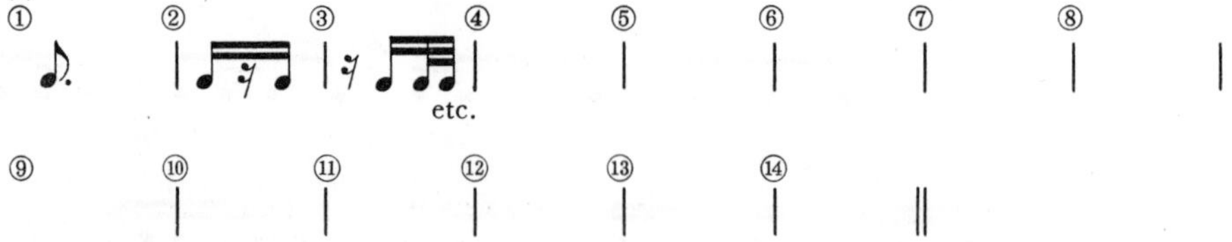

(b)

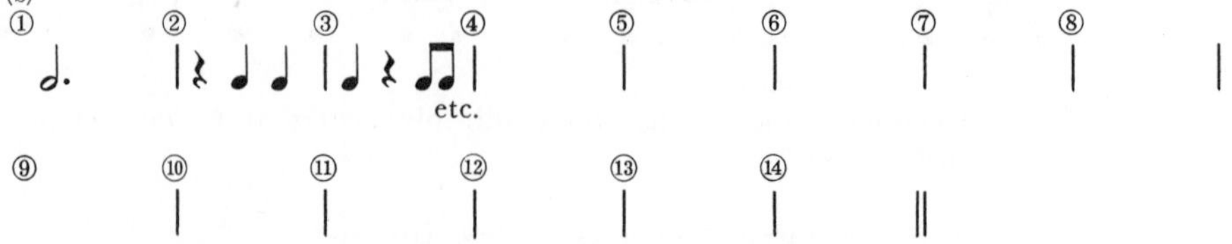

9. Listen while short sequences of the patterns in Problem 8 are intoned. Sing them back and then notate them. Check your results.

(a)

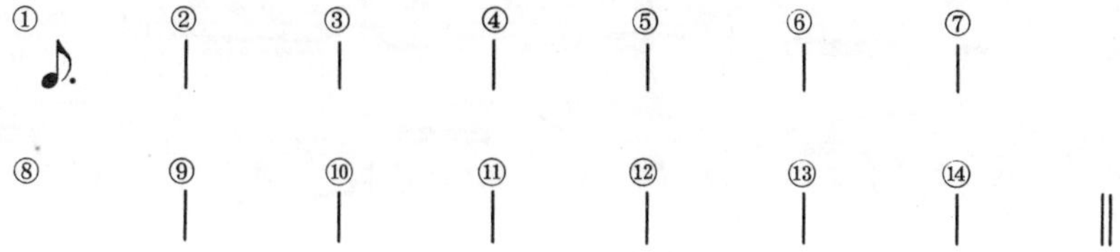

(b)

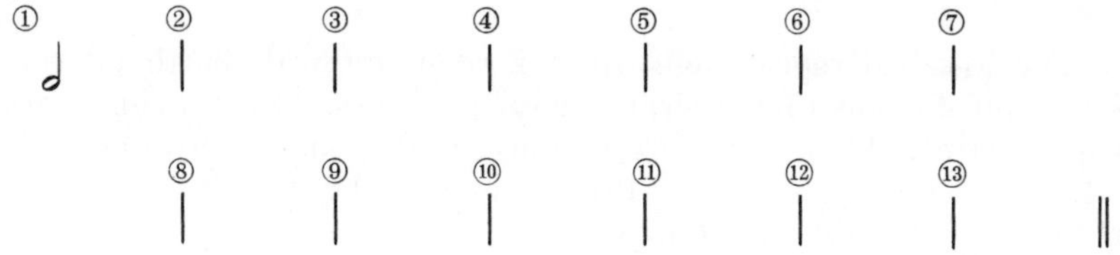

Our discussion of the notation of rhythm is almost complete except for some brief observations regarding a few additional signs, notational principles, and practices. Not all music begins on a downbeat, that is, with a complete measure. When a composition begins on an upbeat, it is traditional for the last measure to be incomplete also—but written so as to create a full measure in combination with the first. (See Ex. 47.)

Ex. 47.

Example 48 also illustrates this principle, and in addition the use of 𝄐 , the *fermata,* or hold. This symbol indicates that the rhythmic flow is interrupted momentarily while the note above (or below) which it appears is sustained according to the wishes of the performer.

Ex. 48.

Ex. 48 continued.

REPEAT SIGNS

The so-called repeat signs are a kind of musical shorthand consisting of signs and symbols that indicate literal repetitions, thus saving space and the copyist's time. These signs take various forms, as in the two tunes in Examples 49 and 50. First compare the two versions of the melody in Ex. 49, (a) being the original and (b), "written out."

Ex. 49.

Note that this simple three-part melody (three phrases of four measures each) is greatly extended by the use of repeats: there are first and second endings plus a *Da capo al Fine* (abbreviated *D.C. al Fine),* meaning to return to the beginning and repeat to *Fine,* the "end." You can see that the first ending is omitted when the phrase is repeated, and that the short-hand version requires only fourteen measures of notation while the written-out form requires twice that much.

In Example 50 the sign 𝄋 appears near the beginning and at the end:

D.S. 𝄋 ; D.S. is an abbreviation of *dal segno,* meaning to return to the sign and repeat thereafter. In this instance, the melody is thus repeated to the *Fine.*

Ex. 50.

Other less complicated repetitions are indicated by the use of 𝄎 , which indicates that the previous beat or measure should be repeated. If it is placed on a bar line, 𝄏 , it indicates that the previous *two* measures are to be repeated. This will become clear if you compare the two versions of the tune in Example 51, the first written out and the second in musical short-hand.

Ex. 51.

OTHER CONDUCTING PATTERNS

To this point, we have concerned ourselves with rhythm patterns whose meter signatures indicate both the number of beats per measure and the beat unit, or in the case of compound meters, the number of beat divisions in a measure and the note value of each. In those instances where the tempo may be quite slow or very fast, it is sometimes convenient to consider as basic a metric scheme something other than that suggested by the meter signature. For instance, Example 52 may be best conceived as having the eighth note rather than the dotted quarter as the beat unit because of the slow tempo and the prevalence of thirty-seconds. In this case, one would say the beat had been subdivided, and would conduct it in six according to this pattern:

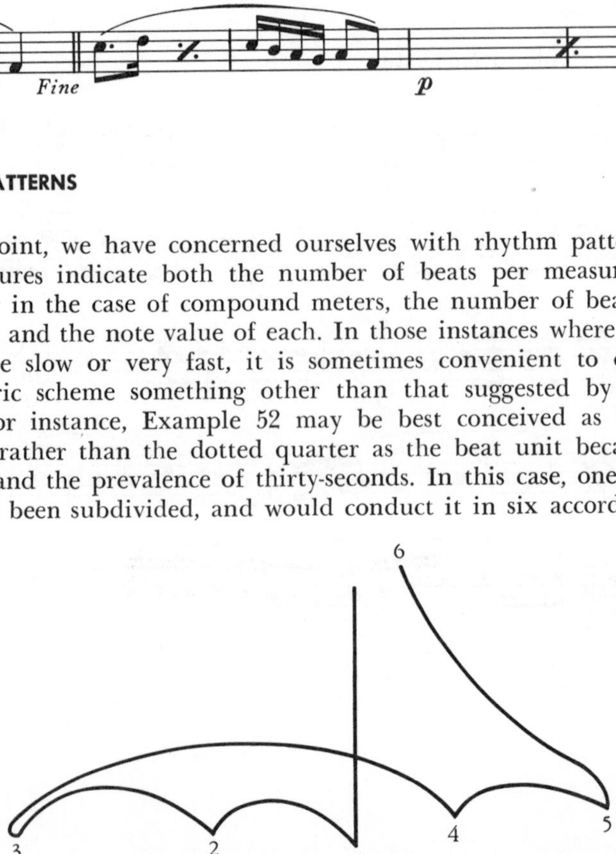

Ex. 52.

The reverse is true when the tempo of a piece is quite rapid and it is easier to sense (and conduct) the metric pattern having a beat unit twice or three times the size of that indicated. Example 53a exemplifies the former, and Example 52b the latter.

Ex. 53a.

Ex. 53b.

The "one-to-a-bar" conducting pattern required for Example 53b is such that after the impact of the downbeat, the arm moves out from the body and then upward in a circular motion in preparation for the next beat. It appears something like this:

DOUBLE AND TRIPLE DOTS

We have learned that a dot is placed after a note to increase its duration by one-half, for example : 𝅗𝅥. = 𝅗𝅥 + ♩ . By adding another dot, a double dotted note results, 𝅗𝅥.. = 𝅗𝅥 + ♩ + ♪ , whose duration is three-fourths of a beat longer than the initial note. The second dot simply adds half the value of the previous dot. And, the same would be true were a third dot added (resulting in a triple dotted note): 𝅗𝅥... = 𝅗𝅥 + ♩ + ♪ + 𝅘𝅥𝅯 . Multiple dots should be used sparingly with notes, since they tend to confuse the beat division. They should not be used at all with rests.

Before proceeding to a discussion of other concepts of pitch organization, intone the rhythms in Example 54 working on each until you have mastered it. Use various tempos. Once you can perform them notate them as they are performed, using a minimum of hearings.

Ex. 54.

(6)

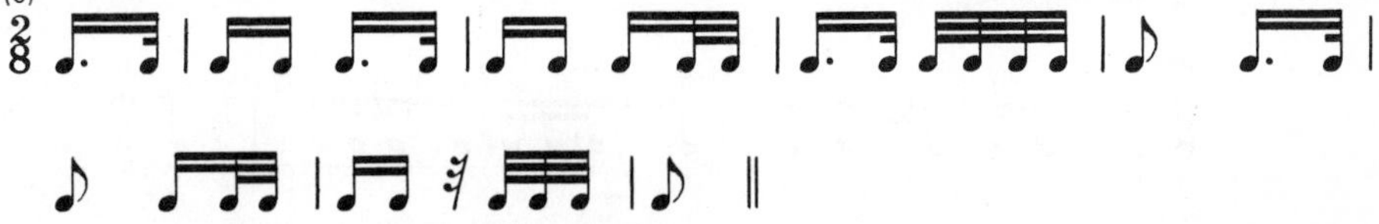

(7)

(8)

(9)

(10)

(11)

(12)

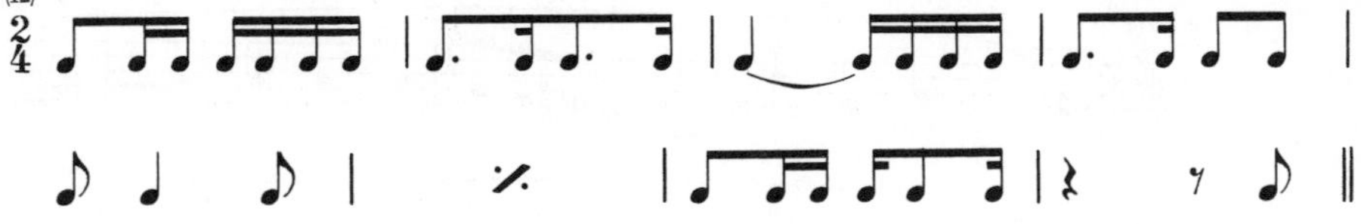

Ex. 54 continued.

(13)

(14)

(15)

SCALE

We have spoken of pitch sets of varying numbers of different pitches—three, four, five, etc.—and we have worked with melodic patterns made of these materials. Let us turn now to a larger ordering of different pitches called *scale*. Scale comes from the Latin word *scala,* meaning ladder, and is used to identify an arrangement of pitches in ascending or descending order. We will concern ourselves momentarily with a particular type of scale made of seven different pitches, each of which is represented by a different letter name. Any seven-tone scale is properly called a *heptatonic scale,* but the form with which we will concern ourselves is a particular type of seven-tone scale, the *diatonic scale,* whose pitches are indicated by seven *different* consecutive letter names, the first seven letters of the alphabet.

Recall in our initial discussion of semitones (see Unit 1, Exs. 33 and 34) that those represented by two consecutive letters were called *diatonic* (*a–b, c–d,* etc.), and those having the same letter name with different accidentals (*a–a♯, b♭–b,* etc.) were called chromatic. In so many words, the diatonic scale contains no chromatic half steps but is made up exclusively of diatonic steps. To clarify this point, study Example 55 which exemplifies a scalar type that is the mainstay of much music of the Western world.

Ex. 55.

D major scale (d^1–d^2)

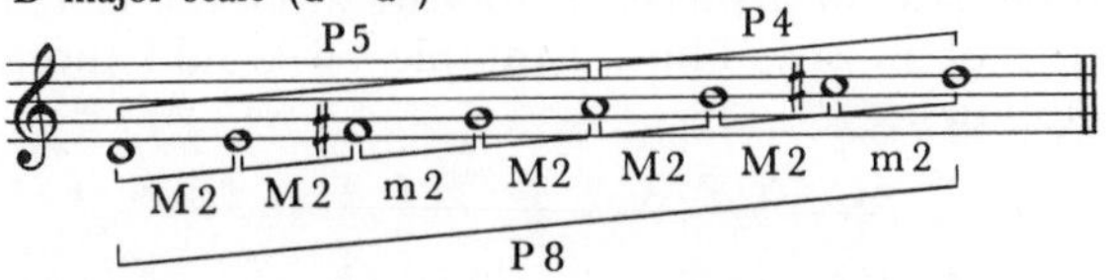

(We should emphasize that scale is an abstraction deriving from music, and not the reverse. We extract scales from a tonal context for purposes of study—writing, hearing, and performing.) In studying this melody, note that we may extract seven different notes and arrange them in ascending order from d^1 to d^2. Too, the particular arrangement of seconds—MMmMMMm (11 1/2 111 1/2 steps)—constitutes a particular kind of diatonic scale, a *diatonic major scale,* more specifically termed the *D major Scale.* (This diatonic scale and its companion, the *minor scale,* soon to be discussed, dominate the music of our culture.)

Lastly, upon listening to Example 55, note that the focal pitch is D, the key note or *tonic.* We say, then, that the piece is in the key of D major, for the derivative scale is the D major scale and the key tone (tonic) is D. In common usage, scale and key are considered to be virtually the same since the former represents the *basic* tonal elements of the latter. However, it should be kept in mind that they are not always synonymous, for various non-scale notes (chromatic variants) may be introduced which do not alter the key. For instance, chromatic variant ($g\sharp^1$) is used in Example 56, yet the tonic D is unmistakable.

Ex. 56.

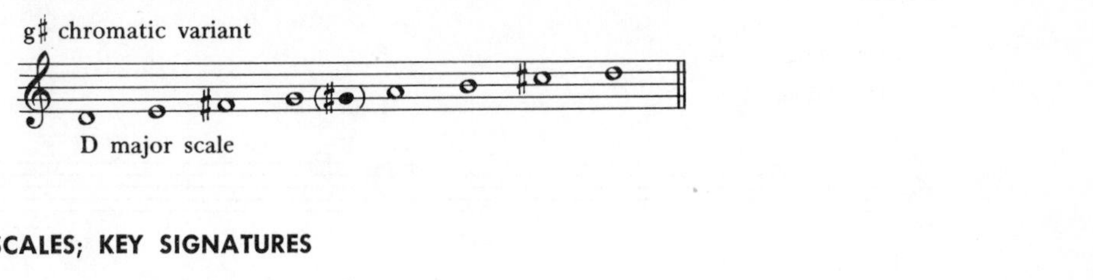

g♯ chromatic variant

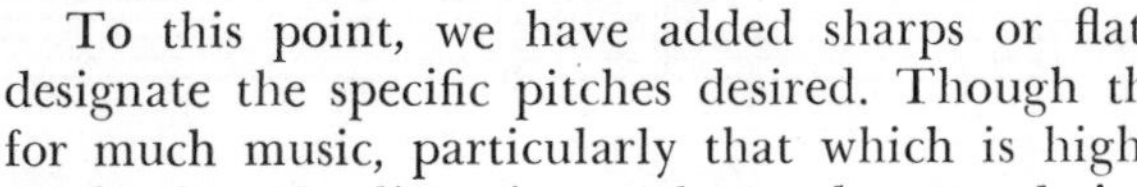

D major scale

MAJOR SCALES; KEY SIGNATURES

To this point, we have added sharps or flats before notes in order to designate the specific pitches desired. Though this is an effective technique for much music, particularly that which is highly chromatic, music that is predominantly diatonic can better be served, in terms of clarity and labor saved, by the use of *key signatures.* A key signature is a capsule summary of the sharps or flats to be used in a piece; it appears after the clef sign at the beginning of each line of music. Thus, Example 56 would more properly have been written as follows:

Ex. 57.

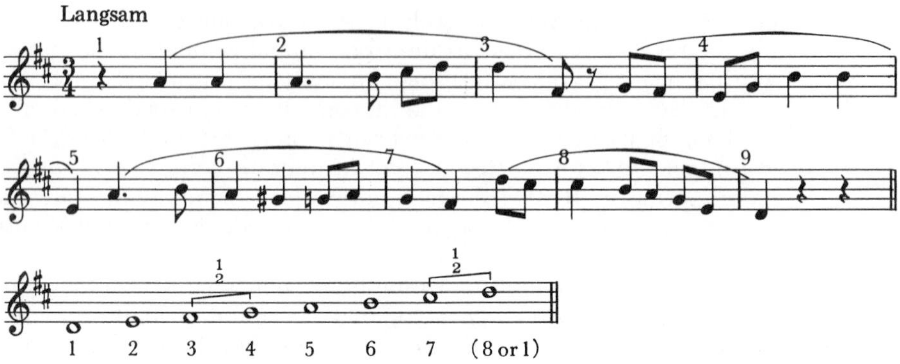

Accidentals in a key signature apply to all subsequent appearances of the designated notes, regardless of octave placement. That is, the ♯ on the fifth line of the signature in Example 57 inflects all *f*'s (measures 3 and 7), including those on the first space; likewise, the ♯ in the third space of the signature applies to all *c*'s within the staff. (Note also that the numbers 1–7 may be used to indicate the degrees of the scale. Numbers are a convenient reference system for identifying the pitches of a diatonic series, and you will need to develop facility in singing them as you progress in music-reading.)

Let us concentrate on the major scale for a moment and practice notating it in various keys, using sharps and flats, not key signatures. Assume that the note given is the tonic pitch (the "key note," or focal pitch). Then, play the scale on the piano and practice singing it with numbers and with "ta." (See Ex. 58.)

Ex. 58.

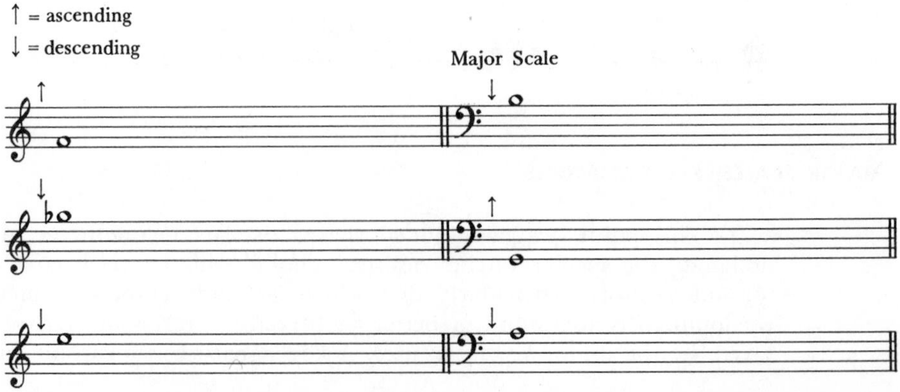

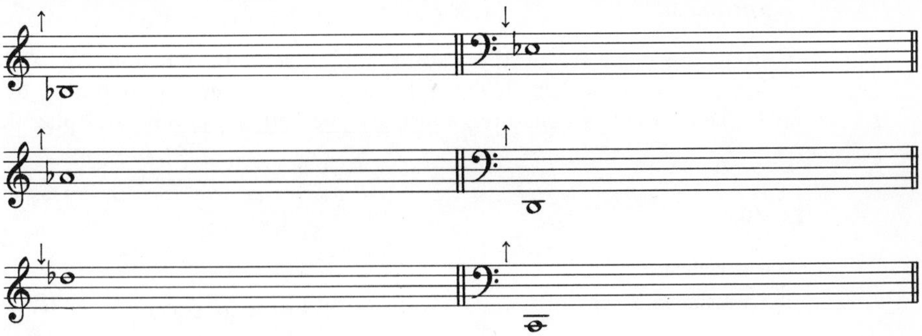

MINOR SCALES

Another family of frequently used diatonic scales is that of the minor scale previously mentioned. There are three scalar members of this family: the natural, harmonic, and melodic minor forms.

The natural minor scale is a close relative of the major scale, for its pitch components are the same. (That is, in Example 59 the pitches of the *D* natural minor scale are also those of the F major scale beginning, of course, on the sixth degree of the scale.)

Ex. 59.

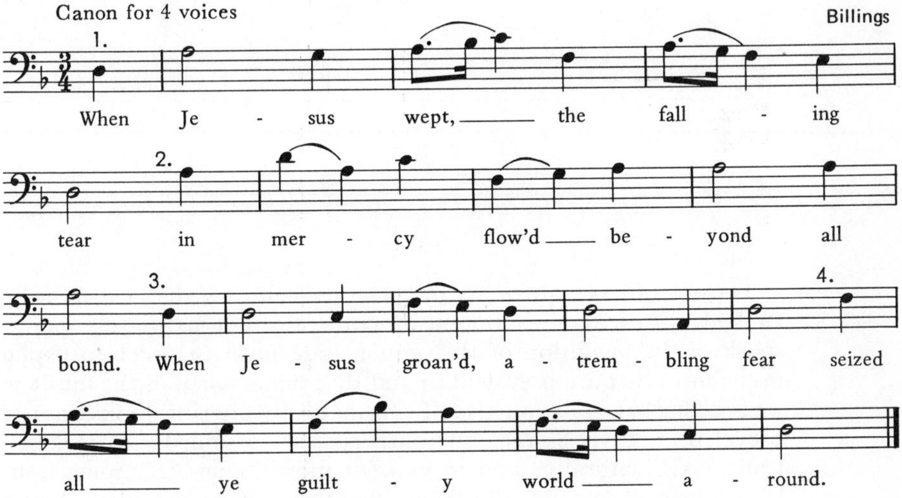

D natural minor scale

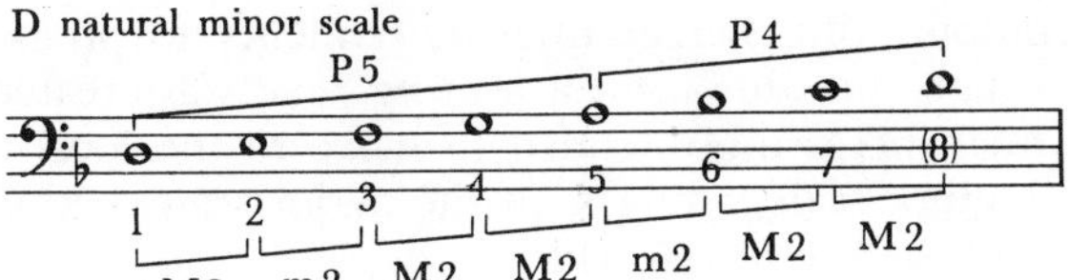

PROBLEM

Study the structure of the natural minor scale in Example 59, and construct similar ones as illustrated in Example 60 in the various keys indicated by the given pitch. (Don't use key signatures, and mark the half steps.) Sing and play them.

Ex. 60.

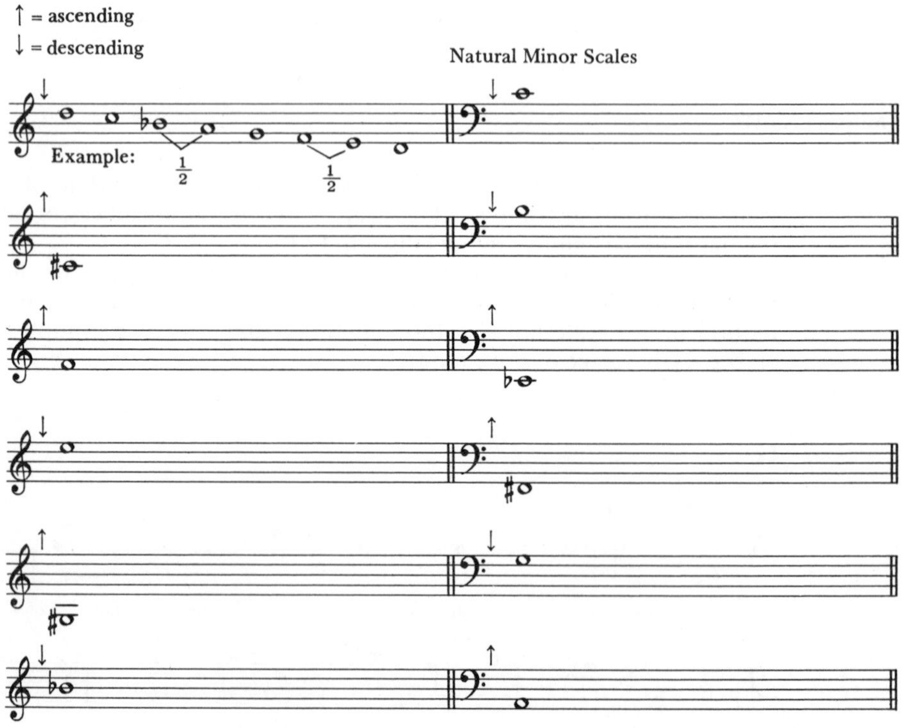

Because of its frequent use in harmonic contexts, the next minor scale to be studied is called the harmonic minor scale. Let us digress momentarily to speak of the evolution of this minor scale form in order to explain certain preferences that are prevalent in and that shape much of the music with which we are familiar. The practice of chromatically altering (inflecting) pitches was prevalent as early as the thirteenth century, assumedly to make the melody lead more "naturally" and to make it more "singable." Some four centuries later, these chromatic alterations had become so prevalent that new scale forms were established that incorporated the most common inflections. By the seventeenth century, the seventh degree of the natural minor scale was regularly raised a semitone, thus heightening its tendency to progress to the next note above. Through this alteration a *leading tone* was created (a semitone below tonic), which increasingly tended to move to the focal pitch (the tonic). The harmonic minor scale, along with the major scale, became central to the harmonic music of the Western world.

Note in Example 61 that the pitches framed by the perfect fifth 1–5 are arranged in a pattern identical to those of the same pitches of the natural minor scale. The difference occurs in the perfect fourth 5–8, where in the natural minor they are m2-M2-M2, and in the harmonic minor, m2-+2-m2. When used, the unique sound of the augmented second between 6 and 7 makes this scale form easy to recognize. However, composers often avoid its use in melodic lines as is the case in Example 61, where one finds no juxtapositions of e♭ and f♯. (In contrast with the other examples, the pitches of this tune exceed an octave, and the tonic lies near the middle of the melodic range.)

Ex. 61.

PROBLEM

As with Example 59, study the structure of the harmonic minor scale and familiarize yourself with its sound; then practice writing, singing, and playing various ones, as indicated in Example 62. Again use no key signatures and identify the half steps and augmented seconds.

Ex. 62.

↑ = ascending
↓ = descending

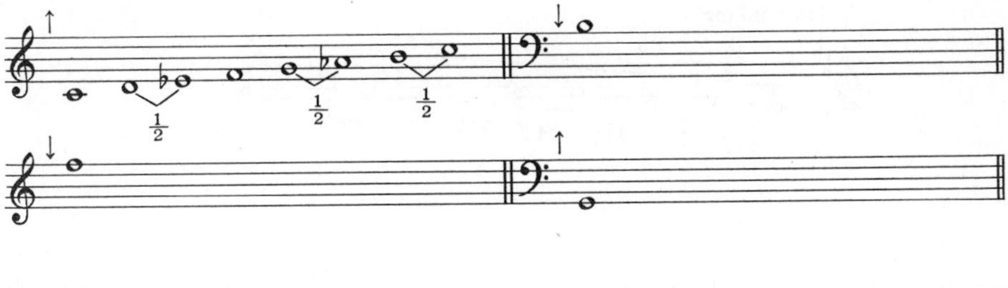

Ex. 62 continued.

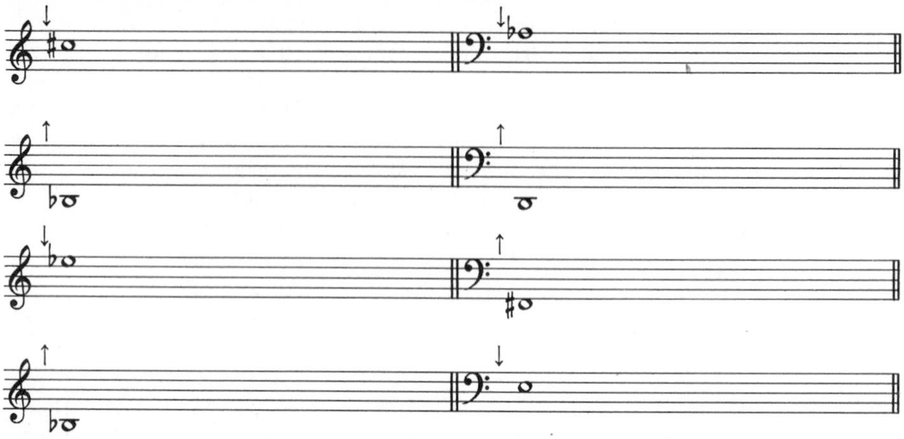

The last diatonic minor scale to be considered is the so-called *melodic minor*. This form represents a further modification of the natural minor scale whereby the "uncommon" skip of the augmented second between the sixth and seventh degrees of the harmonic minor scale is made more "singable" by an upward inflection of the sixth degree, thus creating the interval of a major second and providing a "smoother" melodic line. As you can see in Example 63, pitches 1–5 are arranged the same as pitches 1–5 in both the natural and harmonic scales (Ex. 59, 61). This scale differs from the first two in that pitches 5–8 are identical to pitches 5–8 in a major scale—that is, M2-M2-m2. (Some authors assert that this form is the ascending form and that the descending form is that of natural minor. Be that as it may, for simplicity's sake we will consider the melodic minor to be but one scale, as in Example 63.)

Ex. 63.

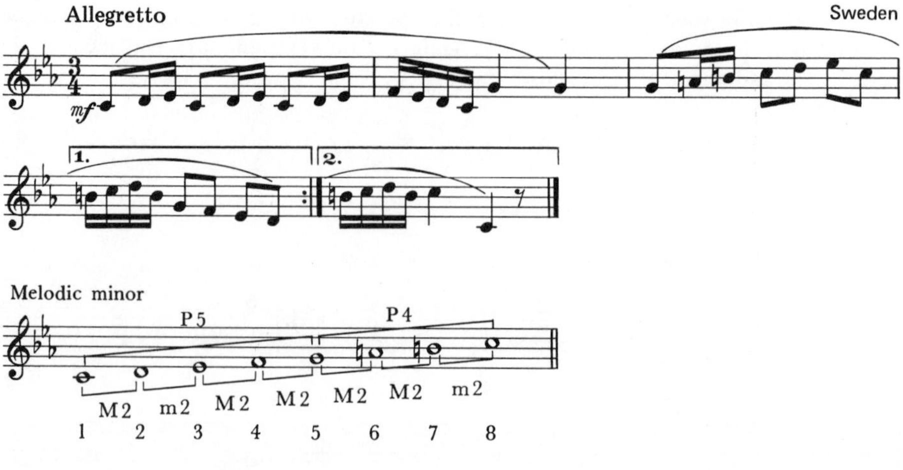

PROBLEM

As before, practice constructing, singing, and playing the scales (melodic minor) indicated in Example 64.

Ex. 64.

↑ = ascending

↓ = descending

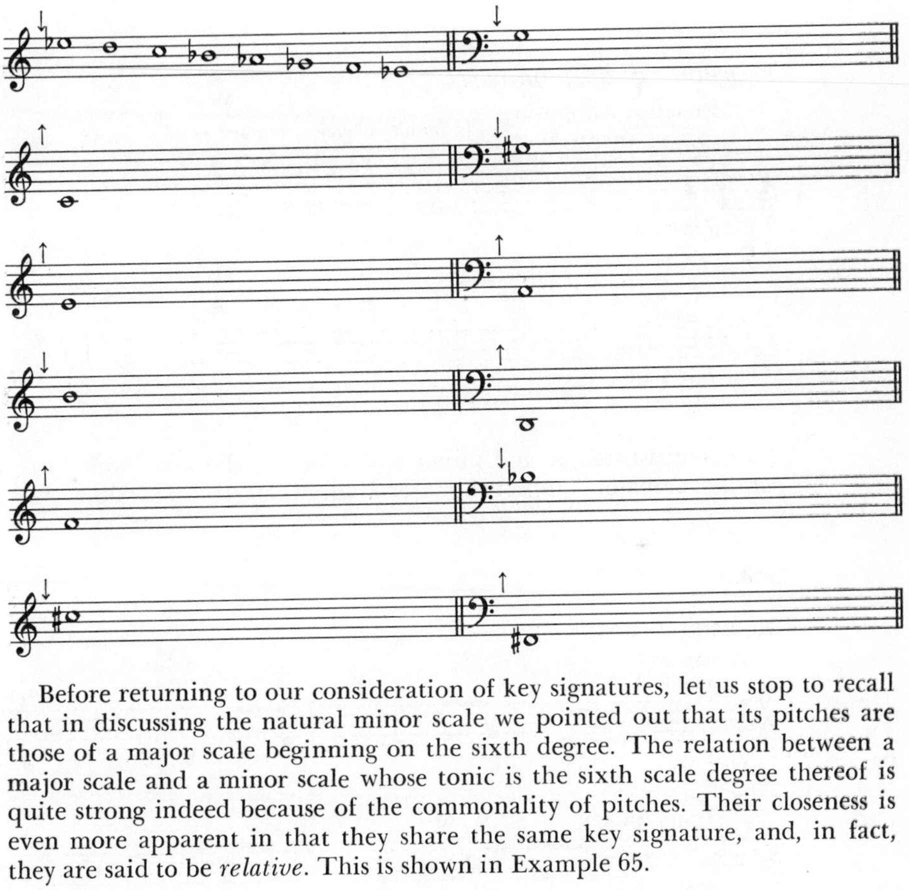

Before returning to our consideration of key signatures, let us stop to recall that in discussing the natural minor scale we pointed out that its pitches are those of a major scale beginning on the sixth degree. The relation between a major scale and a minor scale whose tonic is the sixth scale degree thereof is quite strong indeed because of the commonality of pitches. Their closeness is even more apparent in that they share the same key signature, and, in fact, they are said to be *relative*. This is shown in Example 65.

Ex. 65.

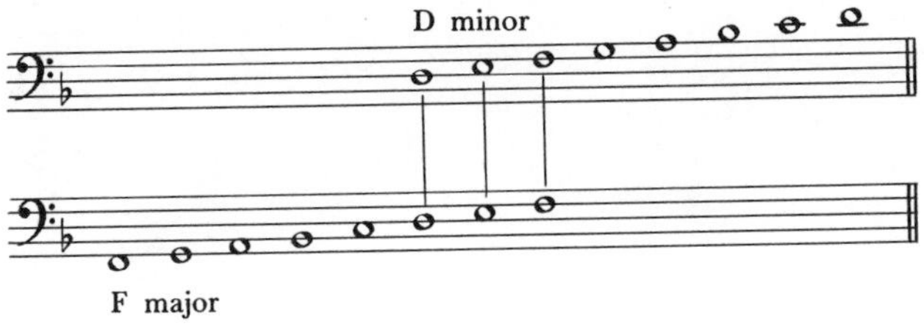

RELATIVE AND PARALLEL SCALES

Major and minor keys having the same key signature are related; that is, one is *relative* to the other: F major is the relative major of D minor, and vice versa (D minor is the relative minor of F major), since both have the same key signature. It is comparatively easy to remember that the relative minor key is always a minor third below the relative major: A major-F♯ minor: B♭-G minor, etc. (See Ex. 66a.)

Ex. 66a.

SYMPHONY IN G MINOR (K.550)

Mozart

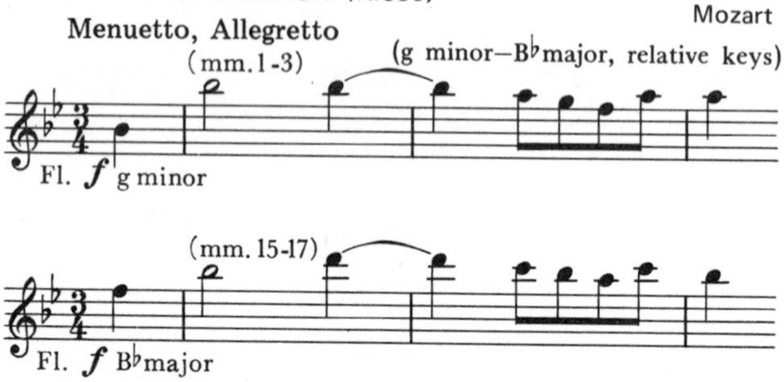

In contrast, major and minor scales having the *same* tonic are said to be *parallel:* C major-C minor, E major-E minor, etc. (See Ex. 66b.)

Ex. 66b.

SURPRISE SYMPHONY

Haydn

MAJOR AND MINOR KEY SIGNATURES

Example 67 shows the key signatures for major and minor keys. Though it would be possible to arrange the sharps or flats of a key signature in various ways, the traditional order is followed here. (This practice, more conventional than otherwise, will become clearer when you consider the subsequent paragraph and diagram.)

Ex. 67.

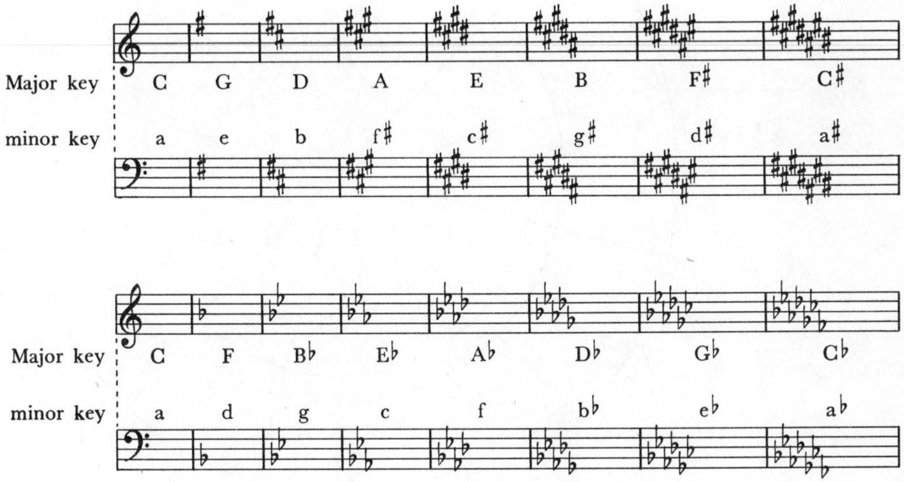

CIRCLE OF FIFTHS

Eventually, the various major and minor key signatures must be committed to memory, but until that time it will be helpful to consider what is commonly known as the *circle of fifths.* The following diagram of the circle of fifths presents keys in "natural" order: increasing by one the number of sharps in clockwise direction, and likewise for flats in the opposite direction. Proceeding clockwise the keys are a perfect fifth apart, and counterclockwise, a perfect fourth. Note that one can also consider this a circle of *fourths* by reading counterclockwise, and that in either direction there are twelve steps around before the circle is closed and the initial key is reached. Study the chart carefully, for it shows both the number of sharps or flats required for a particular key, whether major or minor.

The designation *enharmonic equivalents* means that in the standard system of major and minor keys, certain keys have exactly the same sound even though one is notated with sharps and the other with flats. In other words, the B major scale and the C♭ major scale actually consist of the same pitches in terms of the sounds produced, even though one is notated with sharps and the other with flats. The same is true of the D♯ minor and E♭ minor scales and others indicated on the following diagram.

CIRCLE OF FIFTHS
Major keys

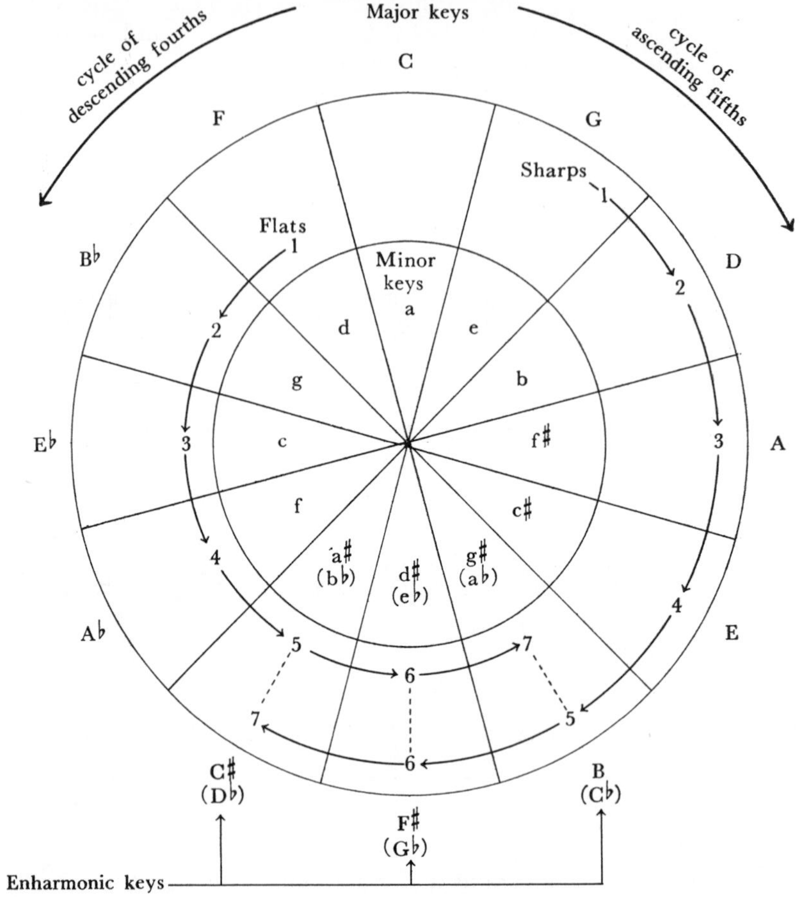

PROBLEMS

1. Below each of the key signatures in Example 68 indicate both major and minor keys.

Ex. 68.

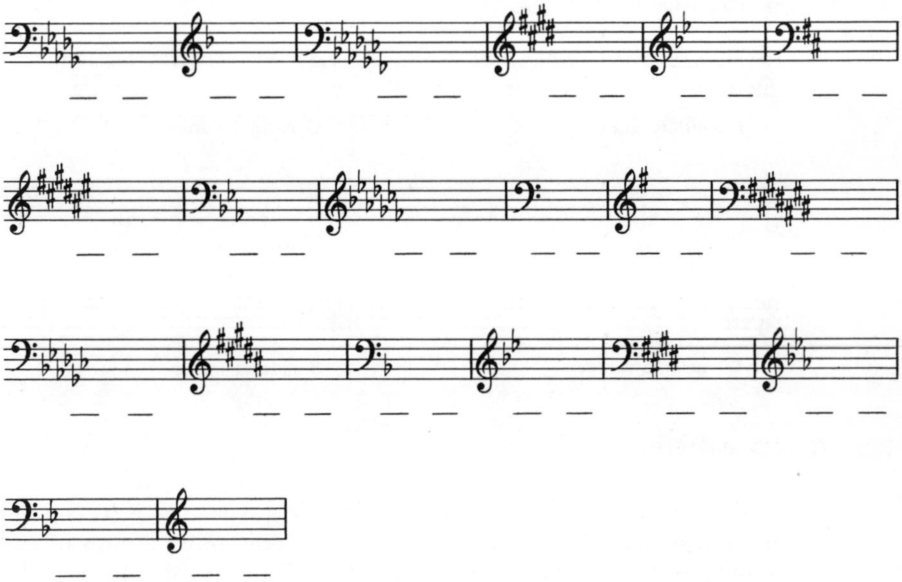

2. Write the proper key signatures for the keys indicated in Example 69.

Ex. 69.

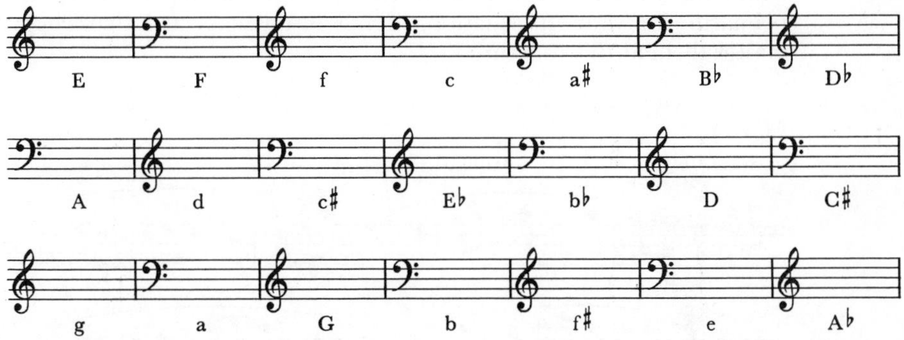

3. Construct the scales indicated in Example 70, using the proper key signatures.

Ex. 70.

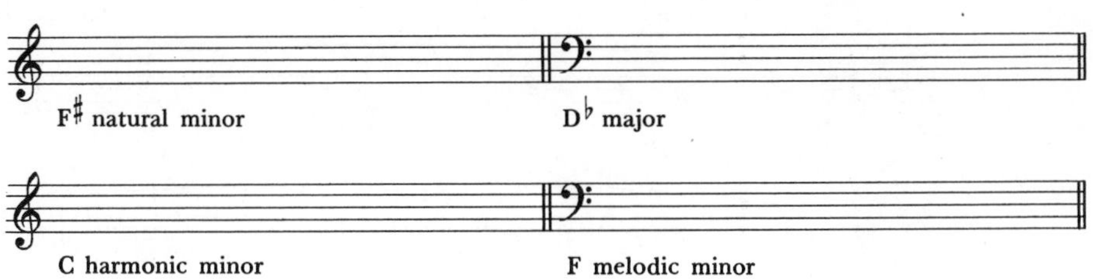

Ex. 70 continued.

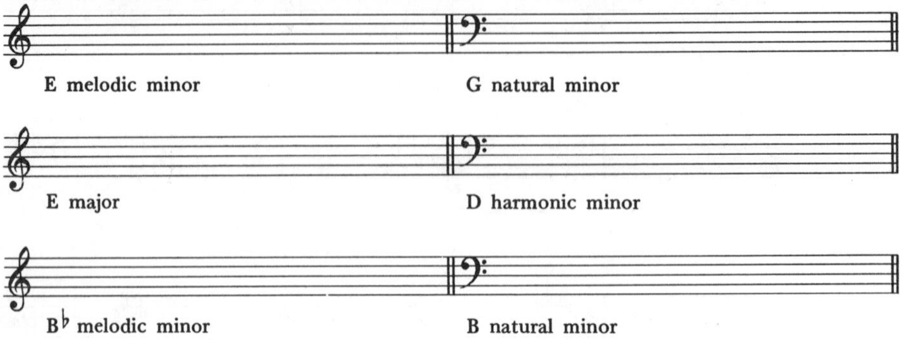

TRIPLETS AND DUPLETS

The meters we have studied have been regular: that is, they resulted from the reiteration of an unvarying pattern of basic pulse groups of twos, threes, or fours–duple, triple, or quadruple beat patterns. Much music, less regular in its rhythmic structure, may contain mixtures of pulse groups of threes and twos, or the reverse; or twos, twos, and threes; and so on. The steady flow of regular divisions of the beat in either simple or compound meters is often "disturbed" by the interpolation of irregular divisions, for example by *triplets* in single meter or *duplets* in compound. Consider Examples 71a and 71b, which illustrate less regular treatment of metric patterns. These are presented primarily for your information, and it is not expected that you completely master them at this juncture.)

Ex. 71a.

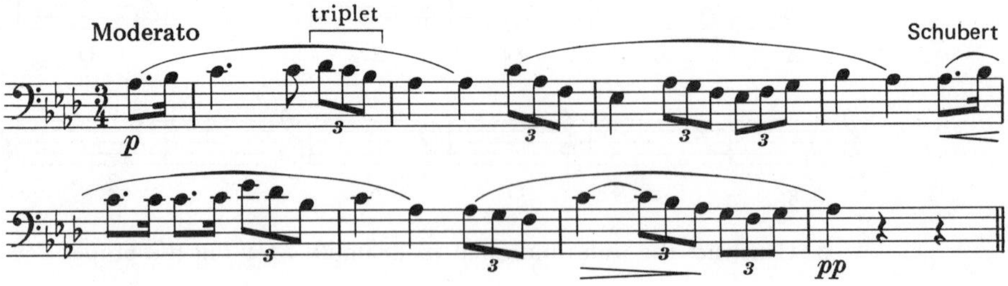

Ex. 71b.

IRREGULAR METER, MIXED METER, AND POLYMETER

The regularity of the basic metric pulse is little disturbed by such infrequent "irregularities"; even less common, at least in music written prior to this century, is the use of meters in which the beat patterns are irregular,— that is, in which the measures are made of combinations of two, three, and four pulses. For instance, two plus three is the metric pattern of Example 72a, and three plus four is the pattern of Example 72b.

Ex. 72a.

Ex. 72b.

Composers often create works in which the metric patterns are changed quite frequently. This technique is often indicated by the use of mixed (multiple) meter signatures (Ex. 73a) or by the interpolation of meter signatures throughout (Ex. 73b).

Ex. 73a.

Ex. 73b.

In more complex schemes, different meters may be simultaneously combined, resulting in *polymeter*. (See Ex. 74.)

Ex. 74.

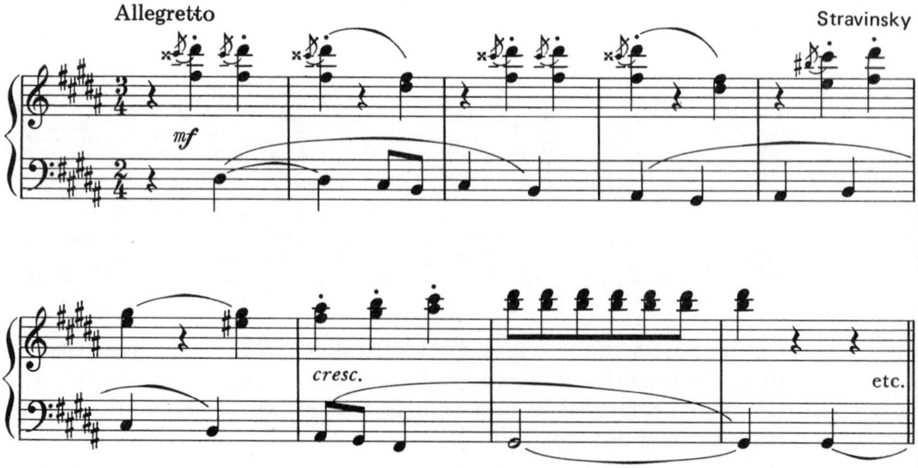

MODES

Returning to our presentation of scale formations, let us become familiar with a term rooted in medieval music: *mode*. In the broadest sense, mode denotes an arrangement of pitches in a scale, and in this regard it is proper to speak of a piece based on a major scale as being in a "major mode," or, if on a minor scale, in a "minor mode." However, in a more specific sense, the word *mode* refers to a particular group of scales having their roots in the music of antiquity. In codifying the music of the medieval church, Gregorian chant, an eight-mode system called "church modes" was formulated. These theoretical abstractions were useful in explaining the development of music from single vocal lines (monody) to combined lines (polyphony), and the advent of chordal harmony. Then the modes fell into disuse, generally speaking, but composers since that time have made occasional use of them; in fact, much folk music and contemporary "pop" music makes use of the so-called church modes. In other words, though the older forms were replaced by the major-minor scale system, they were not eliminated entirely, and they continue to live in the minds of composers who turn not only to the future but also to the past for their tonal building materials.

Theoretically, a mode may be built on any one of the seven tones of a diatonic series. The result will be seven different arrangements of whole and half steps—that is, seven different modes, as indicated in Example 75. The proper names of these modes derive from the Greek.

Ex. 75.

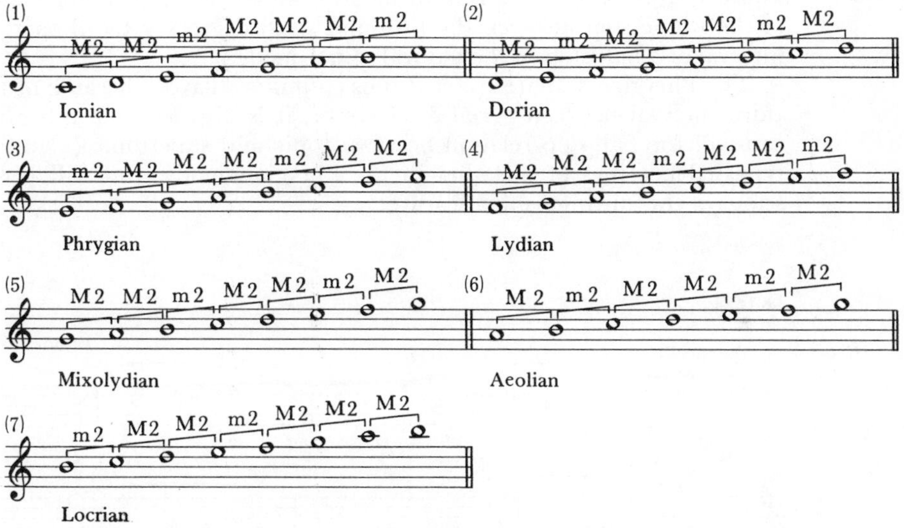

We will eliminate the Ionian and Aeolian modes from consideration because their patterns are those of the major and natural minor scales. Further, the Locrian mode is almost never used, probably because the relation between its first and fifth degrees is not a perfect fifth. (This reason will become more clear after we study harmony and tonality.) Let us turn then to the four modes that appear with some frequency in the general literature of music: Dorian, Phrygian, Lydian, and Mixolydian.

Consider Example 76, a folk tune in the Dorian mode. Sing it and listen to it as you follow its movement, paying particular attention to the "minor" flavor heightened, of course, by the absence of the half-step relation between degrees 7 and 8, commonly called the *leading-tone* relationship. (Recall that the seventh degree of a major scale has a strong tendency to "lead" to the eighth (first) degree, the tonic.)

Ex. 76.

DORIAN

Sea Chanty

You can differentiate the Dorian mode from the natural minor scale because of the whole step between the fifth and sixth degrees. (Recall that this is an interval of a half step in the natural minor mode.)

The Phrygian scale (Ex. 77) also has a minor "flavor" because of the minor third interval between 1 and 3. However, it is distinct from other modes because of the half-step relation between tonic and supertonic (1 and 2). Upon repeated hearings of melodies in the Phrygian mode, you will become conscious of this distinguishing feature.

Ex. 77.

Allegretto

Anon. (13th Century)

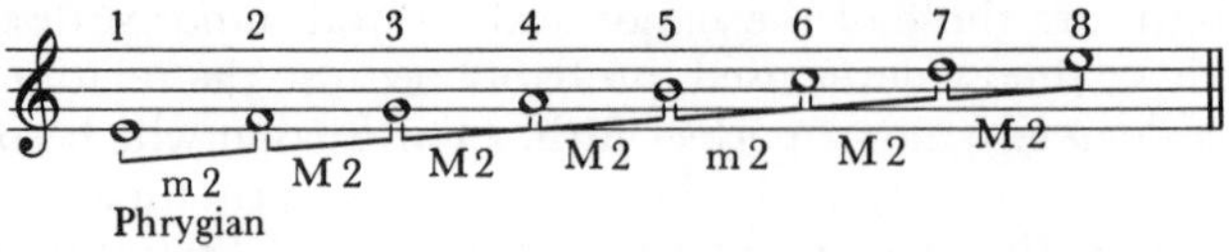

The Lydian mode (Ex. 78) has a "major" sound because of the major third between 1 and 3, which is true of the major scale. Its most distinguishing features are, however, the tritone existing between 1 and 4 and the half step between 4 and 5.

Ex. 78.

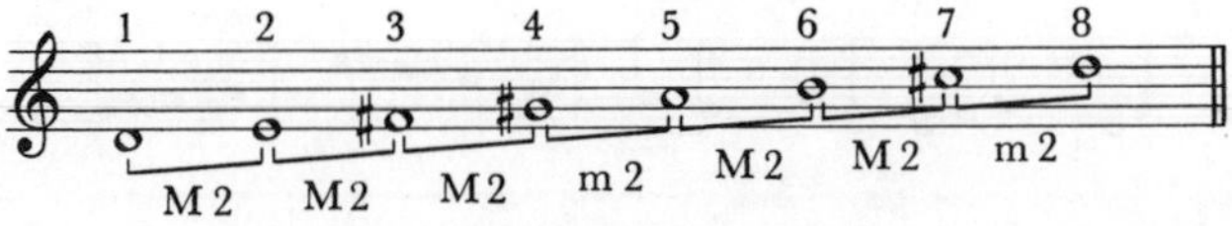

The Mixolydian mode (Ex. 79) also shares this "major-mode" quality, again because of the major third between 1 and 3. Its unique sound results from the lack of the leading-tone half step between 7 and 8, which, of course, differentiates it from the major scale.

Ex. 79.

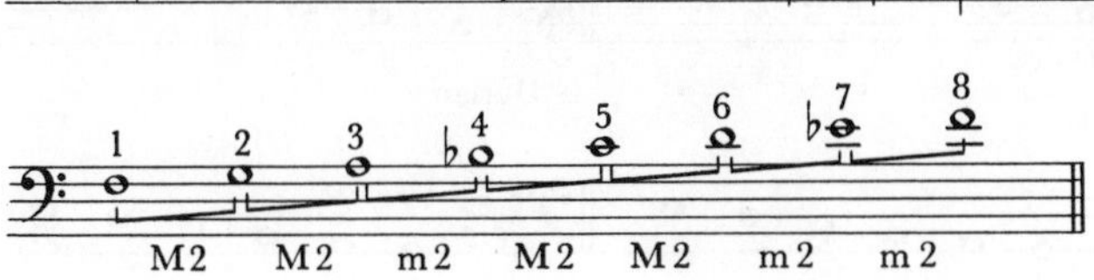

As mentioned earlier, the Aeolian mode (Ex. 80) is identical in structure to the natural minor scale and, hence, requires no further explanation.

Ex. 80.

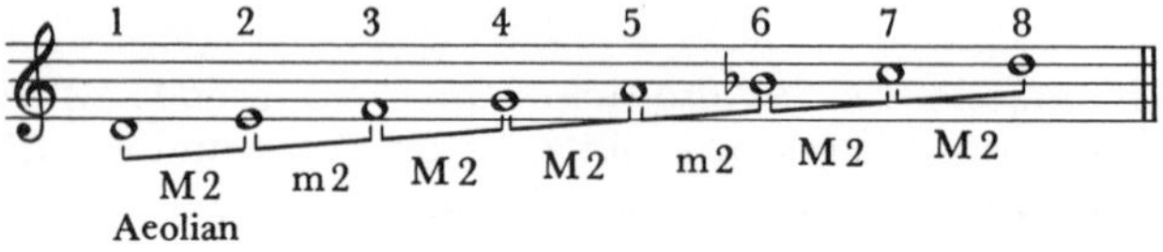

With the addition of the Locrian mode our diatonic series of modal scales is complete. However, it should be obvious in light of some of the preceding examples that any one of the modal forms can be constructed on any of the degrees of the chromatic scale. In other words, any one of the twelve notes of the chromatic scale may serve as tonic, and the choice of the signature appropriate to each is determined on the same basis as the choice for major and minor scales. That is, one must determine the arrangement of whole and half steps peculiar to a particular mode, and use the pattern of flats or sharps in the signature appropriate to that pitch sequence. Some find it helpful to think of the modes as being built on various degrees of a major scale—Dorian on 2, Phrygian on 3, Lydian on 4, and Mixolydian on 5. Thus, a Dorian mode on G would be thought of as being built on the second degree of the F major scale; or Phrygian on G♯, the third degree of E major; etc. (See Ex. 81.)

Ex. 81.

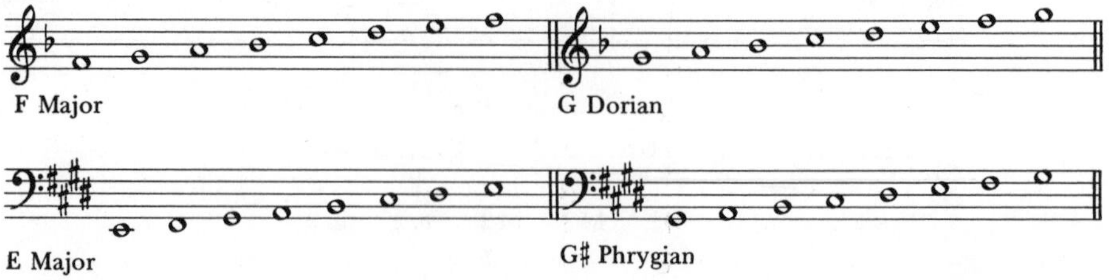

Though it is not necessary that you thoroughly master all of the modes at this time, consider for the moment two problems that will better familiarize you with these scales.

PROBLEMS

1. Construct the modal scales indicated in Example 83, using sharps and flats and assuming the tonic to be the pitch given.

Ex. 82.

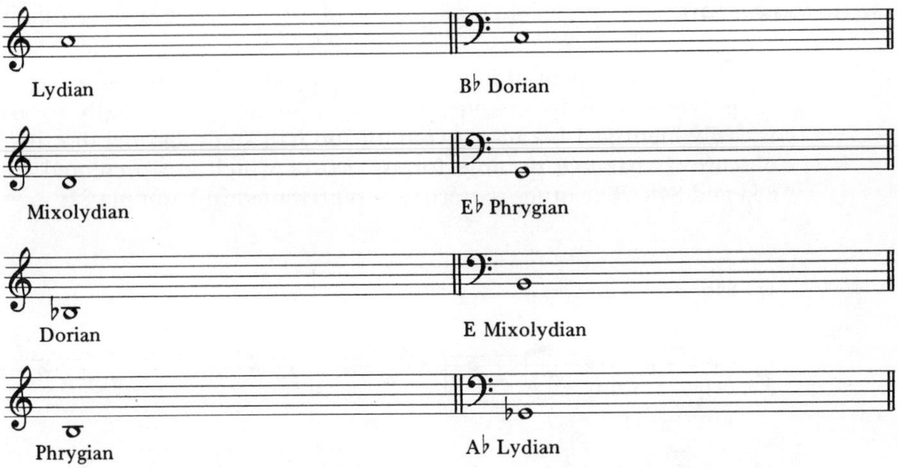

2. Further construct the modal scales in Example 83, using the appropriate signature.

Ex. 83.

Modes with signatures

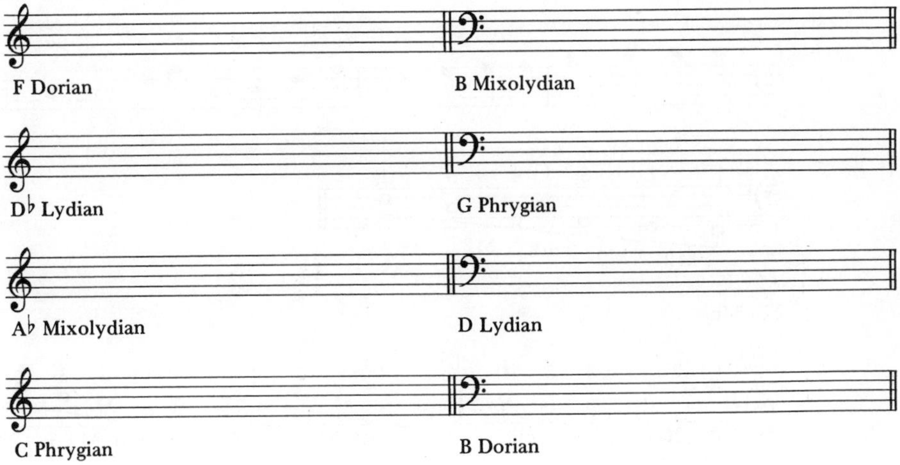

The variety of possible scales is sizable indeed, even if one is limited to diatonic scales of seven members. Nevertheless, although composers have had virtually unlimited choice in regard to scale selection, their practice has generally been confined to those few forms discussed thus far. Let us turn to briefly consider other forms with which you will become acquainted as you study further.

PENTATONIC SCALE

The five-note pentatonic scale is a gapped scale that has existed for a long time. One detects its presence in folk music and occasionally in art music. It is easily identified because it contains no half steps and because it is relatively obscure. It has five possible forms, two of which are presented in Examples 84a and 84b. The other patterns are represented in Example 84c.

Ex. 84a.

Ex. 84b.

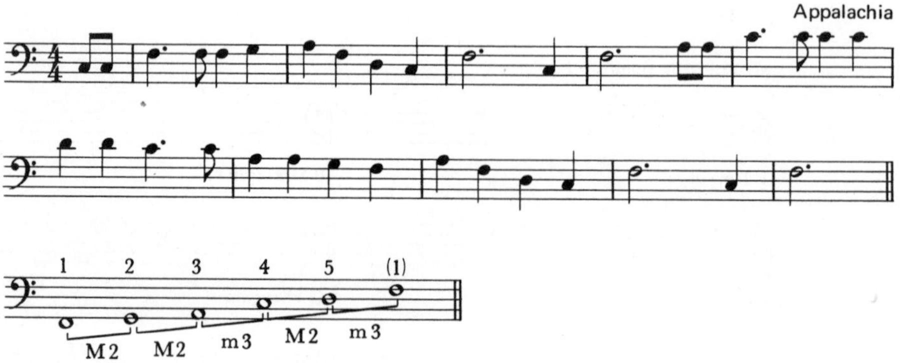

Ex. 84c.

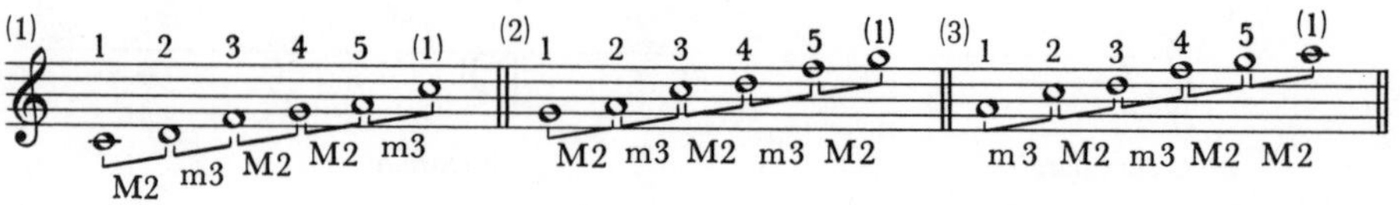

Familiarize yourself with these various types, but most important, learn to recognize the sound of these scale forms, which is characterized by *leaps* between various adjacent tones.

CHROMATIC AND WHOLE-TONE SCALES

Brief mention should be made of the chromatic scale and the whole-tone scale, which are illustrated in Examples 85 and 86. The former (Ex. 85[a]) comprises twelve notes, each being a half step removed from its neighbor. (Note that there is only *one* form, for regardless of which pitch is selected for the beginning one, all will contain the same set of pitches.)

Ex. 85.

Chromatic Scale

(a)

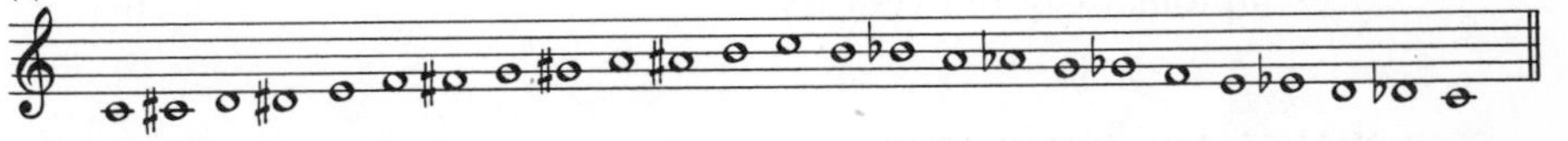

(b)

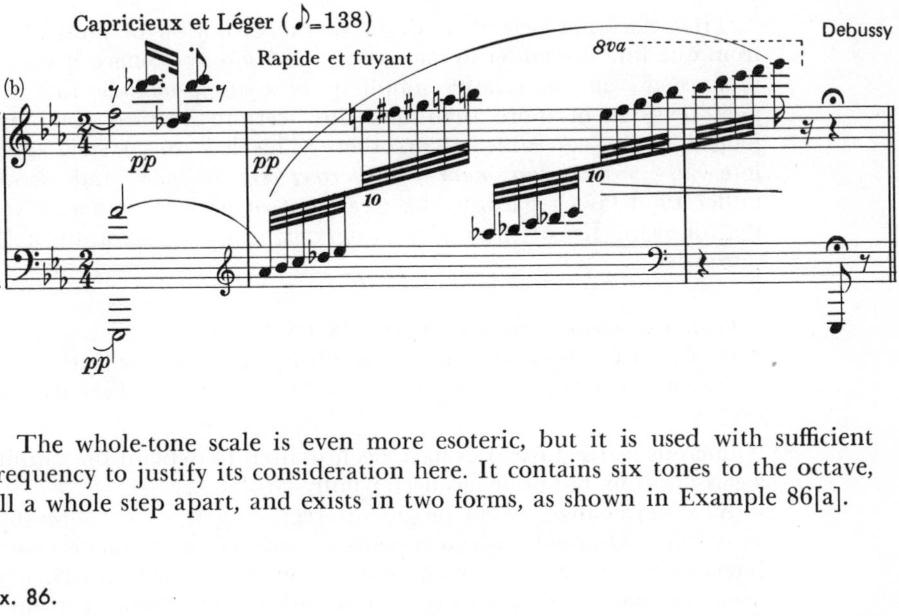

The whole-tone scale is even more esoteric, but it is used with sufficient frequency to justify its consideration here. It contains six tones to the octave, all a whole step apart, and exists in two forms, as shown in Example 86[a].

Ex. 86.

Whole-tone Scale

(a)

Ex. 86 continued.

(b) **Modéré** Debussy

The use of this scale in works created near the end of the nineteenth century contributed to the weakening of the major-minor scale system that had reigned for well over three hundred years. Because of its tonal vagueness (lack of strong tonal polarity), it became a useful tool in breaking the tyranny of the major-minor tonal system that had dominated music so long, and in so doing it prepared the way for the musical experimentation that was to become so symptomatic of our century.

CONSONANCE AND DISSONANCE

Time does not permit a review of the evolution of musical organization from one line (*monody*) to many lines (*polyphony*). Suffice it to say that as it progressed from the relative simplicity of a single melodic line to more complex textures of more than one line, certain vertical combinations were judged more "agreeable" than others. This led to a system of categorizing intervals—*perfect consonance, imperfect consonance,* and *dissonance*—and rather rigid laws regarding the treatment of each. Familiarize yourself with the following list of the various intervals, classified according to these three categories.

Perfect Consonances—unison, P4, P5, P8
Imperfect Consonances—M and m thirds, and M and m sixths
Dissonances—M and m seconds, M and m sevenths, and the tritone

Numerous learned treatises have been written to explain the rationale of such a classification, but none has been wholly satisfactory.

As tastes change, so do judgments regarding what is "agreeable" or "disagreeable." Although such judgments are subjective, the fact remains that some intervals are more agreeable or stable (consonant) than others, which in contrast are considered relatively unstable (dissonant). Some persons have theorized from various scientific bases (mathematical, acoustical, and psychological) with equally imperfect results; nevertheless, the very basis of harmonic music is the ebb and flow produced by the tonal movement between dissonance and consonance—that is, between points of harmonic instability or tension, and stability or repose. Let us abandon such theoretical considerations to turn to more immediate matters regarding harmonic structures.

As was mentioned earlier, the traditional classifications of consonance and dissonance have lost much of their meaning. Therefore, the needs of the contemporary musician are better served, perhaps, by a consideration of relative degrees of consonance or dissonance, as illustrated in the progression of the intervals in Example 87 from stability to instability.

Ex. 87.

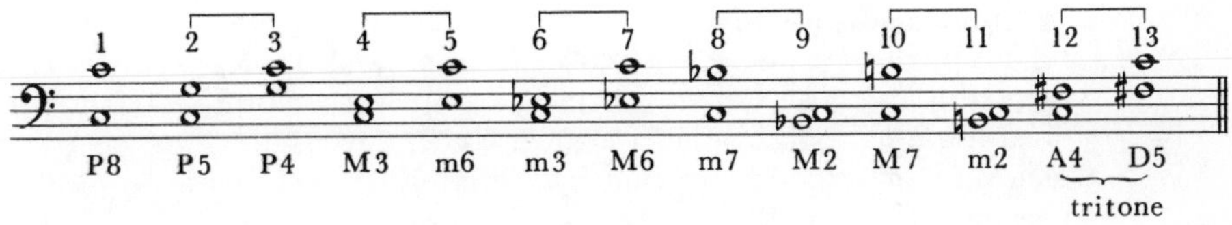

Determine for yourself where the juncture between consonance and dissonance occurs, and, for that matter, the relative stability of one interval compared to another.

COMPOUND INTERVALS

Intervals exceeding an octave are called *compound intervals,* and are named and classified the same as their equivalents within the basic octave. For example, a ninth is an octave plus a second; that is, it is a "compound second," which is a dissonance and may be either major or minor. Likewise, a tenth is a consonant "compound third," which is also either major or minor. For practical reasons, the concept of compound intervals is limited to ninths, tenths, elevenths, and thirteenths.

Lastly, it should be observed that intervals are invertible: the relative position of the constituent pitches may be reversed by moving the lower tone up an octave, or the upper one down an octave. This will become clear if you return to Example 87 and compare pairs of intervals, beginning with 2–3, 4–5, etc. You can see that through inversion, a fifth becomes a fourth, a third becomes a sixth, a seventh becomes a second, etc. Further, such invertible pairs form an octave; and major intervals become minor, and vice versa. Perfect intervals that are inverted become other perfect intervals; augmented intervals become diminished, and vice versa.

PROBLEM

Create and identify the intervals that result from inverting the intervals in Example 88, according to the examples given.

Ex. 88.

(A) Lower note an 8ve higher

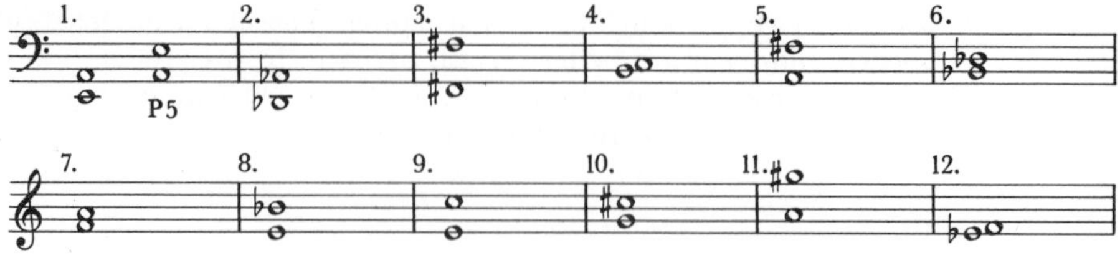

(B) Upper note an 8ve lower

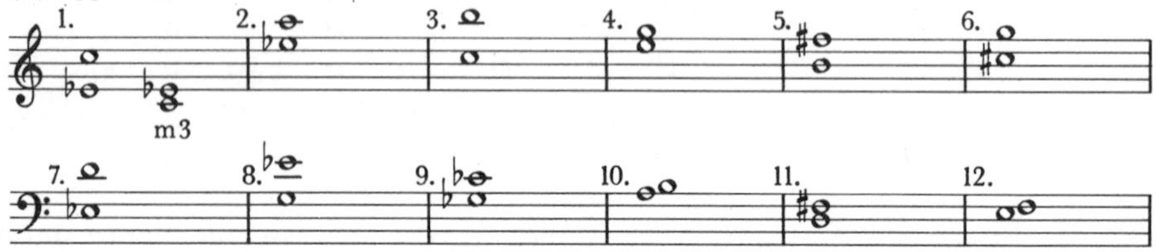

MOVABLE CLEFS

To close our discussion of rudiments, consider one other matter that has continued to vex students of music through the years—movable clefs. By now, we are all familiar with the two clefs most commonly used: the treble and bass clefs. At one time they were movable, that is, they appeared in various positions on the staff. Nowadays, the treble clef (*g clef*) and bass clef (*f clef*) are fixed, as we have seen. However, there is one other clef that is currently used, the *c clef,* which is movable and is used to fix *middle c* on one or the other of the five lines of the staff. Its use arose, supposedly, from a desire to avoid excessive numbers of added ledger lines, and, thus, to simplify the problem of music reading. In old music, whenever the line exceeded the range of the staff, the clef was moved or replaced by another type. The result was satisfactory in one way, but the challenge to the skill and perseverance of a student unschooled in the reading of music with movable clefs was sizable indeed. It is gratifying to know that a musician today must cope with but four clefs, generally speaking, and no more. Earlier, he might have been faced with the realization of music containing a variety of clefs, as suggested by Example 89.

Aside from the bass and treble clefs now in common use, one finds quite prevalent usage of the *alto clef* and *tenor clef,* the remnants of the movable c clef of older days. The alto clef fixes c^1 on the middle line of the staff, and is used most frequently to notate viola parts (hence, it is often called the *viola clef*). The tenor clef (c^1 fixed on the fourth line) is used most often for the upper range of the cello, bassoon, tenor trombone, and other instruments of similar range. Acquaint yourself with these clefs, and concentrate on mastering the alto clef in particular since you will be reading scores of many works involving the viola. Remember that the converging lines of the c clef indicate middle c (c^1), and then practice reading with this in mind until mastery is achieved.

Ex. 89.

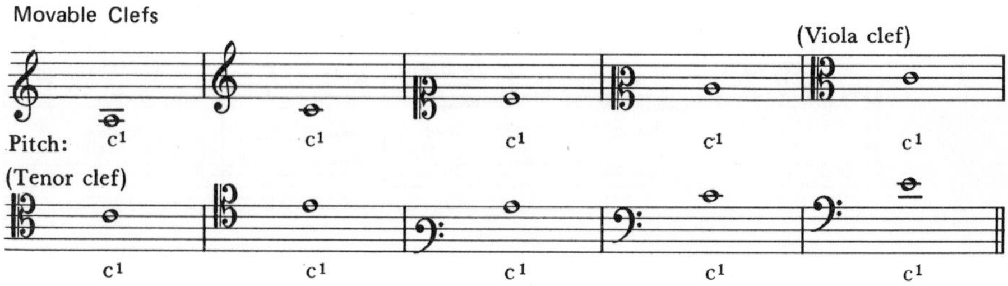

PROBLEMS

1. Transcribe Examples 90 and 91 onto the treble clef on the staves beneath.

Ex. 90.

Ex. 91.

2. Transcribe Examples 92 and 93 onto the clefs indicated.

Ex. 92.

Ex. 93.

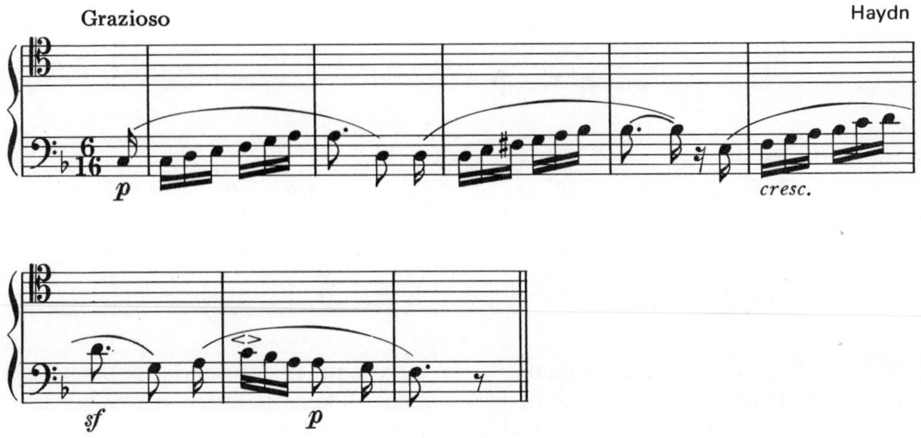

3. Sing Examples 94 and 95, first using pitch names, and then "ta."

Ex. 94.

Ex. 95.

In this brief summary of the rudiments of music, it has been impossible to dwell on any matter in great detail. There is much yet to be learned—new vocabulary, concepts, techniques, and skills. So, we encourage you to review carefully and systematically the materials presented in Units 1 and 2, to ensure the thorough background that will make more readily accessible the more challenging materials yet to be presented.

unit

3

ANALYTIC CONCEPTS

INTUITION VERSUS ANALYSIS

Many musicians, especially those in training, fail to understand the goals and practical values of musical analysis. Far too often, analysis is viewed as a kind of academic routine to be endured during apprentice stages of musical life and quickly abandoned upon graduation to musical maturity, the sooner forgotten the better. Unfortunately, such an outlook is not completely without justification in view of what many beginning musicians have been taught in the name of musical analysis.

Analysis, at best, can be a useful tool for performers and conductors in providing rational bases for the decision-making and interpretation that are essential parts of musical performance. Furthermore, analysis provides guidelines for stylistic interpretation and comparison, as well as for the exploration of music old and new, by ear or by score study—guidelines that can and should be essential tools for informed musicians. At worst, analysis is reduced to such curricular time-killers as tabbing each and every chord in a Bach chorale or Beethoven piano sonata with a roman numeral, as if doing so were the equivalent of a meaningful explanation of the various relationships and patterns found in the music.

Analysis should bring out what mere surface reading commonly fails to reveal. It demands perceptive reading of both gross and detailed elements in a composition, coupled with a grasp of those processes and considerations that provide workable bases for analytical decisions and performance. The basic concepts of musical organization, such as unity, variety, repetition, and change, are rather generally and objectively agreed on; the realization of such conceptual guidelines for musical analysis often involves subjective decisions, however. Analysis, like performance, demands both objective and subjective considerations; it is *not* scientific.

Sidney Foster, the artist-pianist, recently observed before a class[1] that a performer must be a master theorist, completely versed in analysis. He then commented on the necessity of carefully analyzing the music that one is to study and perform. Unfortunately, many novice musicians disdain systematic analysis of the type alluded to by Sidney Foster, in favor of *intuition*—preferring to interpret music "as they feel it."

In Unit 6 we will relate musical analysis to performance. In the present unit several analytical procedures and considerations are mapped out and applied on a limited scale. Assuming that intuition and feeling are essential facets of any musical task—listening, performing, or analyzing—take the challenge offered by such informed artists as Sidney Foster and try to develop analytical insights into music that may prove to be helpful, if not invaluable, to *your* music-making.

BASIC MELODY

Most musicians are, as performers, primarily concerned with the realization of *one musical line;* obvious exceptions are pianists, organists, guitarists, xylophonists, and certain others. But as singers, clarinetists, trumpet players, and string players we deal essentially with one line. This does not mean that we should concentrate in practice and performance on that single line to the extent that we are not aware of other parts or accompaniments. It does mean that the one-line player must be able to both interpret and understand the materials and structure of his part as well as its relation to those operating with it. In this discussion we will deal initially with the former consideration, postponing the latter.

One of the most essential suppositions of musical analysis, one easily documented in the writings of such outstanding musician-theorists as Heinrich Schenker, Paul Hindemith, Leonard Meyer, Arnold Schoenberg, and others, is the notion that musical form—musical shape or design—operates and is perceived on different levels; that is, that there are, in effect, various dimensions of musical time-passing or motion. The span from opening to close represents one level of musical time-passing; the progress from note to note represents another very different level of musical motion. Between these levels we perceive a level of musical motion that marks the passing of the most significant formal events in a composition, as charted by such occurrences as beginnings and endings of phrases and sections, cadences, climaxes, points of decisive change, and others. It is this level of musical perception that is generally regarded as most significant in the creation of musical shape and structure. The details of most compositions can frequently be understood as a product of the elaboration (working out) of musical structure. It is through awareness of the interrelation between structure and detail that analysis becomes meaningful; too often analysis has been predicated on description of activity at only one level rather than on recognition of the relations between different levels. *Basic-Melody* analysis relates melodic structure and detail in the musical line.

---

[1] I.U. Theory. Sophomore lecture.

Example 1 is the melody of a familiar song by Simon and Garfunkel. Like most traditional melodies, and many contemporary ones too, this piece illustrates several basic tonal materials and organizational techniques. The most significant component of the piece's structure is its clear adherence to tonality, in this case the key of E[2] minor.

Ex. 1. "Scarborough Fair"—traditional.

Tonality frame

Several interacting factors are responsible for our perception of E as the *tonic,* or *central tone,* of this melody. In the first place, E is the opening and closing note; it provides a clearly stated point of pitch reference at the melody's beginning. Furthermore, E is firmly emphasized at subsequent measures in the melody, such as measures 4 and 5, 13, and 18. E is confirmed as tonic in the cadence at measure 21. In each of these occurences, E is imprinted on our hearing by virtue of an agogic (durational) accent or a downbeat (metric) accent. As the melody unfolds the note *e* quickly assumes a role in the melodic structure not equaled by any other pitch. Notes that for various reasons assume such prominence are traditionally called *tonal centers* or *tonic* pitches. It's easy to see how a singer performing a melody such as this can utilize the tonic as a ready aural reference for preparing entrances or finding other related notes in the melody.

Note that both e^1 and e^2 are prominent in this melody; taken together, these two pitches form the most stable interval relation available, that of the perfect octave. Clear evidence for the stability of the octave can be found in

---

[2] Lowercase letters denote pitch names and uppercase letters denote the names of major or minor keys.

the overtone series, in which the octave is the most prominent interval of all. Note the location of the two *e*'s shown in Example 1 in the overtone series built on E, presented in Example 2.

Ex. 2. Lower partials of an overtone series on E.

Scanning Example 1, it is easy to see that the tonic octave e^1–e^2 provides a framework, a floor and ceiling, for the melody. The brief occurrence in measure 20 of d^1, *e*'s lower neighbor, in no way detracts from the importance of the E octave. Tonal melodies frequently reveal a similar low-high projection of the tonic octave. In other melodies the *dominant* octave often plays a similar role.

The dominant note is also a very stable tonal element, deriving its stability from its strong relation to the fundamental as the second most prominent member of the overtone series. See Example 2; note the prominence of *b*, the dominant of E. It's easy to see how prominent *b* is in Example 1; its importance in the melodic layout is secondary only to *e*. In melodies that do not span an octave from tonic to tonic or dominant to dominant a tonality frame is formed by the span of a fifth or twelfth (an eighth plus a fifth) from tonic to dominant; far more rare, but possible as well, is a tonic-to-mediant tonality frame spanning a major or minor tenth. Tonal arrangements such as these help create the feeling of tonality that is prevalent in most traditional melodies. We will call such tonic (or dominant) octave spans a *tonality frame*. The tonality frame frequently creates a very basic component of tonal melodic structure, acting as a kind of scaffold for the support of other structural and decorative materials. Read the melodies in Example 3, most of which incorporate tonality frames based on either tonic or dominant octaves; also note any examples in which *no* clear tonality frame is present.

Ex. 3.

(a) Mozart

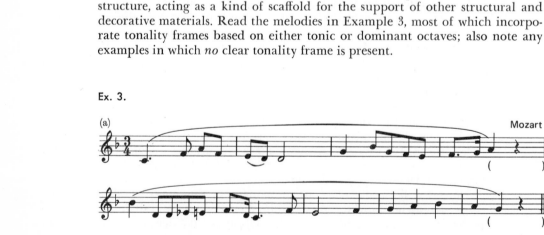

Violin Concerto No.1 in D, Op.19

Andantine sognando Prokofieff

(b)

Concerto for 2 Clavier and Orchestra, II

(c) Adagio ovvero largo — Bach

(d) Trouvère Song

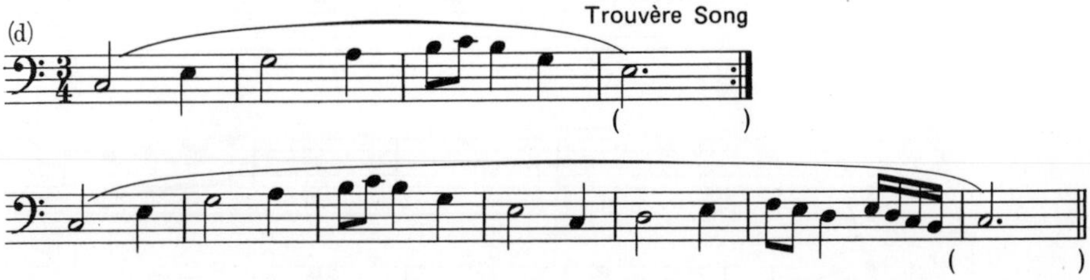

(e) Traditional

Now check your ability to identify the tonality frame of a tonal melody by reading the music in Problem 1a and showing the tonality frames in the space provided. Check your answers.

PROBLEM 1a

Analyze the tonality frames of these melodies.

(1) Beethoven

Tonality frame

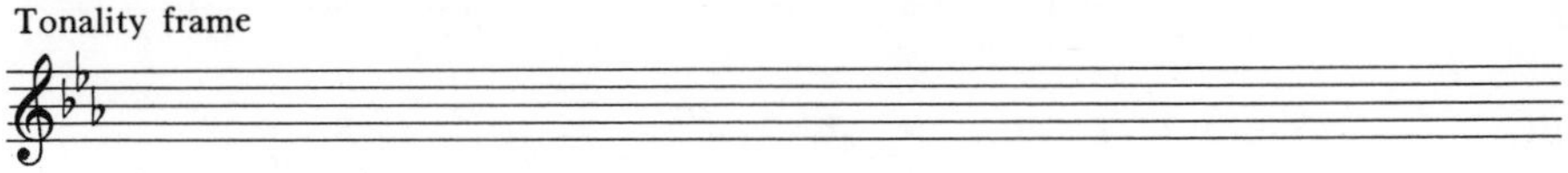

Problem 1a continued.

(2) Schubert

Tonality frame

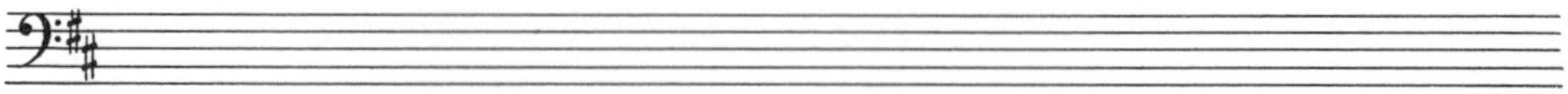

(3) Schumann

Tonality frame

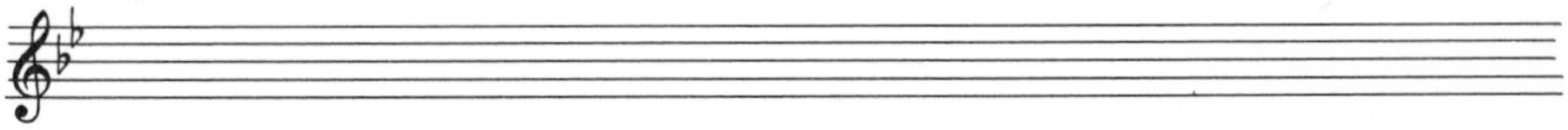

PROBLEM 1b

Complete the melodies begun below, using both materials that are given and some of your own invention. Employ the keys and *tonality frames* indicated after the key signatures. Write melodies that you can sing easily; fill the blank measures. Sample solutions are provided; consult them.

(1) **Moderato**

(2) **Lento**

(3) Allegro

PROBLEM 1c

Listen to melodies composed for Problem 1b by other members of the class, if possible. Try to develop your tonal memory by (1) singing the tonality frame after the melody is played, and (2) writing down the completion of the melody from dictation.

Range and Tessitura

The *range* of a melody denotes the absolute high-low span. The range of "Scarborough Fair" (Ex. 1) is from d^1 to e^2, that is, an octave and a major second (in all, a major ninth). This contrasts with the octave tonality frame of the same melody. Any melody exhibits range; some melodies reveal no distinct octave tonality frame as such.

PROBLEM 2

Determine the range of this melody:

Down in the Valley

Folksong

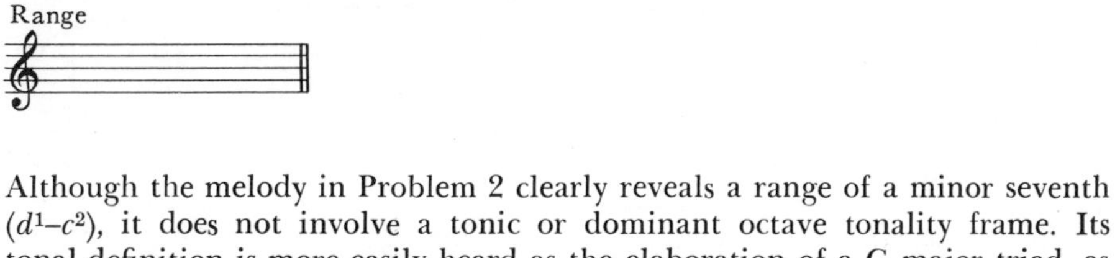

Range

Although the melody in Problem 2 clearly reveals a range of a minor seventh (d^1–c^2), it does not involve a tonic or dominant octave tonality frame. Its tonal definition is more easily heard as the elaboration of a G major triad, as noted in the melody's opening. This important phase of melodic tonality will be explored at length shortly.

Reference is often made by singers, and other musicians as well, to the *tessitura,* or general *lie,* of a melody or extended melodic passage, such as an aria or an entire operatic role. Tessitura refers to the high-low area *typifying* the overall activity of a melody, that part of the register that is most used for the melody. This contrasts with the *range,* which denotes the absolute high and low pitches—even though such pitches might only occur once or twice in an extended section. It is not always possible or relevant to attempt to distinguish between range and tessitura; however, the contours of many melodies are such that the distinction may be meaningful, as in the case of the melody in Example 3.

Ex. 3.

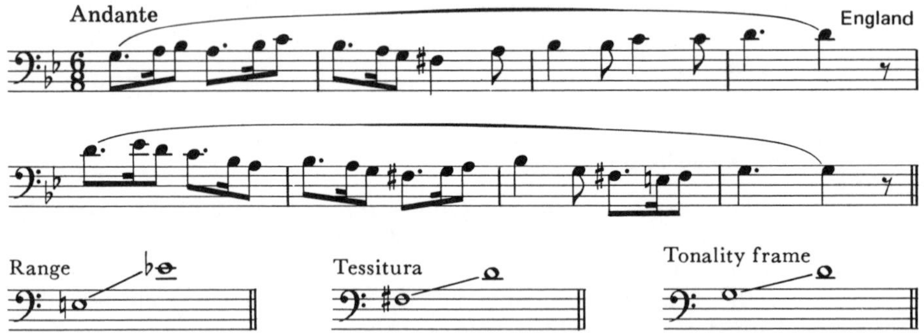

PROBLEM 3a

Indicate the tessitura, range, and tonality frame for the following three melodies:

PROBLEM 3b

Which of the melodies in Problem 3a reveal octave tonality frames?

Triadic Outline

A significant basis for the recognition and delineation of tonality in melody occurs in the form of direct and elaborated outlines of the tonic triad, the triad involving the stable scale degrees *1*, *3*, and *5* (and their octave duplications). Many theorists have pointed to the relation of such triadic outlines to the natural properties of sound found in the harmonic or overtone series. Compare the opening of the National Anthem to the natural overtones of C major. (See Ex. 4.)

Ex. 4. National Anthem and C harmonic series.

Of the twenty-five notes in the passage quoted, all but five (marked *x*) coincide with prominent, stable members of the harmonic series. There can be no question but that the accessible key feeling of the National Anthem, obviously intended to be within the tonal grasp of virtually any ear–trained or untrained, professional or amateur–is in part due to the simple pitch relations stated at the outset of the tune, which form a cliché that has been evidenced to one degree or another in virtually every musical period of the past thousand years.

Both major and minor triads have been given such melodic treatment in tonal music; however, only the major triad can be seen as a direct duplicate of tones of the harmonic series.[3] The minor triad, an exact mirror of the interval format of the major (Major = Mm thirds while Minor = mM 3rds, in

---

[3] The minor third of the C-rooted triad does not occur as a prominent partial.

that order), must be regarded as an artistic rather than "natural" phenomenon. Augmented and diminished triads, though having obvious characteristics in common with the major and minor triads, do not create tonal stability and do not occur as tonic triads outlining degrees 1, 3, and 5 of the major or minor scale.

We can recognize linear triadic patterns in numerous shapes. Our perception seems to be so attuned to triadic figures that any of those shown in Example 5 can be easily interpreted as an inversion or variant of a fundamental arrangement of a major triad. Each of the arrangements shown here occurs in its parallel minor form as well. Familiarize yourself with these by ear through playing and singing, so that recognition becomes automatic.

Ex. 5. Familiar linear arrangements of major triads.

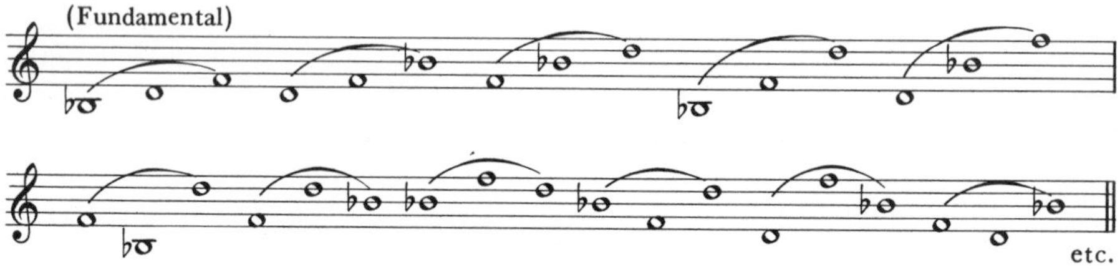

When the members of a triad occur in immediate succession, direct triad outlining results; when *other pitches intervene* between triad members, elaborated triad outlining is the result. Both of these processes are of crucial importance to the delineation of major and minor keys in tonal melody.

PROBLEM 4

Locate and circle examples of direct major or minor *tonic* triad outlining in the following melodies. Sing or play each melody.

(1) Bach

(2) Haydn

(3) Brahms

Articulations of tonic triad tones in melody represent an important aspect of key delineation even when such triadic pitches are embellished by other intervening pitches. From a different point of view, it is easy to see that strategic occurrences of members of the tonic triad mark the progress of the melody that follows.

Ex. 6. Bach: Mass in B minor, *Gloria in excelsis.*

Because of their relation to the tonality of the melody, not to mention their placement on accented beats, the notes *d, f♯*, and *a* create a stable and easily heard structure for the measure-by-measure, beat-by-beat filling-in and elaboration that constitutes the detail of the melody's contour and rhythm. No direct triad outlining is found in the melody, but there can be little question about the importance of the D major triad as an underpinning for it; the process is one of staggered, that is, delayed, triadic outlining.

In many melodies, both direct and elaborated triadic configuration occur; sometimes one overlaps the other. Almost any tonal melody reveals triadic configuration or elaboration in one form or another. Only the rarest of tonal melodies fails to reveal motion from one to another tonic triad degree. The stability of key of a given passage or melody is related to the prominence and frequency of appearance of tonic triad tones.

Compare the two melodies in Example 7 in terms of key feelings. Example 7a is a simple elaboration of the triadic tones *f, b♭*, and *d*. Triadic members *f, a♭*, and *c* are far more subtly concealed and elaborated in Example 7b, with the result that tonal feeling is more subjective, resting precariously between F minor and A♭ major.

Ex. 7a.

Ex. 7b.

PROBLEM 5

Pitches of various tonic triads form the structural bases of the melodies that are shown below; on the staff beneath each melody, sketch the triadic members that are elaborated. The position on the lower staff should coincide with the location of the structural pitch in the melodic line above. Connect the structural pitches by beams, as shown in Example 7, notating each pitch as an open note.

(a)

(b)

(c) France

In all likelihood you have noticed, in dealing with the preceding examples and problems in this unit, that tonic triadic outlines frequently overlap; in other words, a pitch that is stated as part of a direct outline, that is, part of the melodic detail, may at the same time represent part of a larger triadic span, a structural pitch. This sort of formal ambiguity is entirely consistent with the fact that musical structure itself is frequently ambiguous. Our perception is constantly affected by the interactions of musical events on different levels. That is why an event that appears initially to affect only detail may, in the light of subsequent events, have to be interpreted as part of a higher level of organization as well.

In Example 8, it is easy to see how the root of the tonic triad of G major functions on different levels: on the one hand, as in measures 1–3, it is part of an opening elaboration of the G triad; on the other hand, it is part of a more prolonged outline of the same triad, formed by the span of the entire first section of the song (mm. 1–12), involving the opening *g* of phrase one, measure 1, the close of phrase one on the triad third, *b,* and the end of the section on the dominant, *d.* The overlapping beams in the graph below the music depict in notation this phenomenon of pitch relations, which can be realized only in sound, and the meaning of which is (at least in part) subjectively perceived.

Ex. 8. Schumann: *Der Zeisig*, Op. 104, No. 4.

PROBLEM 6

Familiarize yourself with the following melody and make a sketch showing triadic outlines and involving both structure and detail, using Example 8 as a model. It is not necessary to attempt to account for all examples of direct triad outlining in this piece, but just those that are overlapped by more structural tonic triad elaboration.

In the preceding discussion and illustrations, we have noted a number of related matters affecting the organization of pitches in tonal music. These considerations have direct bearing on our perception of tonality, and it should be clear that they frequently interact and overlap. The three-stage analysis shown below the melodic line in Example 9 reflects the application of these considerations to the sketching of the tonal structure of a melody.

Ex. 9.

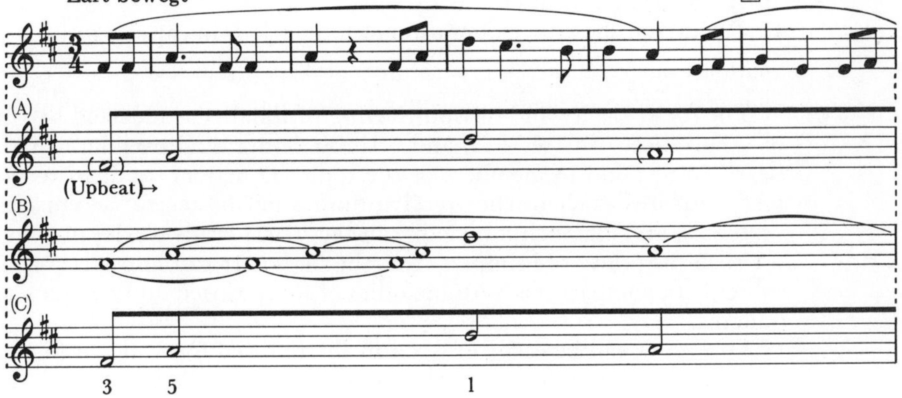

Ex. 9 continued.

Analysis of Tonal Structure in Three Steps

A. Terminal pitches and tonality frame; in capsule form
B. Tonic triad outlines in detail
C. Reduction showing elaboration of tonic triad; in capsule form

The tonal clarity and obvious feeling of tonality is reflected by the number of occurrences of notes 1, 3, and 5 throughout. Well over half of the pitches heard correspond to members of the tonic (D major) triad; in ten of the sixteen measures, such pitches receive durational or metric accents, as in measures 1, 9, and 12. Such a melody can serve as a ready model of tonal melody; for such purposes, the simpler it is, the better. It can also serve as a basis for subsequent comparisons with melodies of more varied and complex tonal components.

Analysis A can be easily grasped in the reduced form shown in Example 9a. The notes that are shown parenthetically in Example 9—which correspond to terminal pitches of successive phrases—are omitted in the reduction (Ex. 9a), as are all *recurrences* of 1, 3, or 5. As no *f*♯'s (3) occur prominently as accented beginning or ending pitches, nor as highs or lows in the melodic range, they are eliminated from the reduction of analysis A. Note that the role of the opening *f*♯ is that of an upbeat, that is, one or more unaccented notes that *lead to,* rather than create emphasis on, a downbeat. The downbeat *a* is of such far greater rhythmic and tonal weight that it alone is retained in Example 9a.

Ex. 9a. Reduction of analysis A: terminal pitches and tonality frame, in capsule form.

(a) Reduced

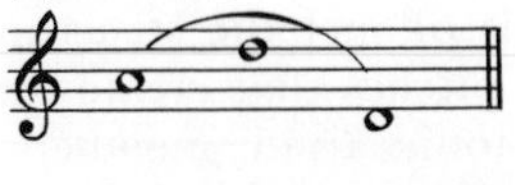

Analysis B is reduced by eliminating immediate restatements of extensions of triadic outline, as occurs with the notes *f*♯ and *a* at the melody's beginning. Triadic tones whose occurrences primarily generate rhythmic interest rather than create points of tonal emphasis—as with *f*♯ and *d* in measure 10—are given minimal attention in the reduction (Ex. 9b), via filled-in note-heads. Doing this helps us to distinguish varying degrees of importance in tonal pitch details. Sing the notes of Example 9b and note the marked feeling of tonality that results; doing so clearly reflects the way in which the melody itself articulates the tonic triad in various phrases.

Ex. 9b. Reduction of analysis B: tonic triad outlines in detail.

(b) Reduced

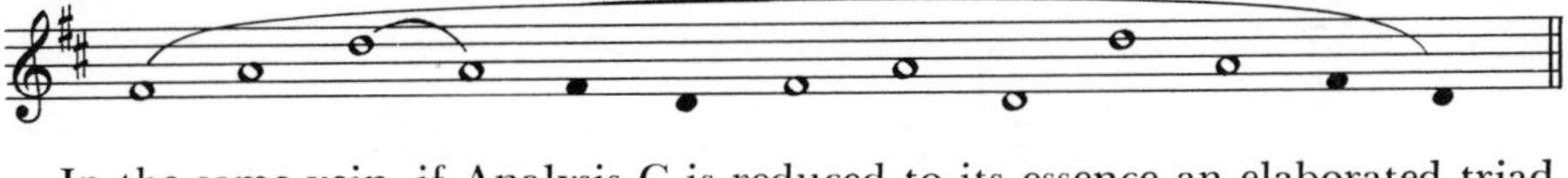

In the same vein, if Analysis C is reduced to its essence an elaborated triad results.

Ex. 9c. Reduction of analysis C: elaboration of tonic triad, in capsule form.

(c) Reduced

Example 9d is a condensed sketch of the preceding reductions combined. All of the activity that occurs within measure 3–13 prolongs the emphasis on d^2. For that reason, the *d* pitch can be viewed as the main structural note of the tonality of the entire span. Note that it is the only pitch that occupies such a position of importance in all three prior reductions. (Ex. 9a–9c).

Ex. 9d. Capsule of Examples 9a–9c.

(d) Capsule of (a), (b) and (c) Combined

This series of analytical steps may appear to be redundant; in fact it is. What is important is that systematic bases for analyzing melodic structure be available and applicable to most tonal music, a great deal of which is far more diversified than the simple song analyzed here.

It is also important to realize that analysis of melodic structure includes many factors other than recognition of those pitches that create tonality. We shall see shortly how pitches other than tonic triad members influence melodic structure and detail—specifically, melodic contour and melodic rhythm —sometimes reinforcing, sometimes embellishing triadic tones.

PROBLEM 7

Analyze the tonal pitch structure of the following melody; model your analytical steps after those in Example 8, the folksong *"Going Home."*

(a) Reduced

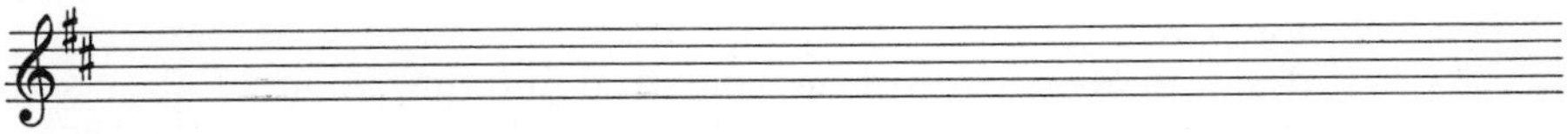

(b) Reduced

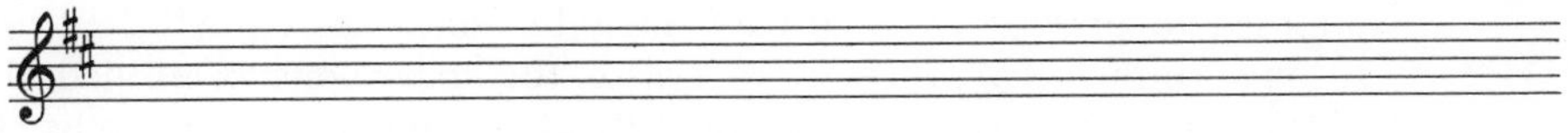

(c) Reduced

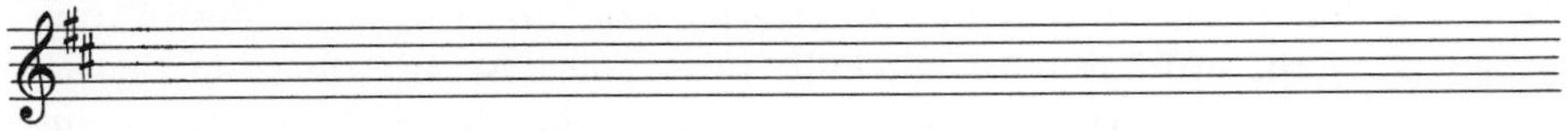

(d) Capsule of (a), (b) and (c) Combined

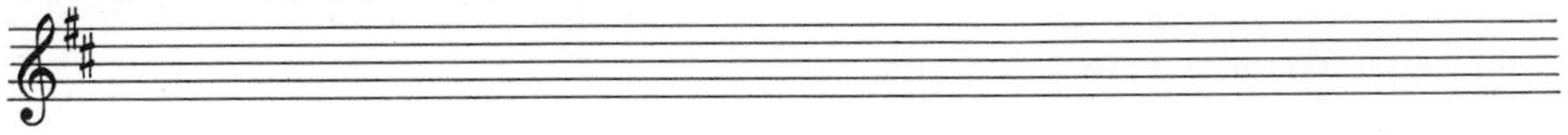

Problem 7 continued.

Solutions

(a)

(b)

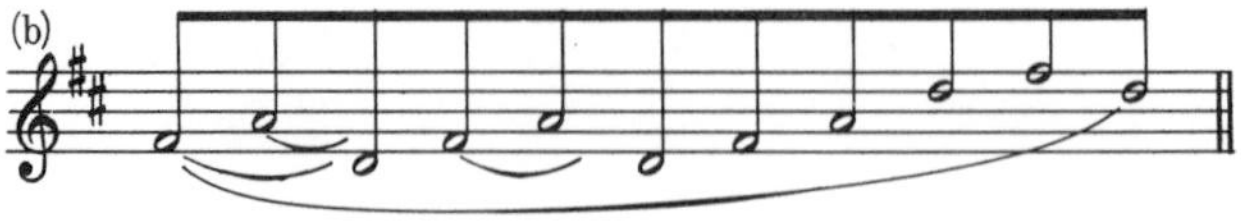

(c)

Despite the fact that it is possible to isolate the various components of a given melody, it is often very hard to account objectively for our individual reactions to a melody or for that matter, a composition. Most musicians seem to experience an essentially affective response on a first hearing; but if our initial responses to melody are largely subjective and affective, our subsequent efforts to remember, comprehend, and explain are more predicated on rational procedures and other, more objective considerations. Frequently, a desire to know more about a particular composition or melody thereof is sparked by a positive emotional reaction to the work: the piece moves us, or a melody in it appeals to us. Sometimes we are attracted by seemingly indefinable characteristics of a line or by its performance. That we react in this way is probably partly responsible for our commitment to music and our strong desire to make music a dominant part of our lives. It seems unlikely that any analytical process will provide a complete basis for the adequate explanation of such responses. Analysis provides bases for understanding musical syntax, structure, and style—that is, the musical signals and patterns to which we react as listeners and which we, as performers, composers, and conductors, must interpret and arrange.

Basic Melody involves an analytical interpretation of the structure of a melody. By structure is meant the *skeletal framework* of the melody—an appraisal of those melodic components whose function is mainly essential as opposed to decorative. The basic melodic tones are embellished and linked through numerous processes to create the marvelous combined illusion of pitch, contour, duration, and timbre that we perceive as melody. The main purpose of making an analysis of a melody's basic pitches is to find out as much as we can about the materials used and their relations in time, as created by the unfolding of a melodic line. There is little question that an awareness of musical syntax can foster insights and decisions regarding interpretation that can be invaluable to the performer. It seems unlikely that a composer would approach melodic composition without some awareness of syntactical relations in his own work.

Melodic Cadence

We determined earlier that the opening and closing notes of a melody are structural; they form boundaries for the entire melodic span. Similarly, the opening and closing notes of the various phrases within a melody are also basic to structure. The main determinants of phrases are cadences, that is, points of pause or inactivity characterized by long notes, rest, or rhythmic repose. The components of melodic cadence are pitch and duration. Phrases are typically characterized by a rather continuous thread of activity and may form musical spans of from one to as many as sixteen measures. In traditional music, four-measure phrases are so common as to be regarded as a norm; to do so may be over-simplification, however. Using the considerations noted here as guidelines to phrase identification will prove sufficient for the present. In subsequent study of melodic design, we will deal more extensively with phrases and phrase relations.

The phrases in Example 10 are indicated by the traditional symbol of a curved line, which denotes a continuing statement or musical "thought." A simple abstraction of the beginning and closing phrase members provides some delineation of the melodic structure.

Ex. 10. "All Through the Night" (traditional melody).

Phrase Beginnings and Endings *

* Not to be confused with a basic melody analysis.

The pattern suggested by this phrase analysis is one that is found in a great deal of tonal music. The opening (repeated) phrase, A, clearly defines the song's tonic, *g*, with its beginning and ending notes. Phrase B represents a digression from the centeredness of the opening, emphasizing *c* as a temporary focal pitch and terminating inconclusively on the leading tone *f*♯. The inconclusiveness of the end of phrase B is emphasized both by a lack of rhythmic pause and by the motion to the leading tone, *f*♯, a pitch that suggests continuation and movement to a goal of the tonic, *g*. Note that the digressive character of phrase B is further suggested by the tritone interval spanned by the first and last pitches of the phrase. The closing phrase, C, re-emphasizes the stability of *g*, which is also associated with the first phrase.

There are many traditional terms for cadences. The expression most commonly applied to such tonic endings is *authentic cadence,* typically represented by motion in the melodic line (main voice or instrument) from 7 to 8, that is, from leading tone to tonic. However, since the term *authentic cadence* assumes a particular kind of harmonic activity in accompanying parts, it seems premature to define melodic cadence on such a basis. For the time being, we will refer to melodic cadences that involve the tonic pitch or its triadic associate, the mediant, as *terminal cadences.* This term simply denotes the finality and completion of *any* cadence on the tonic, regardless of its location in the melody. The phrases in Example 11 feature terminal cadences.

Ex. 11. Terminal cadences in tonal music.

My Country, 'Tis of Thee

(a)

Way Back Home in Indiana

(b)

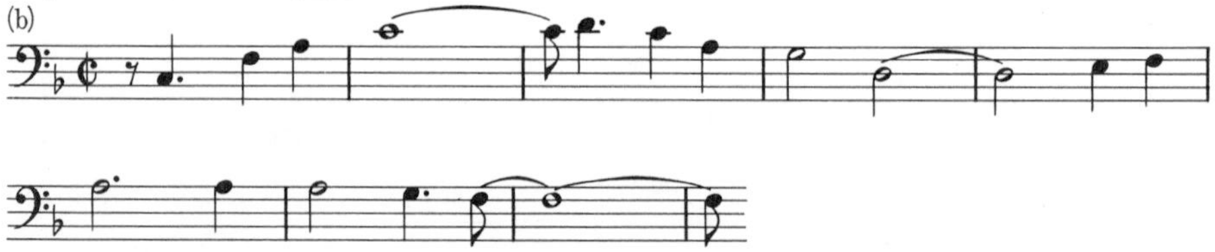

Piano Sonata in C, No.15, Trio (transp.)

(c) Haydn

Op.28, I

(d) Beethoven

Prelude, Op.28, No.4

Chopin

Cadences on the mediant, though described as terminal, are obviously less stable than those defining tonic per se. Because of its close intervallic relation to the tonic, however, cadences on the mediant sound essentially complete. For purposes of differentiation we will refer to cadences on the tonic as *perfect terminal cadences.* Cadences on the mediant are described hereafter as *imperfect terminal cadences.* In later study, the parallel between this distinction in melodic closure and harmonic cadence will become evident.

As a rule, cadences on scale degrees other than tonic (or mediant) evoke a different response from the listener and serve a different function in melodic design. Such phrase endings imply *noncompletion;* they are *open,* so to speak, with the resulting expectation by the listener of *more to come.* The traditional name of half-cadence for such patterns, like those of the terminal group, derives from harmonic action. To avoid such assumptions for the time being, we will describe such open endings as *progressive cadences.* We shall see, furthermore, that such a description can be more useful in dealing with harmonic matters and full textures than such terms as *authentic* and *half,* with their traditional biases and limitations. This is true in particular of the study of cadence in more recent music, as well as a great deal of music written prior to the seventeenth century. Any melodic cadence on the supertonic, leading tone, subdominant, submediant, or subtonic is progressive. (We shall deal with cadences on the dominant subsequently.) Familiarize yourself with the progressive cadences in Example 12.

Ex. 12. Progressive cadences.

Sonata in C Minor, K.457, I

Mozart

Sonata in B♭, K.570 (Finale)

Mozart

Ex. 12 continued.

Op.2, No.3

(c) Adagio

Beethoven

(Supertonic)

Missa Prolationum, Kyrie II

(d)

Ockeghem

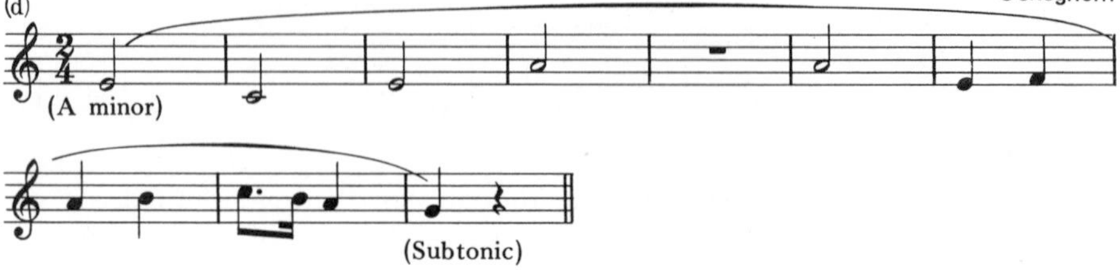

(Subtonic)

The terms describing melodic cadence presented above are based solely on the relation of the cadence pitch to tonic in tonal music. It should be noted that such limited description fails to account for a component of cadence as crucial as pitch, if not more so—namely, rhythm (or its absence). In reviewing Examples 11 and 12, it's apparent that the degree of conclusiveness, or lack of it, of a given cadence is as much related to the durational prominence (length or placement, or both) of the cadence pitch as is the relation of the cadence pitch to the tonic. In Examples 11a and 11b, for instance, the conclusiveness and terminal effect of the cadence notes is in part due to their relatively long duration. The rather inconclusive effect of the melodic cadence on $d^2\sharp$ in Example 11c is, by the same reasoning, a result of short duration.

The progressive cadences in Example 12 reveal a similar relation to rhythm. The listener's expectation for continuation is in each excerpt a product of both pitch and rhythm. Note that a further rhythmic distinction should be made on the basis of metric position, that is, the arrival of the cadence pitch on a strong or weak beat. Comparing Examples 12a and 12b, it is easy to see that the strong beat arrival of the cadence note in the former is more definitive than the "last-gasp" arrival on *e*♭ in the latter. Other factors such as dynamic change, rise or fall (direction), and intervallic pattern of the cadence as well (usually a product of the last two pitches in the phrase) clearly affect our perception of melodic cadence.

None of the cadence types noted above relates specifically to the *dominant* scale degree. Melodic cadences on the dominant are usually progressive; but in some instances the dominant note is heard as the fifth of a tonic triad outline, and creates an impression of somewhat weak conclusion similar to that of the imperfect terminal cadence on the mediant. The dominant's progressive effect, however, is analogously heightened by its frequent occurrence as part of a triadic outline centered on a dominant root. Final cadences on the dominant pitch are usually imperfect terminal. The cadential ambiguity of the dominant pitch in melodic contexts reflects its frequent role as a secondary focal pitch in tonal music. Because the dominant note shares membership in both the tonic and dominant triad outlines, the two most stable and key-defining in tonal music, its role in melodic tonality, is more susceptible to contextual interpretation than any other pitch. Cadences on the dominant may be interpreted as either terminal or progressive, based on context.

Ex. 13. Tonic triad (outline); dominant triad (outline).

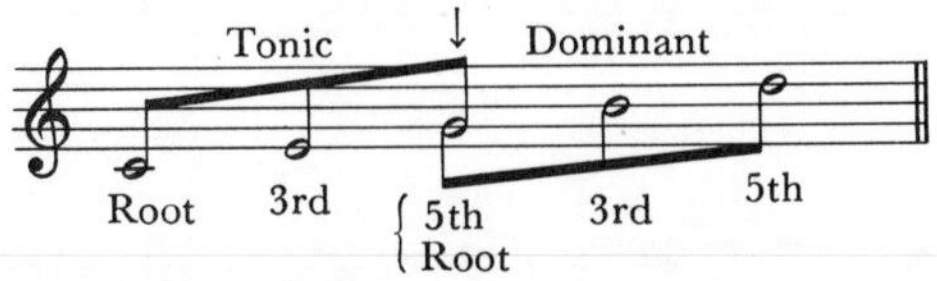

The excerpts in Example 14 suggest the variety of cadence treatments commonly given the dominant note. Because of this variety, it is all the more important to note carefully the pitch materials used in the approach to the dominant cadence.

Ex. 14. Melodic cadences on the dominant.

Violin Concerto — Beethoven

(a)

Bellini

(b)

(c) — Bach

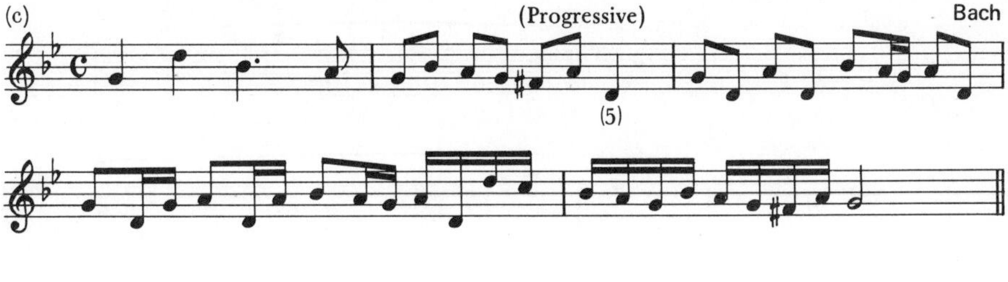

Ex. 14 continued.

Seaman's Song

Kyrie IV; Cunctipotens (III)

PROBLEM 9

Discover each cadence type used in the following melodies, and write the appropriate name at the points provided. Play or sing each melody before completing the analysis.

Violin Concerto No.1 in D, Op.19

Andantino

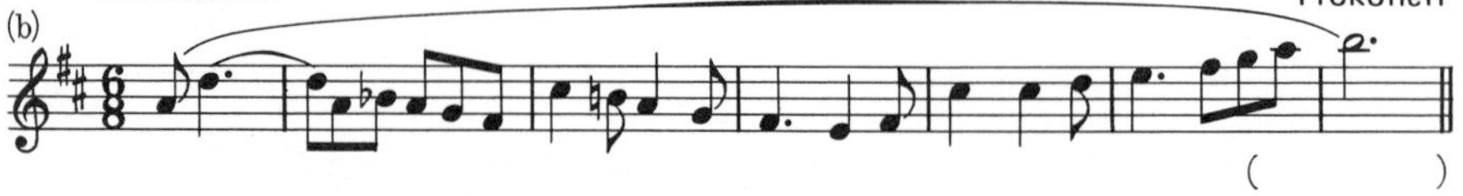

Concerto for 2 Clavier and Orchestra, II

(c) Adagio ovvero Largo

Trouvère Song

(e) Traditional

Contour

Musicians commonly speak of a musical line. In doing so, they tie together successive pitch relations—the horizontal element of music—to an aspect of graphic art. The imagined line depicts melodic contour, the rise and fall of successive pitches. As the word contour suggests, most musical "lines" are more curved than straight, and a drawn line depicting the linking of two points in a melody, a beginning and cadence point, is seldom a direct one.

The illusion of melodic motion is a product of the interaction of pitch and duration. We can depict graphically the contour of a line, representing its relative pitch distances. We can similarly represent the successive durations of the same line. It must be emphasized that the interaction of pitch and duration is only reflected in actual musical notation. Isolating both the contour and rhythms of a melody, though frequently informative, can never yield the picture of what is heard that notation does, for notation presents a simultaneous picture of pitch and rhythm (and other elements too).

We dealt previously with range and tessitura, range representing the extremes of melodic contour, and melodic contour showing the filling-in of the highs and lows that create its range. Example 15 shows how the range of a melody is elaborated by the rise and fall of melodic detail and is thus a product of the various directions and patterns within its boundaries.

Ex. 15. Mozart: Symphony No. 40 in G Minor, *Menuet*.

The contour detail of this melody fills in its d^1–d^2 tonality frame, pinpointing various members of the tonic triad along the way. The process by which the details of melodic contour frequently elaborate and link members of the tonality frame and of the tonic triad is virtually axiomatic in much tonal music. In Example 16 note the role of tonic, dominant, and mediant notes as cornerstones of melodic contour. In later analyses we will assume that you recognize such relationships.

Ex. 16. Examples of melodies with tones of the tonic triad as prominent parts of the contour.

Op.28 in D Major, I

(a) Beethoven

Trouvère Song

(b)

(c) Haydn

In all of the excerpts in Example 16, tonic, dominant, and mediant pitches are prominent as contour extremes. The tonality of each line is quite clear. Melodies (a) and (b), however, unfold the most easily recalled contours; this is true in part because they are composed of essentially step, or *conjunct,* motion. Excerpt (a) opens by stating all of the notes of the D major scale within the descending span from dominant to dominant. The importance of *steps*—the smallest, most accessible intervals—cannot be overestimated. Steps are essential components of melodic contour. Melodies that consist mostly of steps present overall contours that are *exact* replicas of their rise and fall patterns, as in the case of the familiar phrase in Example 17.

Ex. 17. Tchaikovsky: Symphony No. 4, II, *Rondo.*

Since steps, more than any other interval, create the links and connections that are the crux of melodic contour, they loom as important intervals in the determination of the skeletal framework called basic melody. As such, they form a significant counterpart to the triadic outlines cited previously. Triad outlines constitute *disjunct* patterns, for triadic tones are separated by leaps. The structure of most melodies comprises combinations of both steps and leaps; we shall see shortly how the two are often combined in such a way that important steps in the contour link members of the tonality frame or tonic triad. First, let's consider a less obvious application of the term *melodic step.*

Step Progression

In an earlier discussion, we dealt with the melody by Bach that appears in Example 18. Initially, we noted that the pinpointing of the important pitches in this melody is effected by the elaboration of an ascending D major triad. A closer look at this melody reveals, furthermore, that the triadic tones *d, f♯,* and *a* are connected by other pitches with adjacent triad members, and in the process steps are formed; these connecting notes assume importance because they fall on the first beat of the measure and are accented. The resulting

Ex. 18. Bach: from the B Minor Mass.

(a) Bach

line, shown at the bottom of Example 18, is a pattern or series of structural or basic pitches that clearly reflects a perceptible framework of pitch and rhythmic detail. Such progressions by *step*—that is, formed by staggered or delayed conjunct motion—are called step progressions. Like direct or indirect triadic outlines, such step progressions form bases for perceiving linear design, contour, and elaboration in works from most periods and styles of music. Step progressions, that is, delayed or elaborated motion by steps, are generally separated by one or more intervening pitches. Elaborated motion usually forms part of linear *detail* and may involve steps, leaps, repeated notes, chord outlining, or combinations of these; they create elaboration and embellishment.

The melodic excerpts in Example 19 contain several instances of step progression. The members of a step progression are shown joined by a beam. Most perceptible step progressions contain at least three notes.

Ex. 19. Melodies containing step progressions.

The Marriage of Figaro, "Se vuol ballare," Act I — Mozart

(b) Purcell

(c) Bach

Ex. 19 continued.

(d) Schumann

Mozart

(e)

Decisions as to where step progressions occur in melodic structure are sometimes necessarily interpretive and subjective; this fact should emerge after you study Example 19. There are, however, several general guidelines that may be observed in making interpretive decisions about step progressions.

In Example 19a, it can be seen that the structure of the aria is based on the elaboration of an ascending-descending step progression that moves from tonic–dominant–tonic. All of the basic pitches in the step progression have in common *strong beat placement.* Most of the successive basic pitches lie a measure apart; this produces a symmetrical, even-paced rhythm of the notes in the step progression. One can easily note the way in which members of the step progression both pinpoint and connect tonic triad members. Some members of the progression seem to function more as passing notes, or connectors, between stable triadic notes, thusly: 1 (2) 3 (4) 5, parenthetical notes representing *passing steps* between triadic members. The hierarchic implications of such a description are apparent, the triadic tones implying a higher level of importance to structure than non-triadic tones. In some analytical theories, especially those of Heinrich Schenker, such distinctions are crucial. (No hierarchic distinction is made in the analysis shown here, as yet.)

The distinction between immediate steps—major or minor seconds in melodic detail—and those of a structural step progression, is exemplified in Example 19b. Only melodic seconds elaborated by intervening activity are shown as creating step progressions here; note that symmetrical rhythmic placement, that is, recurring arrival on the same beats of successive measures, is an important feature of many step progressions. The importance of step progressions diminishes somewhat in proportion to the absence of even occurrence and placement of the steps involved.

In Example 19c we felt it important to show the dominant note, *B,* as part of a progression leading to a cadence on the supertonic; obviously, this introduces an asymmetrical element into the rhythm of the step progression, since the concluding pitches lie only one beat apart.

Example 19d reveals the distinction between simple step or conjunct motion in melodic detail (mm. 1–8), and pitches forming the underlying melodic contour, the basic pitch line (mm. 9–12). The latter are usually separated by at least one intervening (passing) step or leap. The step progression is completely symmetrical in terms of rhythmic placement of the notes therein.

Example 19e shows a kind of pitch organization suggesting two simultaneously heard levels of activity in the form of two step progressions, a so-called compound step progression. Study this excerpt and see if you agree with the analysis. Obviously, the illusion of two levels of step-controlled activity is a product of the chord outlining or "harmonically motivated" melody found here, a kind of arpeggiation quite well-suited to the keyboard.

All melodies do not contain clear step progressions. However, it should be clear that step progression, along with the elaboration of pitches of the tonic triad, constitutes a very important analytical-interpretive tool for the evaluation of melodic structure.

Step progression frequently provides a structural framework for melodic elaboration in compositions revealing little or no homage to traditional tonality. Such is the case in Example 20.

Ex. 20. Heiden: *In Memoriam* (SATB) mm. 209–17.

PROBLEM 10

Plot the step progressions that occur in the following melodies; do not bother to indicate step relations of fewer than three successive members. Use the same procedure as shown in Example 20.

Adeste Fidelis

(a)

Problem 10 continued.

Piano Sonata, K.333, I Mozart

Recognizing such melodic components as terminal pitches, tonality frame, tonic triad elaborations, and step progressions provides criteria for the interpretation of linear structure, the skeletal contour of melody; this skeletal outline represents a background against which the *details* of melody, the melodic foreground, weave embellishment and decoration. The latter level of activity, which is the most immediate one, quite often traces a contour that is far more elaborate and complex than that of the skeletal level noted above. Both the basic melodic contour (background) and the detailed contour (foreground) are shown in Example 21. The interaction of the two designs is engaging, and such interaction of contours is often a factor in the creation of effective melody. It is by no means always present, however.

Ex. 21. Bach: Concerto in D Minor for Two Violins, I.

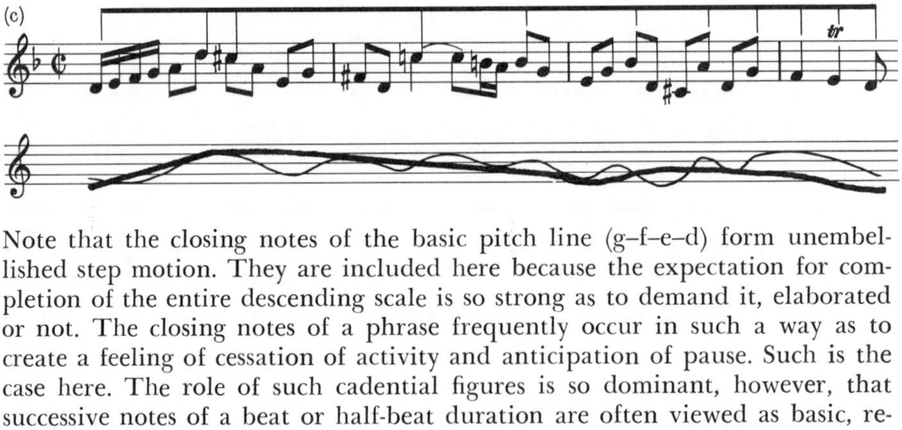

Note that the closing notes of the basic pitch line (g–f–e–d) form unembellished step motion. They are included here because the expectation for completion of the entire descending scale is so strong as to demand it, elaborated or not. The closing notes of a phrase frequently occur in such a way as to create a feeling of cessation of activity and anticipation of pause. Such is the case here. The role of such cadential figures is so dominant, however, that successive notes of a beat or half-beat duration are often viewed as basic, regardless of their simple and direct intervallic step-pattern. The ear must be the final determinant.

Elaborating Basic Pitches; Decorative Activity

We have established that musical organization, in this case melodic, operates on different hierarchical levels. We shall see in later study that such a concept is operative in virtually all musical parameters, as well as other areas of pitch deployment, especially harmony. The differentiation of structural levels of melody is to a great extent the result of rhythm: pitch and rhythm interacting to create melody.

There are, in the main, three kinds of melodic or linear activity that embellish structural pitches; they are briefly illustrated in Example 22.

Ex. 22a. Note repetition.

Ex. 22b. Step motion decorating one or connecting two (or more) different basic (structural) notes.

Ex. 22c. Skip motion embellishing one or connecting two (or more) different basic pitches.

Combinations of these processes often occur in melodic elaboration, as shown in Example 23.

Ex. 23.

A note that embellishes *one* basic pitch is called a neighboring tone, abbreviated n.t.; a pitch that connects by step two or more basic pitches is known as a passing tone (p.t.); and a note that embellishes others by skip is called a secondary pitch (s.p.)[4] As such, they generally reflect chord outlining or arpeggiation of one sort or another. Example 24 includes a variety of decorative techniques, shown in the analysis below the music.

Ex. 24. Melodic decorative techniques.

PROBLEM 11

Find and identify all passing and neighboring tones in the melody that follows.

4 These are also called chordal associates.

*Anticipations—discussed subsequently.

PROBLEM 12

Find and identify all secondary pitches that occur in the preceding melody; consider both pitches of relatively short duration that are approached or left by skip, e.g., the *a*♭ in measure 2, as well as notes that are members of elaborated triads, e.g., the *g* and *b*♭ in measure 9.

PROBLEM 13

In the space provided, reduce the melody to those notes which in your view represent the simplest skeletal basis or the melody.

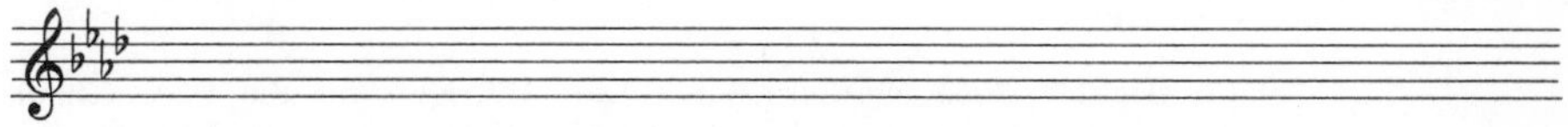

There are several other names for various types of decorative activity that have traditionally been used in analytical description. Such terms as escape tone (sometimes called *échappée*), anticipation, appoggiatura (often called leaning tone), *cambiata,* suspension, and others denote specific types of decorative patterns commonly associated with activity in two or more parts. What is important at this juncture is that you firmly grasp the general concept of melodic step-decoration.

The neighboring-tone figure involves motion by step away from and returning to a basic pitch. It is also possible to create neighboring decorations of basic pitches that involve step relations in but *part* of the decorative pattern. For example, in many instances the basic pitch is embellished by a neighbor of short duration that is subsequently left by a leap. Several instances of such treatment occur in Example 25.

Ex. 25. Rameau.

The notes marked n.t. clearly decorate the dotted eighths that precede them; however, no subsequent return to the basic pitches takes place. These notes (sometimes called escape tones, or *échappées*) are nonetheless neighbor embellishments of more important tones; their melodic function is primarily rhythmic, since they have little effect on melodic contour or tonality. For the time being, such notes will simply be called neighboring tones.

Another example of neighboring or step decoration occurs in a more noticeable role, that of an accented upper or lower neighbor. The tendency of such notes to move or resolve to basic pitches is frequently related to their tonal stability. This applies particularly to those constituting members of the tonic or dominant triads, that is, 1, 3, and 5 in a key. In the melody in Example 26 accented neighboring tones characteristically embellish more stable key members. Such notes are often called appoggiaturas.

Ex. 26. John Lennon and Paul McCartney: "Yesterday."

Both of the notes marked n.t. have in common a lack of step approach; they are, in effect, neighbors approached by leap. The e^2 in measure 3, though similar in effect, is reached from the step above and functions slightly differently in context, though its role is clearly that of an upper step embellishment of the d^2 that follows.

The second pitch of the melody begun in Example 27 serves as a step embellishment of the dominant, *b*, that follows. Such understanding demands an awareness of the tonality of the melody that helps provide a basis for "prehearing" the line.

Ex. 27. Legrenzi.

The tendency of decorative pitches to move to stable members of a tonality is often more pronounced when decorative pitches occur as chromatically altered (mutated) pitches. In many cases, chromatic step embellishments act as temporary leading tones, that is, ascending half-step progressions, to basic notes. Example 28 reveals several such figures.

Ex. 28. Brahms.

As in a great many passages, the use of melodic decorative figures in this melody reveals the incorporation of certain characteristic decorative figures as patterned bases for stylistic and formal unity. Indeed, the appeal of the opening motive with its chromatic neighbor embellishment, restated sequentially in measure 2, seems to typify and characterize the melody as a whole.

Rhythmic Displacement; Suspensions

In Unit 1 of this book we mentioned a rhythmic process called displaced accent, that is, syncopation. Perhaps the most common form of rhythmic displacement occurs when durational accents, accents attributable to contextual long notes, arrive on weak beats or parts of beats. Rhythmic displacement of durations the equivalent of or longer than the basic duration occurs in Example 29.

Ex. 29. Austria.

Rhythmic displacement is frequently combined with a particular kind of melodic step motion in such a way as to produce a kind of melodic delay called a *suspension*. The suspension figure amounts to the rhythmic extension of a note beyond the point of its anticipated motion to a succeeding pitch a step below or above. Such rhythmic delays produce durational accents by virtue of the fact that arrival on a strong beat is delayed to the succeeding weak beat, the anticipated movement coinciding with movement by step on the succeeding weak beat. The melodic suspension is illustrated in Example 30.

Ex. 30. Undecorated melodic movement by suspension

We shall see in later study how melodic suspension was incorporated into polyphonic music so as to emphasize the point of delay with a particular harmonic (dissonant–consonant) succession, as shown in Example 31.

Ex. 31. Suspension in two voices.

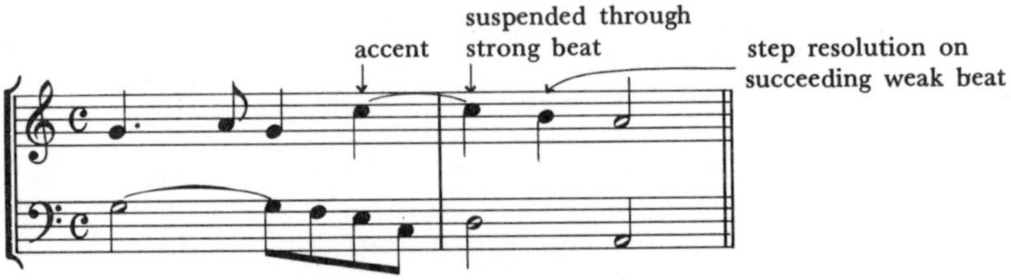

The point of the present discussion is to acknowledge melodic suspension as an important technique for elaborating step movement in a single line, the suspension itself forming a rhythmic delay of the step connection of two basic pitches.[5] In Example 30 the basic pitches elaborated are c^2 and the succeeding b^1. Several suspensions are illustrated in Example 32. Note carefully that in some cases the delay is broken by re-articulation at the point of the suspension. The suspension figure is, in fact, one of the most recurrent forms of decorative activity in a great variety of styles; its effect, without question, is essentially *rhythmic*.

Ex. 32. Melodic suspensions.

(a) Waltz Op. 129, No.4

(b) Op.17, No.9, I

---

[5] Notes interpolated between a suspended pitch and its note of resolution a step below.

(c) Mass in C minor: *Et incarnatus est*

Mozart

(d) K.428, II

Andante con moto

Mozart

Decorative pitches called *anticipations,* most often approached by step but occasionally reached by leap, appear frequently in melody as presoundings of basic notes. Anticipations are usually of short and unaccented duration, and are used most often, perhaps, to "preannounce" cadential notes. Example 33 illustrates anticipations, abbreviated *ant.*

Ex. 33. Schoenberg: Piano Concerto, Op. 42, I.

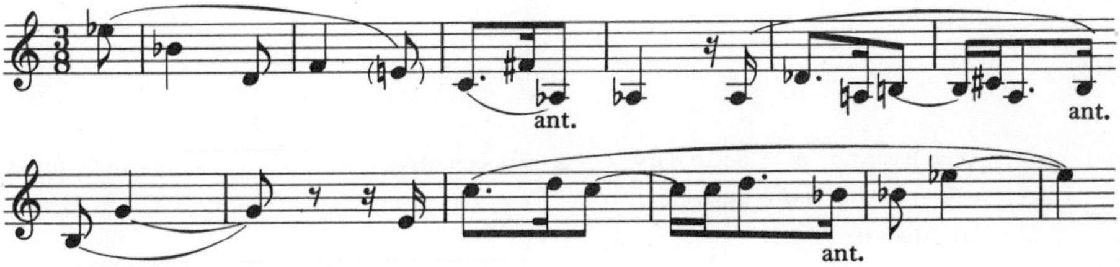

Used by permission of G. Schirmer, Inc.

At this point we should remind ourselves that although it may be theoretically possible to identify every pitch of a melodic passage as basic, secondary, or some specific type of melodic decoration, such is not the goal of linear analysis. The descriptive terms introduced so far, and others as well, are meant to be definitive terms that the analyst can use when labels are helpful in meaningful description of and communication about melodic style and structure. Such labels are not ends in themselves. Perform the extended melodic excerpt in Example 34, and familiarize yourself with its patterns and materials. Note the analytical discussion following the excerpt; then turn to Problem 14, applying similar considerations. Be prepared to discuss your own analysis of Problem 14.

Ex. 34. Sample analysis.

Suite for Cello No.3, Prelude

Bach

Ex. 34 continued.

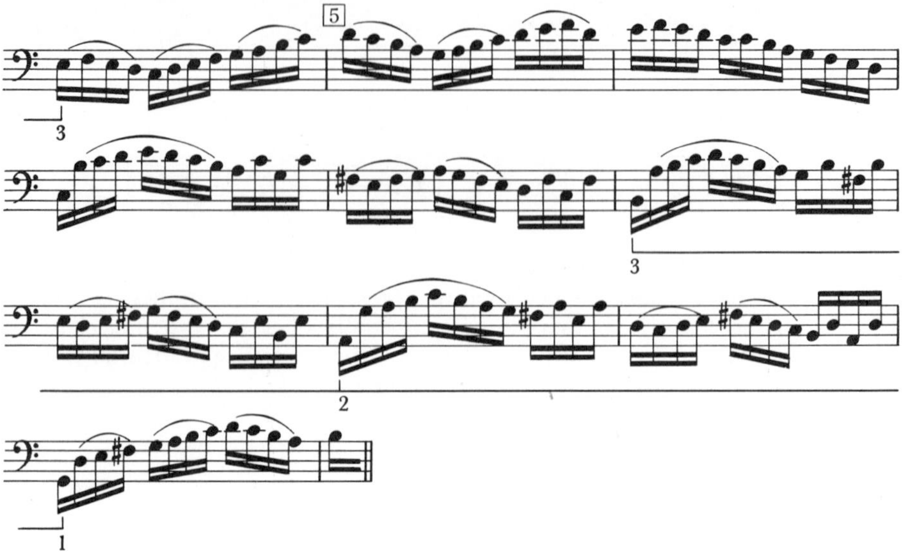

o = Basic ● = Secondary ♩ = Decorative ⌐¬ = Step progressions
⌒ = One basic pitch

(a) Analysis

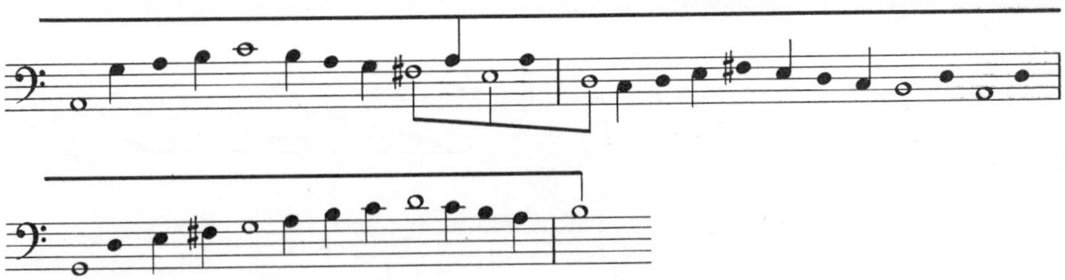

(b) Reduction (c)

Several brief observations can be made as a result of the analysis:

1. The division of the passage into two tonal centers—*C* in measures 1–7, and *G* (the dominant of *C*) from measure 8 to the cadence in measure 14—is heightened by step progressions joining mediant to tonic (3 to 1) in both tonalities.
2. Decorative activity is typically a result of passing and neighboring tones; secondary pitches generally form parts of triadic outlines.
3. The latter part of the passage is marked in part by the short descending step progressions filling in a third, as in measure 8. These provide a gradual intensification of linear activity and interest.
4. Basic pitches inevitably fall on the first beat of every measure, as well as within various measures; rhythmic displacement is not a feature of the passage, as suggested by the symmetrical placement of basic pitches.
5. The reductions (b) and (c) represent an interpretation of the passage as an ascending line from *c* to *b*, connecting the 1, 3, and 5 tones of C major and moving to the key of G. In reduction (c), the tones *d*, *f*♯ and *a* are considered as large scale passing steps connecting *c* and *g*, with both *e* and *b* being viewed as secondary pitches.

Listen to a reading of the passage and see to what degree the analyses reflect your interpretation of the structural elements of the piece.

PROBLEM 14

Sonata No.3 for Violin in F, II, mm.1–20

Handel

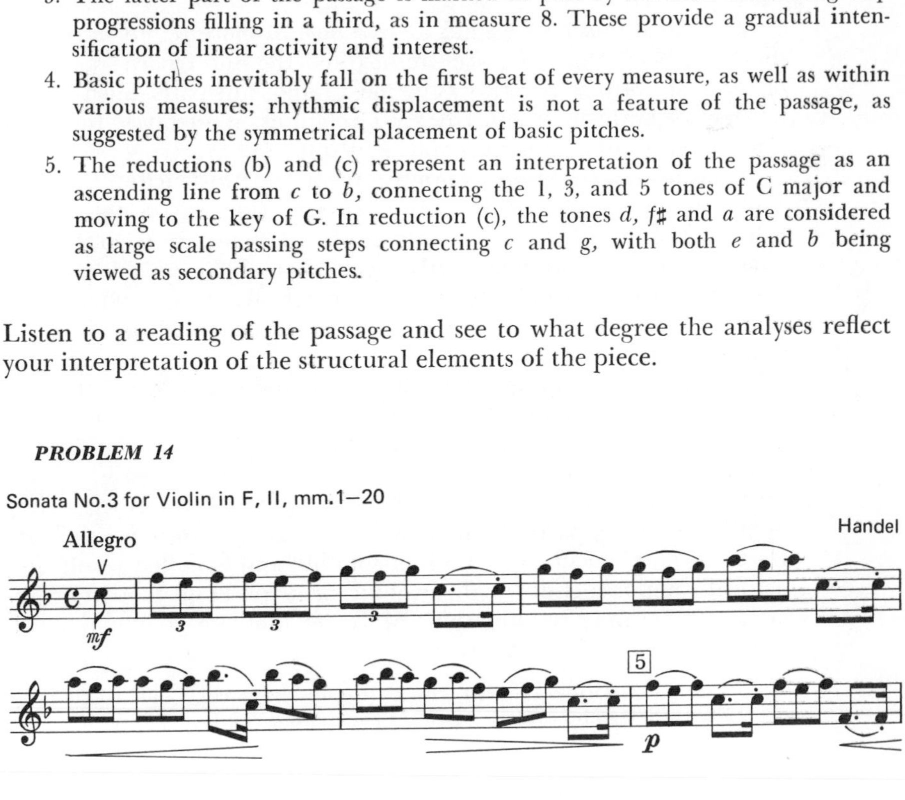

Problem 14 continued.

TWO-VOICE CONTRAPUNTAL FRAMEWORK

Most tonal music, as well as a great deal of more recent music, is composed in such a way that *two voices,* most often the outer parts—soprano and bass, or top and bottom—constitute the most important parts. Such importance is a product of both pitch and rhythmic relations; it involves, furthermore, both linear-contrapuntal and harmonic principles and processes.

It has been a tradition in musical-theoretical instruction to predicate most study of tonal music on the acquisition of skill in (if not mastery of) the rules of thumb and "general principles" of four-part (chorale-style) writing. The assumption has apparently been that the acquisition of mastery of "marching four voices along"[6] results magically in an understanding of the composition and structure of tonal music; unfortunately, such has not proven to be the case.

In this segment of our study, our aim is to develop bases for assessing structure in tonal music of a wide variety of textures, four-voice included. One such useful basis for systematic and comparative study within a wide spectrum of tonal music is afforded by the two-voice framework; this is a term used by Hindemith[7] to describe the two dominant voices in a given texture, usually the outer parts. Most tonal music reveals a distinct polarity of outer voices, a complementary relation of soprano and bass that results in part from natural components of tonal-harmonic principles and in part from recurring kinds of rhythmic combinations of voices that are common to virtually all

---

[6] See the Preface to Leonard Ratner's *Harmony; Structure and Style.*

[7] See Hindemith's *Craft of Musical Composition,* Vol. I.

music. Example 35a presents several measures from "Penny Lane," a familiar song by John Lennon and Paul McCartney. The two-voice frame of the arrangement shown in Example 35b consists simply of the melody and the bass, which are also shown below the music in Example 35a.

Ex. 35a. Lennon and McCartney: "Penny Lane" (mm. 1–8).

Ex. 35b. Two-voice frame of "Penny Lane."

If we focus on the two-voice frame of this passage we can easily see the essential elements of the arrangement, one that may be generally described as consisting of a main voice (the top), and a lower one (bass) whose role is supportive or accompanimental. Viewed rhythmically, the framework presents an opening pattern of two against one, "2 to 1", in that the main voice moves in durations that are half the value of the accompaniment. The pattern is broken in measure 5. The various two-part rhythmic combinations that typify polyphonic music are often called *species,* simply meaning types or patterns—in this case—of combined rhythms. One of the most fundamental considerations of any two-voice framework is that of the particular rhythmic species involved. In many cases more than one combination, sometimes several, will be found. An understanding of the combinations of rhythms that organize any counterpoint, that is, voice-leading, must precede considerations of pitch or other parameters. Furthermore, the ability to grasp the rhythmic relations of parts will enable you to deal with all music, past and present, to a greater extent than will mere understanding of tonal pitch materials and relations. The various rhythmic species are enumerated and then illustrated in the examples below.

First species (Ex. 36) refers to note-against-note rhythm in which identical note values are combined in tandem.

Ex. 36. First-species counterpoint.

Chorale 102 (outer parts) Bach

Second species (Ex. 37) designates movement in a rhythmic relation of 2 to 1.

Ex. 37. Second species.

Well-Tempered Clavier, Book I: Fugue in E Major

Bach

Third species (Ex. 38) involves a 4 to 1 rhythmic relation: 3 to 1 is often regarded as third species as well.

Ex. 38. Third species.

(a) Op.109, II

Beethoven

(b) Op.110: Fuga

Beethoven

Fourth-species counterpoint (Ex. 39) pertains to a rhythmic or metric *displacement* of one member of a first-species relation, frequently producing suspensions in the displaced voice.

Ex. 39. Fourth species.

Op.124, No.4

Schumann

Combinations and changes of species, typical of most music, are described as fifth species; note the various combinations that occur in the two-voice frame in Example 40, which illustrates fifth-species.

Ex. 40. Fifth species.

Le Nuove Musiche: Madrigal

Caccini

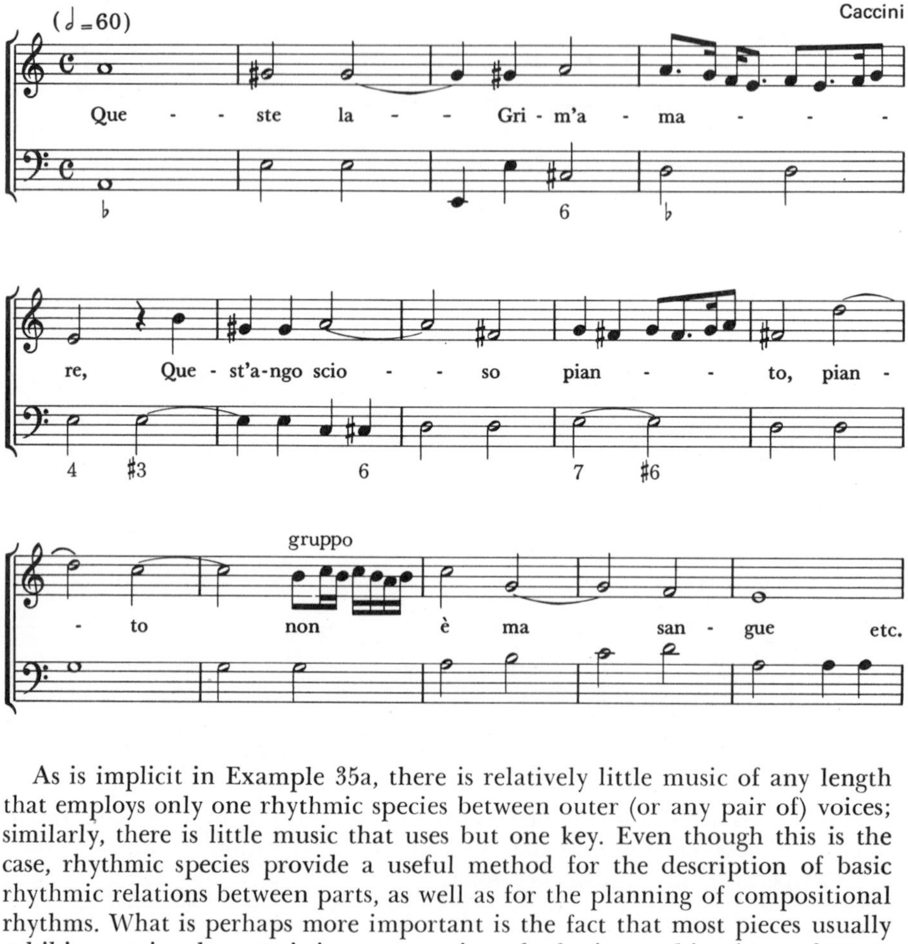

As is implicit in Example 35a, there is relatively little music of any length that employs only one rhythmic species between outer (or any pair of) voices; similarly, there is little music that uses but one key. Even though this is the case, rhythmic species provide a useful method for the description of basic rhythmic relations between parts, as well as for the planning of compositional rhythms. What is perhaps more important is the fact that most pieces usually exhibit certain characteristic or recurring rhythmic combinations of parts which in turn may become important in large-scale formal designs.

PROBLEM 15

After each of the short excerpts below identify the prevailing rhythmic combination, often called *rhythmic association,* of the passage. Make a mental note of any other species that occurs.

(a) Beethoven

(b) *Symphony of Psalms,* II, mm.10–13 Stravinsky

(c) Handel

(d) Brahms

*Consider only outer parts.

Problem 15 continued.

(e)

Bach

Any rhythmic combination of parts can be varied or given breathing room by incorporating temporary inactivity—*rest.* Unbroken periods of one species of rhythm are commonly enhanced by periodic rests in one or another part. This is virtually axiomatic for vocal music because of the physical necessity to pause for breath, but similar breathing points are typically found in instrumental compositions as well, as noted in Examples 41 and 42. The former is from a vocal work, and the latter, a keyboard composition in which the prevailing second-species counterpoint is enhanced by rests in the lower voice. Such rest modifications as the one in the Bach excerpt do not impair the recognition of prevailing patterns of movement, the supposition being that the ear will tend to mentally continue a pre-established pattern unless a markedly different one is introduced. As a result, one may assume that measure 5, for instance, represents a continuation of second-species rhythm despite the second-beat rest.

Ex. 41. Lassus: Motet (textless).

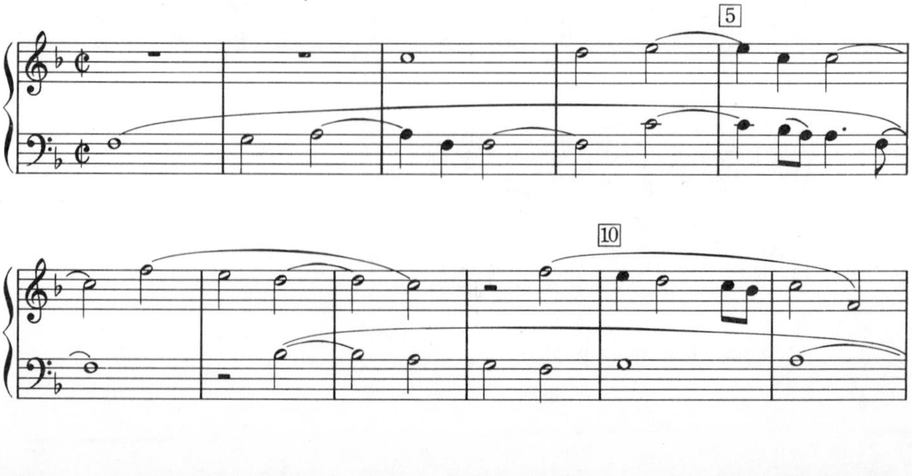

Ex. 42. Bach: Partita in C minor, *Menuet*.

The Brahms piece in Example 43 shows several ways in which the rhythms of the two-voice outer framework often relate to those of other parts of the texture. Obviously, the framework, though it provides a pitch-rhythm scaffolding for the complete texture, is not in itself complete in works of more than two parts. In many pieces, the rhythmic content and organization of the other voices help clarify, define, and complement the outer voices, just as do the various pitch materials; such is the case in the following work.

Ex. 43. Brahms: Chorale Prelude for Organ, Op. 122, No. 6: O *Wie Selig Seid Ihr Doch, Ihr Frommen.*

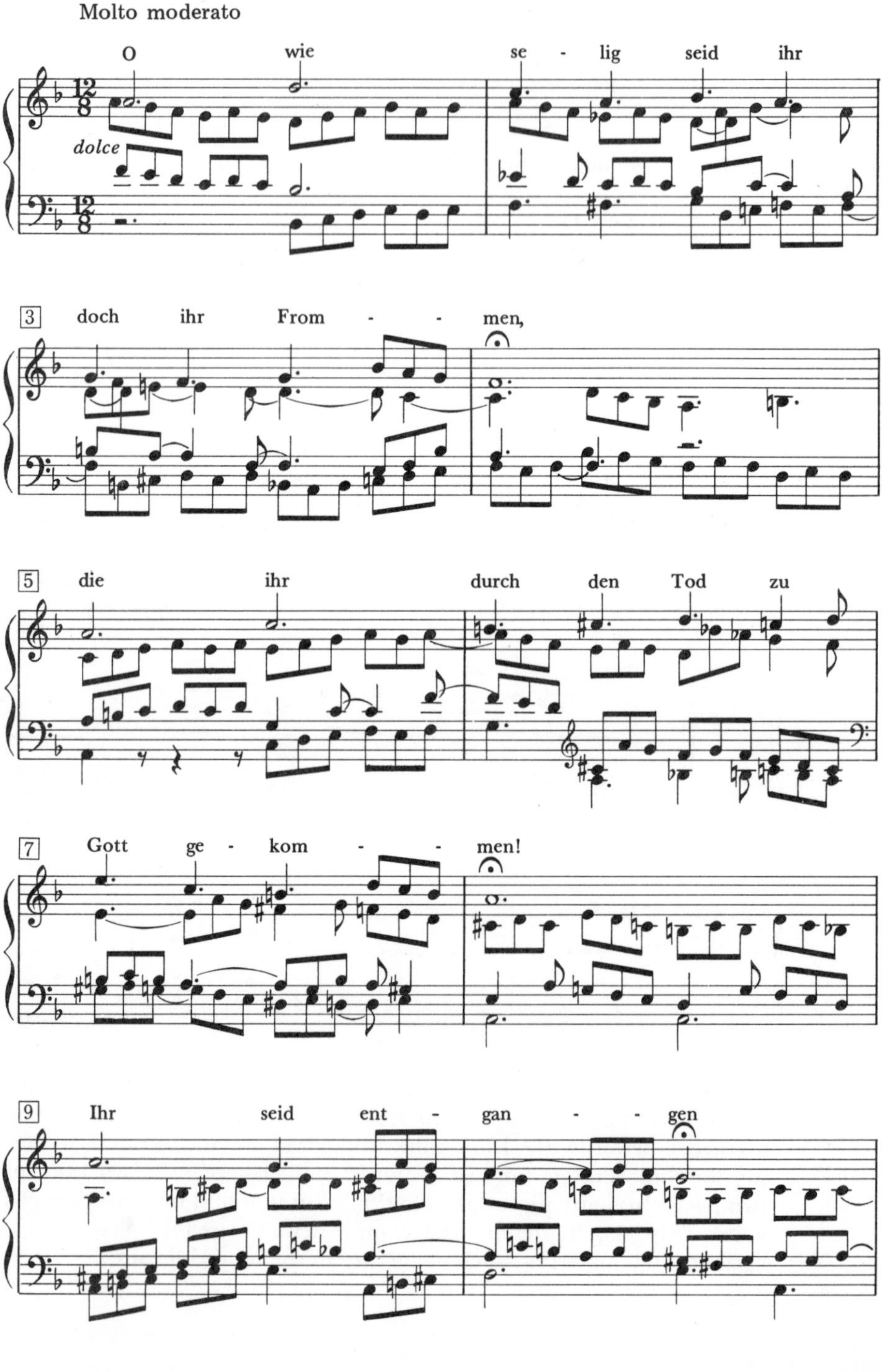

In this piece the counterpoint of the outer parts is mainly first-species, third-species (3 x 1), and occasional patterns of 6 x 1, as in measures 1 and 5. There are no durations or figures found in the outer parts that are not presented at some point in the interior voices. For example, note that the rhythmic displacements in the bass, measure 7, are found in the alto in measure 3, tenor in measure 5, and soprano in measure 13. More important, the overall rhythmic continuity of the prelude is a product in part of the shifting of note-by-note rhythm in eighths between various voice couplings, as in measures 1, 5–6, 9–10, and others. The main voice (cantus) and the bass interact constantly with the inner voices in creating a coherent rhythmic shape. Were this not the case, the piece would consist rhythmically of a series of starts and stops, as suggested by the outer-voice rhythms of measure 2. A good picture of this rhythmic interdependence of parts can be gotten by vocalizing the rhythm of this piece without singing pitches. As you do so, listen to the way in which rhythmic activity and various species migrate from voice to voice. Such processes are the essence of interesting and effective part-writing. Herein, the overall integration of rhythm is so effective that the dominance of the main voice is a product more of pitch-related features than those of rhythm.

Pitch Relations in the Two-Voice Frame; Materials

The materials and principles discussed here in regard to two-voice pitch relations are limited to those associated mainly with traditional tonal music, that is, music adhering to tonality (in terms of mode, as well as traditional major-minor key). Many of the considerations regarding the handling of tonal materials in traditional music have important extensions to and corollary developments in non-tonal music. Tonal music, however, is still the musician's main referent for the solution of problems concerning perception, interpretation, and performance, and it continues to form the greater part of the performance repertoire.

The harmonic staples of the two-voice frame are essentially simple consonant intervals, namely, octaves, fifths, thirds, and sixths (and their octave duplications). Intervals such as seconds, fourths, sevenths, and virtually all diminished and augmented intervals come into play as a product of contrapuntal and decorative activity, linking and embellishing stable intervals.

Considering a passage from Brahms' Romanze it's easy to observe the dominance of simple harmonic staples such as eighths, fifths, thirds, and sixths in the outer-voice frame of the piece. Compare the complete texture (Ex. 44a) with the realization of its framework (Ex. 44b).

Ex. 44a. Brahms: Romanze, Op. 118, No. 5.

Ex. 44b. Two-voice frame of Ex. 44a.

The satisfactory harmonic effect of such a framework is partly due to a number of carefully implemented principles, listed on page 175.

1. A varied selection of harmonic intervals is used.
2. Simple consonances predominate.
3. Intervals emphasizing the tonic and dominant degrees begin and close the excerpt, helping to define the key of F Major.
4. Intervals whose *roots* involve either tonic or dominant notes begin and close the passage, further pinpointing the tonality.
5. A consistent and unobtrusive pattern of note-by-note rhythm is maintained. As a result the important line in the middle parts, reinforced by octave doubling (duplication at the interval of an octave), is easily projected and heard.

The counterpoint—that is, voice-leading—in this two-voice frame also exhibits several essentials of effective composition. Note that the step motion of the top part balances the more disjunct activity in the bass. Furthermore, considerable use of contrary motion—that is, voice-movement in opposite directions—is found. This helps create contoural independence and interest in the framework's parts.

Parallel motion—motion maintaining the same harmonic interval with parts moving in the same direction—is not found in this passage's outer voices. Similar motion—motion of voices in the same direction (up or down) by *different* intervals—occurs in the second half of measure 1. Note how much care the composer has taken to minimize the impact of the octaves and fifths, intervals of minimal harmonic interest and direction and of maximal tonal stability, by reaching them through contrary motion and thereby de-emphasizing their impact. These procedures are virtually axiomatic to effective voice-leading. There are, however, a number of mitigating situations to which we shall turn shortly. Example 45 further confirms, though in a contrasting style, several of the procedures cited in Example 44; familiarize yourself with this example, and, using its two-voice frame as a basis, decide to what degree the preceding statements apply here as well.

Ex. 45. Mendelssohn: Sonata for Cello, Op. 58, III.

Eliminate this lower doubling in the frame.

Ex. 45 continued.

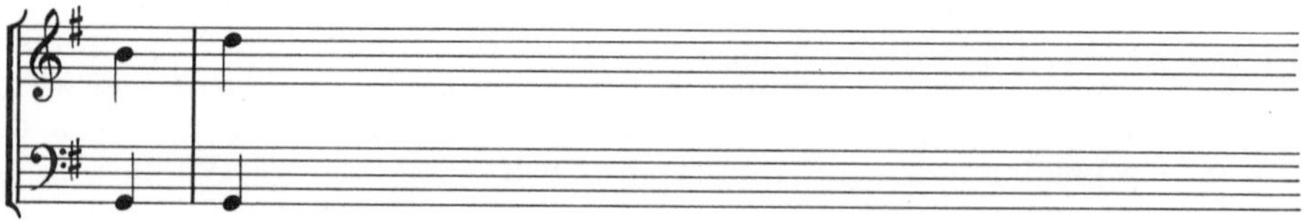

PROBLEM 16

Continue the two-voice-frame reduction of Example 45, begun below the excerpt, eliminating the lower doubling of the bass. Analyze and label all the harmonic intervals of the frame. Then, perform the following functions, based upon your study of this frame:

1. Designate measures containing parallel, similar, and contrasting motion.

2. Indicate the tonality frame of the upper voice.

3. Name three measures in which leaps in one part are offset by steps in the other.

4. Circle on the music an occurrence of an anticipation in the main voice.

5. Identify the measure in which a dissonant interval appears between the main voice and bass of the frame, and the type of melodic elaboration occuring in the main voice at this point.

The details of instrumental textures such as that shown in Example 46 are often such that the components of the two-voice framework are less easily perceived than in less elaborate compositions such as the Mendelssohn piece cited in Example 45. The two-voice frame is composed of two lines, that is, *melodies.* The perception of musical structure can be greatly enhanced by increased melodiousness of any note succession constituting a part or voice.

The opening twenty-three measures of Chopin's Mazurka, Op. 24, No. 2 (Ex. 46a), are typical of many keyboard (or other instrumental) pieces whose elaborations are such that the melodic profiles of the outer parts are not obvious. The texture of the piece consists mostly of a main voice, the top part, and an idiomatic accompaniment. The latter is made of repeated chords, and changes to a waltz-style accompaniment figure at measure 21. This figure consists of an accented bass note followed by two after-beat chords which supply the components of the chord initiated by the bass note. The sonorities in this piece are all triadic.

Ex. 46a. Chopin: Mazurka in C Major, Op. 24, No. 2.

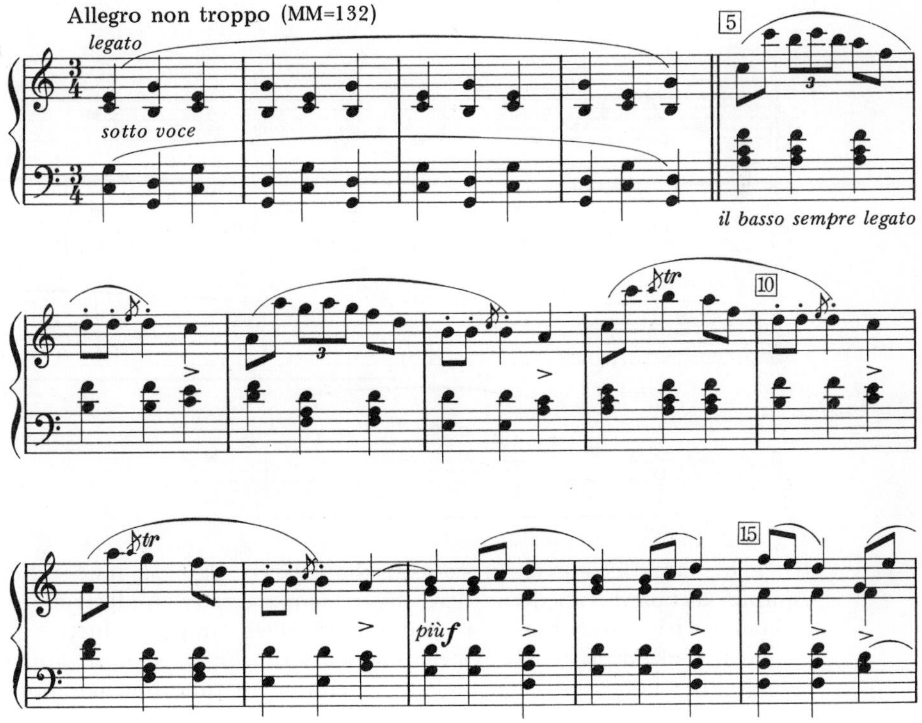

Ex. 46a continued.

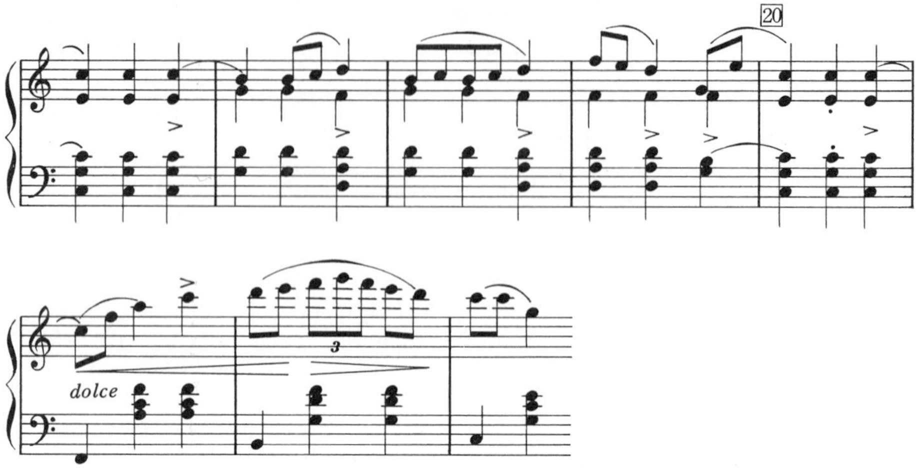

The melodic characteristics of the upper voice are quite apparent; singing the line, an expressive and lyrical melody, makes this quite clear. An interpretation of the structure of this voice is shown in Example 46b.

Ex. 46b.

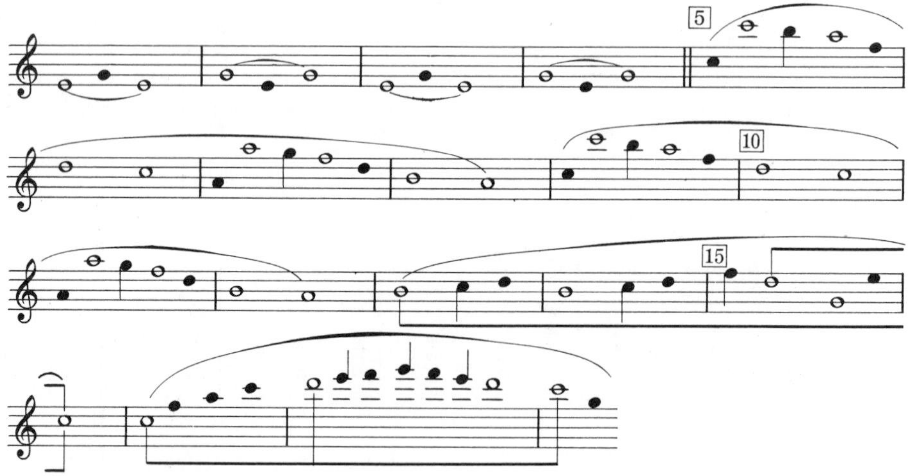

The main decorative process in the bass is that of note repetition, a simple keyboard expedient here, by which a steady, underlying pulse (associated with dance music) is maintained. Two simple reductive principles make a realization of the linear elements of the bass more apparent: (1) eliminating note repetition and (2) extending in time the bass notes, beginning at measure 21, that are understood to govern a full measure,[8] and which pinpoint the root or third of the triad that occurs during the measure.

In Example 46c the bass of Example 46a is shown as a simple melodic line. Its rhythm and contour are of decidedly less interest than the main voice that the bass supports, but it forms nonetheless an acceptable melody, one that will combine to make effective two-voice counterpoint with the main voice, as shown in Example 46d.

Ex. 46c. Unelaborated bass of Ex. 46a.

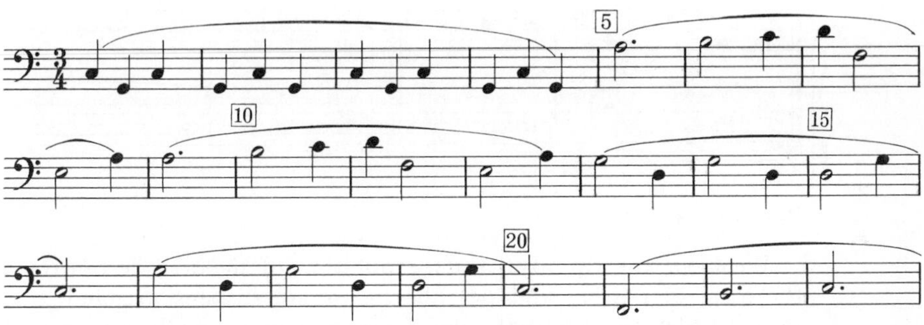

The voice-leading found in this framework (Ex. 46d), like most well-written music, adheres to a number of simple fundamentals of counterpoint. Steps in one voice commonly balance leaps in another, as in measure 5. Contrary motion is predominant, especially toward the ends of phrases (or phrase segments), as at measures 6, 8, and 22. Note further the variety of harmonic intervals heard, despite the prominence of simple harmonic staples. Taken as a whole, this mazurka is good evidence of the simplicity of the underlying harmonic and contrapuntal structure of a great deal of tonal music, the elaborations of which are unique, engaging, and expressive.

Ex. 46d.

*Simplified.

[8] This is further implied by the pedal indications.

Ex. 46d continued.

Decorative Detail

We have already taken up the question of melodic decorative activity in the form of passing and neighboring tones, suspensions, and anticipations; in particular the essential role of the step in controlling such activity. The effect of decorative activity is essentially unchanged insofar as it operates in two-voice frames, but the consideration of a second part necessitates that the main referent for decorative description be *harmonic*.

In tonal music, simple consonant intervals usually form the core of harmonic structure in the two-voice frame, as we have seen, and decorative activity should be viewed as elaboration of such materials; such decorative activity frequently involves harmonic intervals such as seconds, sevenths, ninths, augmented and diminished intervals. Musicians have traditionally called such intervals dissonances, although to do so at this point in time calls into question so many factors related to musical style, context, and interpretation that this term has little meaning for most of us. To pursue this question a little further, familiarize yourself with Example 47.

Ex. 47. Haydn: Symphony No. 22 in E♭, I (two-voice frame).

You can see at a glance the way in which harmonic staples, namely, thirds, fifths, sixths, and octaves, fall on each beat of the passage, providing a solid and clear harmonic framework. Note the overall movement in the key from tonic (*e*♭) to dominant (*b*♭), clearly pinpointing the tonality by means of a I-to-V progression. The details of this passage show clearly how the supporting rhythm (third-species counterpoint) in the bass is fashioned with passing tones. Almost every second eighth note forms a step connection between two basic notes a third apart. Often, it is through such patterned treatments of passing notes that secondary parts take on significant melodic identity, assuming roles of complementary melodic voices in the texture, rather than merely filling up space and time with contrived motion.

Neighboring and passing tones create considerable decorative play in the following keyboard passage by Haydn (Ex. 48a). Note carefully measures 3, 5, 8, and 10 of the example in which neighboring tones fall on the beat and form dissonances with the accompaniment. Compare the reduction in Example 48b to the music in Example 48a for a clearer picture of the essential simplicity of structure of the piece. The elaboration of this and countless compositions like it is predicated almost entirely on step decorations of simple triadic frameworks.

Ex. 48a. Haydn: Piano Sonata in E Minor, III (1778).

Ex. 48a continued.

Ex. 48b. Reduction to basic pitches of two-voice frame.

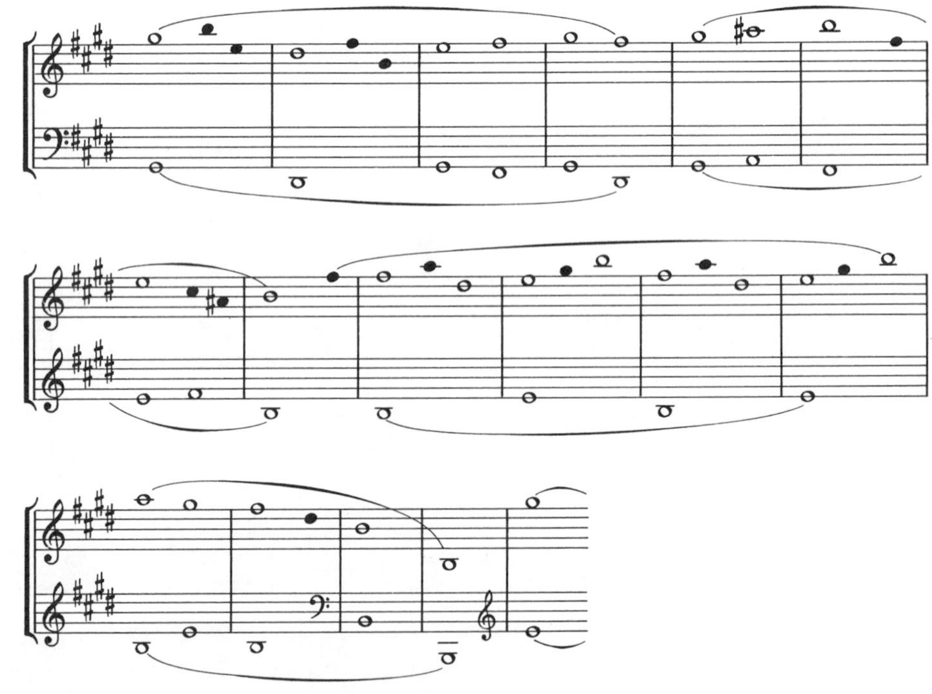

The voice-leading so expressively elaborated in Example 49a shows the importance of step decoration in weaving a contrapuntal texture; lower neighboring tones are the most characteristic decorative patterns here. The three-voice texture of the example is fashioned around two fundamental voices. Third species counterpoint is dominant here. Compare the music with its two-voice frame (Ex. 49b).

Ex. 49a. Bach: *Well-Tempered Clavier*, Book I, Prelude No. 9 in E Major.

Ex. 49b. Two-voice frame.

*The dotted line shows the continuation of a basic pitch via a change of register.

Contrapuntal pieces such as the one in Example 49a generally reveal a basic frame that is a result of shifting activity between two leading members of a texture of several (three to five) competing parts. The limitations of performance and perception generally preclude a concentration of melodic activity in more than two simultaneously dominant voices. Test the validity of this statement by studying the five-part writing in Example 50.

Ex. 50. *Cipriano de Rore* (madrigal).

In general, the parts operate in note-against-note, or first-species rhythm, in the passage. The *cantus,* the top voice, tends to lead much of the time, while the *bassus* provides both harmonic stability and occasional points of melodic interest as well, as in measures 18–20. All five voices are used together very sparingly; when they all sound, as in measures 12–14, the two-voice frame is mainly a product of the outer parts, the inner voices supplying both harmonic support and imitative contrapuntal activity of secondary importance. Note, however, the variety of rhythmic species found in such passages. Such contrapuntal activity demands the stability provided by a simple two-voice frame. When such contrapuntal-harmonic frameworks are not perceptible, confusion and unclear design may result. This composition lacks the unequivocal key definition of much eighteenth-century music, but its contrapuntal dependency on a simple, consonant tonal framework is nonetheless present.

Several assumptions that are important concomitants of the analysis of most tonal music underlie this unit of study. First, most tonal compositions, regardless of the medium of performance or type of texture involved, reveal an essential framework composed of their outer voices. The basis of such a framework is rhythmic, melodic, and harmonic. Second, just as a single line of music may be reduced to a line of basic notes that form its structural underpinnings, two combined voices may be similarly reduced to a structural frame that accounts for both harmonic and melodic activity. Furthermore, several interacting parts may be fashioned from far fewer fundamental lines of rhythmic and pitch *motion.* Such elaborative or accompanimental procedures as pedal points, note repetition, arpeggiation, and the like are seldom part of the essential lines of musical motion. Third, several kinds of decorative activity that provide step embellishment of structural tones—such as passing and neighboring motion—have been noted. Subsequent study will involve further analysis of these and related processes, particularly as they involve the harmonic materials and structure that we shall consider in the following section on harmony.

To review, turn to Problem 17, the solution of which will afford a clearer picture of the relations among the various items discussed to this point.

PROBLEM 17

Complete the various analytical tasks listed below, after familiarizing yourself carefully with the musical excerpt that follows.

Piano Sonata No.2 in G, II

Haydn

Problem 17 continued.

1. Reduce the passage to a two-voice frame, eliminating octave doublings in the bass.

2. Make a basic pitch analysis of the upper voice.

3. Account for all decorative activity in the main voice in measure 1 to the first beat of measure 8. Label each decorative pitch on the music.

4. Cite at least two examples of on-the-beat harmonic dissonances formed by outer voices in which the bass is an articulated suspension, specifying measure numbers.

   ____

5. Locate and mark two significant step progressions in the main voice.

6. Find at least five occurrences of elaborated triad outlining and five occurrences of simple triad outlining; name the measure(s) and the particular triad and triadic quality involved.
   Sample: measure 12, B♭ major (simple)
   measure 1, G minor (elaborated)

7. Show the tonality frame of measures 1–6 of the top part.

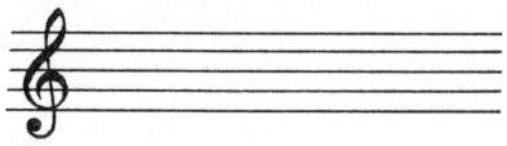

8. What type of decorative activity most characterizes this excerpt as a whole?

   ____

9. What rhythmic species prevail in the piece? ____________________

10. At measure 10, the key of the piece shifts from G minor to B♭ major; the subsequent portion of the example is clearly contrasted with the prior one; in what way is this exemplified by the top voice's activity?

HARMONIC CONSIDERATIONS: TRIADS AND SEVENTH CHORDS

Triads have served as fundamental harmonic materials since the fifteenth century; even in the present day of experimentation and novel compositional procedures, tertian chords operate in one way or another in a great deal of music. This is particularly true as regards much traditionally-based concert music, a great deal of jazz, most commercial and pop music, church music, and folk and educational music. Many composers continue, despite the wide spectrum of possibilities, to exploit triadic sonority in numerous and often very imaginative ways, and it seems likely that triads will appear on the musical scene for a long time to come. Indeed, despite numerous innovative and in many cases strikingly effective developments of non-tertian chords, triads are so ingrained in our whole musical experience, from childhood on, that their total replacement by any alternate, unified harmonic system representing more than a flurry of activity seems doubtful. The aim of this brief study of triadic harmonic materials is to establish a basic understanding of their use in tonal music rather than to *master* their manipulation in composition.

Perhaps the most unique aspect of triads, one that really differentiates triadic use from that of non-tertian chords, lies in the flexibility of arrangement and ease of recognition we attribute to them through our acceptance of the theory of invertibility of triads, a theory associated mainly with the eighteenth-century French theorist Jean-Philippe Rameau. Study carefully the chart of vertical arrangements of a D major triad, shown in Example 51. Sing or play each of the chords until you absorb the sound.

Ex. 51. Various arrangements of a D major triad and its inversions.

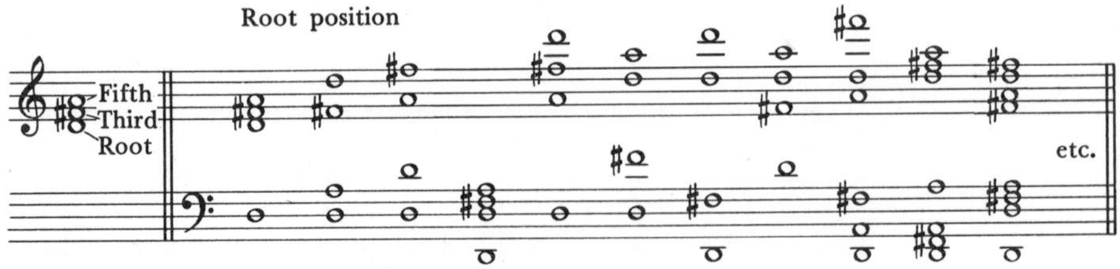

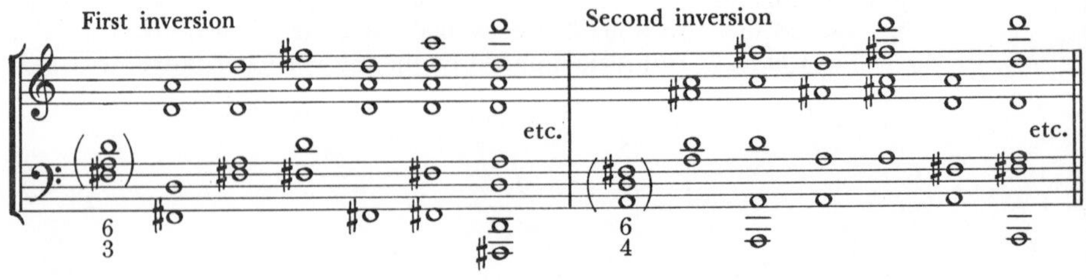

Note that each category of sonorities has a different lowest pitch—*d, f♯, a*—that helps differentiate one from the other. Moreover, those with the root, *d,* as lowest tone are particularly important because they represent what is generally considered to be the natural tonal ordering called *root position.* The three general triadic forms are: root position, that is, any arrangement of a given triad with the root as the bass or lowest sounding member; first inversion, that is, any arrangement with the chord third, here *f♯,* as the bass—resulting in the vertical combination of a sixth and a third above the bass ($^6_3$)—and second inversion, that is, any deployment of the chord with the fifth sounding below the other chord members, and resulting in a ($^6_4$) vertical combination. Obviously, there are numerous ways of spacing (arranging above the bass in vertical order) the chord tones of root position or either inversion. Only a smattering of possible arrangements appear in Example 51. Note, however, that each deployment has certain unique sound characteristics, such as breadth of spacing, close upper parts above a bass, emphasis on high register, and so forth. Play over the samples in Example 51 and substitute f-naturals for all f-sharps; the resulting chord is a D minor triad, one whose quality, that is, composite interval effect, differs markedly from the D major triad. Note that the minor triad *d–f–a* reverses the interval format (M3-m3 spanning a perfect fifth) of the major triad, the minor triad comprising a *minor* third and major third spanning a perfect fifth. (The generalizations about inversions of major triads apply equally to minor triads.)

The tones of the D minor triad do not all coincide with those of an overtone series based on the same fundamental, namely because the chord third, *f,* is not a prominent member of the D harmonic series. Consequently, the minor triad, despite its obvious significance in virtually all tonal music, cannot be viewed as a "natural" harmonic entity. That the chord is constituted entirely of simple consonances may explain in part its acceptance by composers as a stable harmonic unit, one quite capable of fulfilling the role of a tonic triad. Read Example 52 and find occurrences of both major and minor triads. This composition, like many pieces forming the core of traditional music literature, is written for *four* parts (or voices): sopranos, altos, tenors, and basses. This being true, it is obvious that one of the three tones of any triad being sounded by four voices must be used twice—that is, it must be *doubled.* In dealing with major and minor triads, the *root* is most often the doubled chord member. Exceptions to the preceding principle are numerous, and the study of chord doubling, spacing, voice-leading, and related questions is usually undertaken in detail. In this unit, such matters are only incidental to the main questions being considered, and as a result they will be given only brief attention.

Ex. 52a. Bach: Chorale No. 244, mm. 1–4.

C minor:

Ex. 52b. Triadic materials from Ex. 52a.

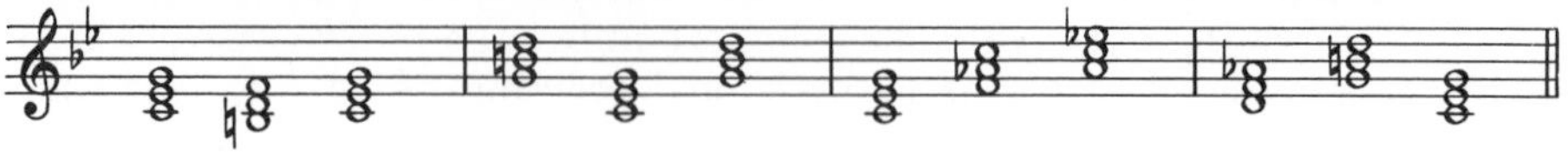

The triads in the Example 52 are, for the most part, easily recognized. This is because the four voices generally sound together as a unit and because the rate of harmonic change—that is, the harmonic rhythm of the passage—duplicates the $\frac{4}{4}$ metrical pulse, a new chord falling on most successive quarter-note beats. In a great deal of music literature, however, the deployment of triadic materials is more subtly veiled in counterpoint, figuration, arpeggiation, and other elaborative compositional techniques, making recognition of the basic harmonic units more problematic, if not ambiguous. The selection of excerpts in Example 53 exhibit a progression from simple to more elaborate employment of triadic materials.

Ex. 53. Excerpts based on triadic materials.

(a) *Ermuntre Dich, Mein Schwacher Geist* — Bach

(b) Piano Sonata I, K.545 — Mozart

(c) Fugue in D Minor — Bach

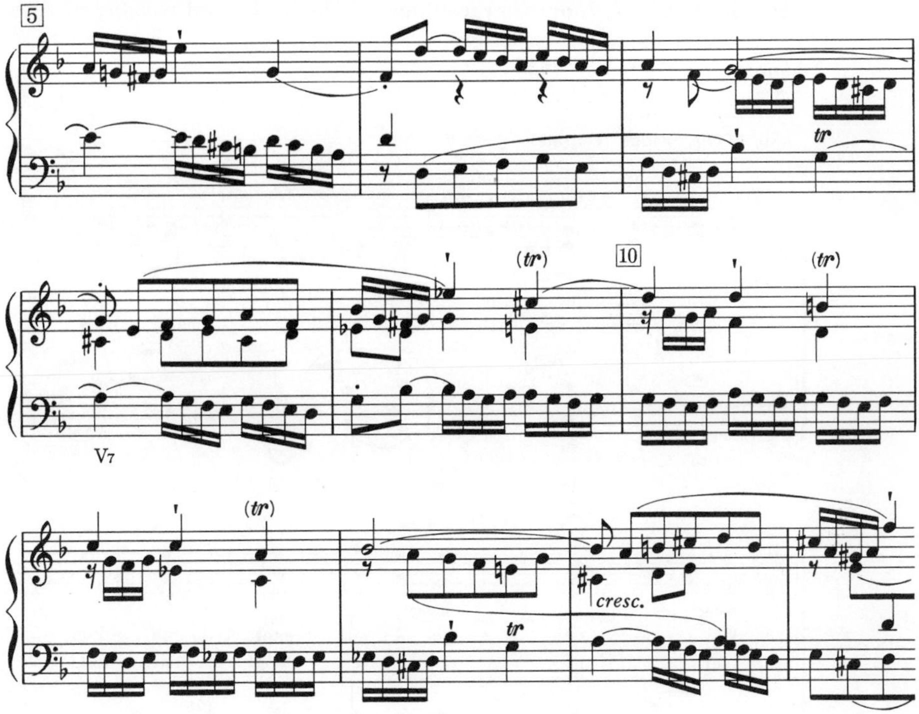

It is apparent that the essential simplicity and plasticity of triadic materials, particularly major and minor, has had an appeal and serviceability to composers that is unexcelled by any other musical harmonic material. This applies to a lesser extent to the diminished and augmented triads (illustrated below), whose role in the repertoire is far more restricted than that of major and minor triads. Both of these triads sound unstable in most tonal contexts, the former containing a tritone, and the latter spanning an augmented fifth, an interval that lacks identity in a key without reference to other factors—particularly melodic direction.

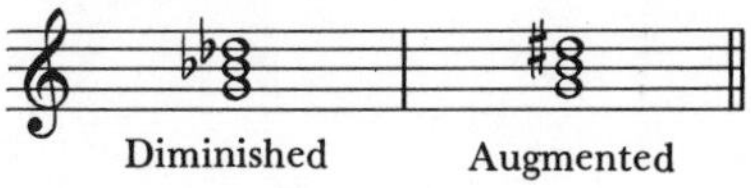

PROBLEM 18a

Sing in a group or play at the keyboard the following Bach chorale. Below the bass indicate the *quality* (M for Major, m for minor, + for augmented, and ° for diminished) of each undecorated on-the-beat triad. Add the appropriate symbols—$\binom{6}{3}$ or $\binom{6}{4}$—for inverted triads immediately following the indication of quality. Then place the symbol *R, 3,* or *5*—representing the doubled chord member of each sonority (triads only)—*above* the respective *soprano* notes. Measure 1 has been begun in the manner described.

Jesu, Meine Freude (chorale)

Bach

PROBLEM 18b

The following excerpt is composed mostly of melodically outlined triads. Read the passage away from the keyboard (silently), trying to hear each chord in your mind's ear. Verify the accuracy of your hearing by playing each measure's chord in a vertical arrangement. Below each measure indicate the quality of the respective chord outlined.

Album for the Young: A Short Study

Dominant Seventh Chord

Of greater consequence than diminished or augmented triads is the family of four-note chords called *seventh chords,* which form simple extensions of the triad. These chords play an important role in defining tonality, in shaping melodies and counterpoint, and generally in expanding the tonal harmonic palette as is found, for instance, in measure 8 of the Bach fugue in Example 53, in which a four-note chord rooted on *a* occurs: 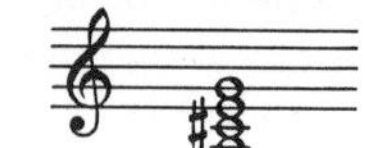

Without question, the most crucial role of all four-note seventh chords is that played by the *dominant seventh* chord, a four-note chord composed of stacked thirds, whose root is the fifth scale degree, the dominant. The important function of the dominant seventh, the V^7 chord, in defining tonality cannot be overstressed. For the time being, recognizing various arrangements and treatments of the dominant seventh chord should occupy our attention. Consider the short excerpt in Example 54.

Ex. 54. Wolf: Goethe-Lieder No. 19.

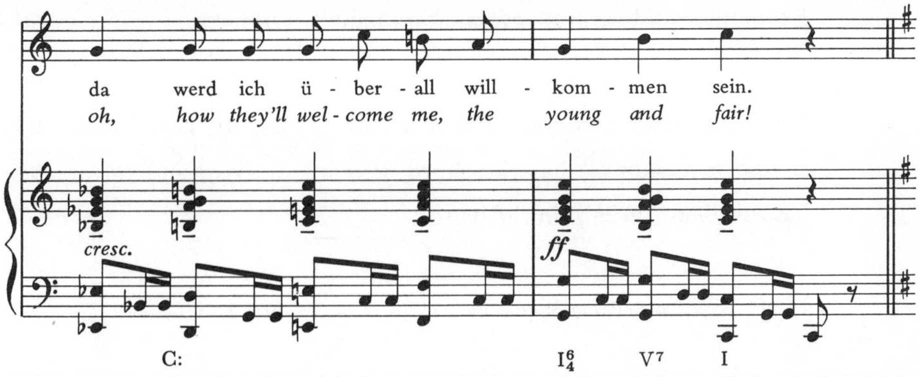

The next-to-last sonority of this excerpt differs from those immediately surrounding it in that it is composed of four different notes; the repeated *d* that falls on the weak part of the beat is part of the same chord. Shown in its simplest tertian (stacked thirds) arrangement, this chord consists of the notes *g, b, d,* and *f:* 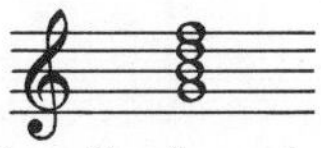 . The root, *g,* is the fifth scale degree of C major, so the chord's function is *dominant.* Unlike the major triad that forms the basis of the sonority, this chord contains unstable intervals, namely the minor seventh from *g* to *f*—root to chord seventh—and the *tritone* from *b,* the chord third and leading tone of the key, to *f,* the seventh of the chord. Most musicians regard this combined effect of a tritone with a dominant root as a prime factor in the establishment of key feeling, which is so important to tonal music in general. Note the resolution of the tritone members as the dominant seventh chord, V^7, moves to the tonic, 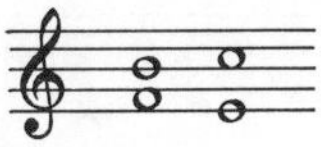 , the leading tone pointing the way to the tonic by an ascending half step, *b–c,* and the chord seventh, *f,* moving in contrary motion to the third of the tonic triad, *e.* This pattern of contrapuntal motion associated with dominant-to-tonic progression is found in most tonal music of the past three hundred years or so. Example 54 contains other variants of the same progression in the keys of *B* and *E♭*. Locate them.

We can describe the dominant seventh as a chord formed by a root, a superimposed, or stacked, major third, a perfect fifth, and a minor seventh. Like other triadic sonorities, it occurs in a great number of rhythmic and spatial arrangements; furthermore, it can be inverted just like simple triads. The three inversions of the dominant seventh discussed above are shown below in their simplest close-position arrangements; the arabic numbers denote the intervals sounding above the bass (or lowest part) for each of the three possible inversions.

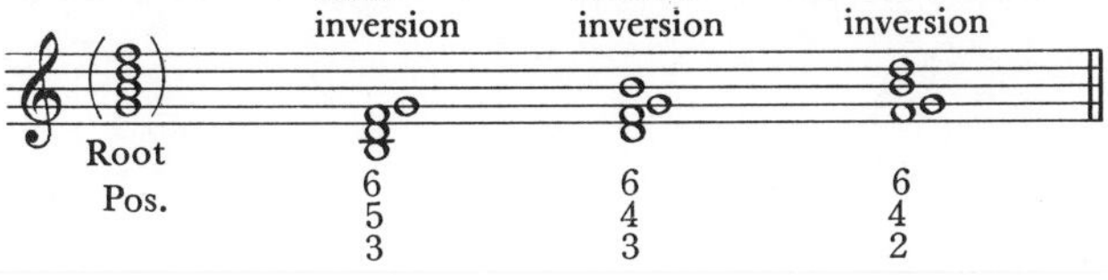

Example 55 illustrates several dominant sevenths in various positions and inversions. The implied keys are shown in large letters. It is essential to remember that *all* chord inversions are determined solely by the chord member in the bass; therefore, first inversion $\left(\begin{smallmatrix}6\\5\\3\end{smallmatrix}\right)$ has the chord third in the bass, second inversion $\left(\begin{smallmatrix}6\\4\\3\end{smallmatrix}\right)$ has the chord fifth in the bass, and third inversion $\left(\begin{smallmatrix}6\\4\\2\end{smallmatrix}\right)$ has the chord seventh in the bass.

Ex. 55. Beethoven: Piano Sonata in G Major, Op. 14, No. 2, II.

It's easy to see how dominant sevenths often influence and shape melodic contour in both immediate and elaborated successions, as in Example 56.

Ex. 56. Bach: Two-Voice Invention in G Minor.

PROBLEM 19

Place a check below the bass of any V^7 chords in the passage that follows, indicating by the appropriate symbols any inversions that occur, for instance, $\begin{smallmatrix}6\\5\\(3)\end{smallmatrix}$ $\begin{smallmatrix}(6)\\4\\3\end{smallmatrix}$ $\begin{smallmatrix}(6)\\4\\2\end{smallmatrix}$.[9] Before the chord indicate the tonic to which it relates. See measures 1–5.

[9] Numbers shown in parentheses are commonly omitted in practice.

Well-Tempered Clavier, Book I: Preludio 7

PROBLEM 19b

Check each measure in which a V^7 chord occurs; above each note of the voice part write R, 3, 5, or 7 to indicate its relation to the chord root. (Do not re-label repeated notes.) Measure 1 is begun as a sample.

"Hark, Hark! the Lark"

Allegro
Schubert
Voice
Piano
p
Fine
Fine
7
3
pp
Horch, horch, die Lerch' im Ä - ther - blau! und Phö - bus, neu___ er -
Hark, hark! the lark at Heav'n's gate sings, And Phoe - bus 'gins___ to
weckt,___ tränkt sei - ne Ro - sse mit dem Thau, der Blu - men - kel - che
rise,___ His steeds to wa - ter at those springs On chal - ic'd flow'rs___ that

Problem 19b continued.

The dominant seventh retains its most characteristic elements: the fifth scale degree root, the leading-tone as the chord third and a minor seventh. The leading tone and chord seventh form a tritone (a diminished fifth or augmented fourth). The chord fifth is sometimes omitted for one reason or another. Furthermore, in many contexts the texture precludes the simultaneous sounding of three or four parts. When such is the case, dominant sevenths are often *implied* by the linear motion of two or more parts; the resulting horizontalization of the V^7 notes, or those of any chord for that matter, in no way detracts from its harmonic significance. Note the implied or incomplete V^7 chords in Example 57.

Ex. 57. Handel: Cantata No. 49.

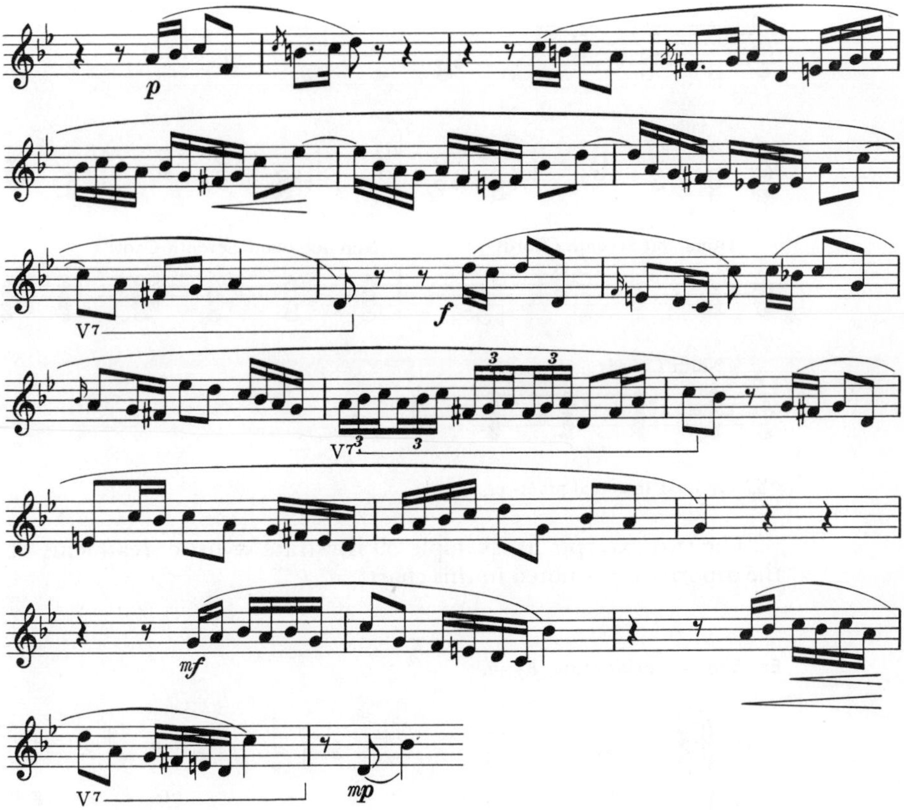

It should be clear that the harmonic materials of traditional music consist of a relatively small nucleus of sonority types, namely, major, minor, diminished and augmented triads, dominant (also called major-minor) sevenths, and the inversions of these. We will not be concerned for the time being with further extensions of triadic sonority, including non-dominant sevenths, ninth chords, thirteenths, and the like; they will be taken up subsequently.

Not all tonal music exhibits a distinct triadic vocabulary; this is especially true of music of the early Renaissance and before. *Diads,* two-note sonorities usually occurring in the forms of simple consonances such as octaves, fifths, fourths, thirds, and sixths, form the harmonic staples of twelfth-, thirteenth-, and fourteenth-century music. In some cases, such materials—thirds and sixths in particular—imply triads. To what extent such interpretations by us are conditioned by familiarity with later, triadic tonal music is by no means clear. The chart of vertical combinations in Example 58 is a capsule summary of the harmonic staples of most diatonic tonal music.

Ex. 58. Tonal harmonic staples.

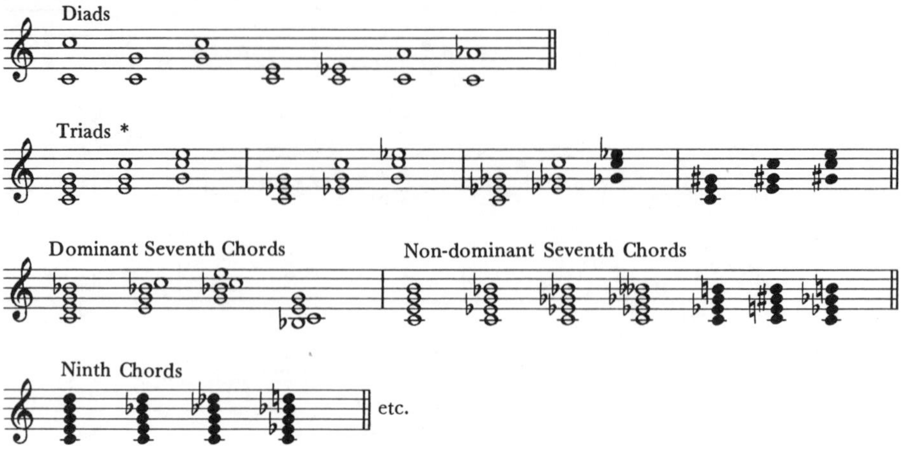

*Rarely used in actual practice.

The two excerpts in Example 59 illustrate stylistic treatments of several of the sonority types noted in this chart.

Ex. 59a. Victoria: Mass, *Kyrie.*

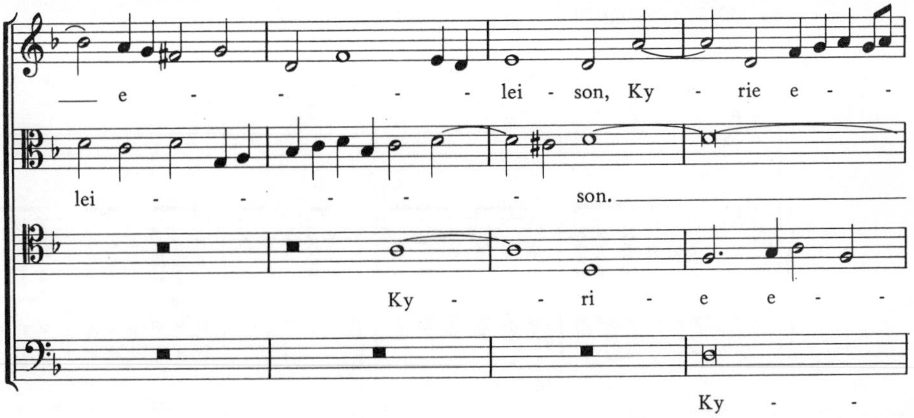

Ex. 59b. Mendelssohn: "Sonata in D Major," Op. 58, I.

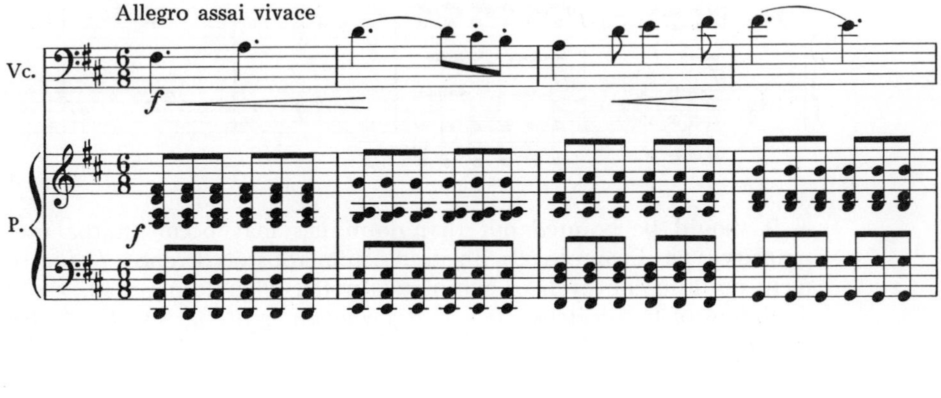

Ex. 59b continued.

It should be pointed out that doublings may occur in the use of any sonority type; Example 59a illustrates numerous occurrences of the reinforcement on different levels of one or two notes. The closing diad, *g–d,* presents doublings of both pitches. It is still a *diad* since it consists of only *two different notes.*

PROBLEM 20

Check the bass note of every accented or "strong-beat" *diad* in the following passage.

Codex Ivrea, Credo

(Father Almighty, maker of heaven and earth, of all things visible and invisible.)

Most music involves harmonic relations and materials of one sort or another, just as it involves linear events, texture, timbre, and other elements. The organization of chords and harmonic progressions in a key, however, is associated mainly with tonal music. Tonal in this usage, however, need not be limited only to music of the eighteenth and nineteenth centuries. As has been indicated, the effect of tonality and the degree to which tonality is operative in music differs markedly among various musical styles.

In our earlier study of melodic structure we noted how such factors as tonality frame, cadence, triadic outlining, and the like contribute to the realization of tonality. Undoubtedly, one of the most persuasive forces in tonal organization is that of triadic function, that is, the relation to a given tonic of the various sonorities with which it interacts. Since triads are associated with their roots, it's a simple proposition to identify the various triads that occur in a key by the scale degree corresponding to the root of each triad. (See Ex. 60.)

Ex. 60. Major scale and corresponding triads:

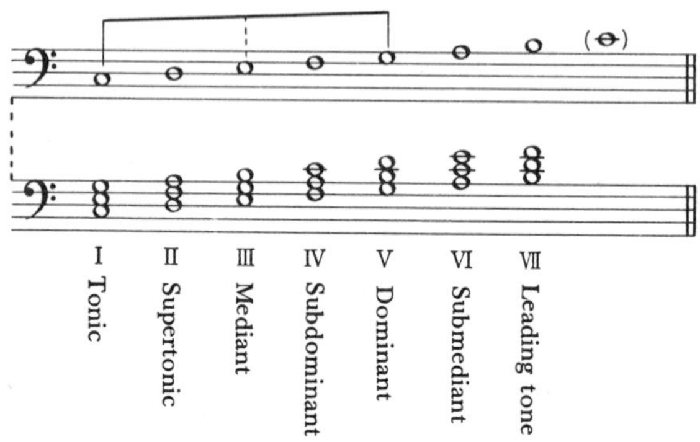

Variable minor scale with corresponding triads.

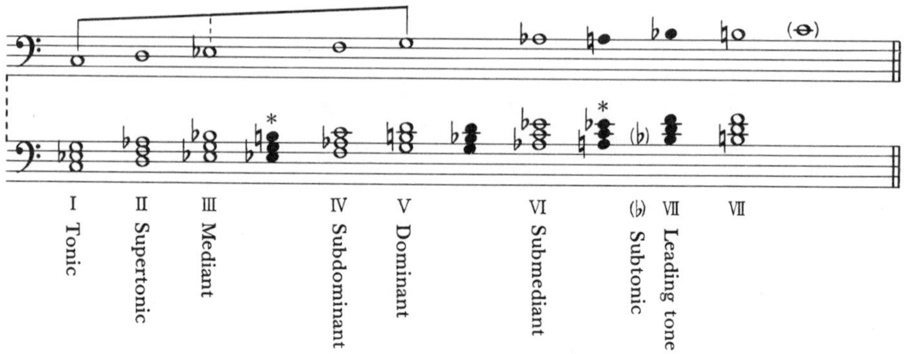

*Relatively infrequently found.

Familiarize yourself with the quality (major, minor, etc.) of the various triads in major and minor keys. Since the determination of tonal structure is primarily a question of the relationship and connection in time of the tonic and dominant, it is to this component of tonality that we shall next turn our attention. Obviously, an ability to differentiate tonic and dominant is predicated to some extent on an ability to recognize any triadic sonority in a given context.

PROBLEM 21

Identify (by writing roman numerals below the lower part) the function (scale degree corresponding to the root) of each *on-the-beat chord* in the following excerpt. Include any dominant sevenths as well. Show appropriate inversions where pertinent. (Do not re-label repeated chords.)

Mazurka, Op.68, No.3 Chopin

Harmonic Progression; Tonic–Dominant Relation

In the beginning of this unit, mention was made of the hierarchical implications of musical structure. Perhaps no facet of music exemplifies more clearly the organization of musical sound on different levels, that is, at different spans of musical time-passing, than harmony. This is easily observed in Example 61a.

Ex. 61a. Clementi: Piano Sonata, Op. 10, No. 1, II.

Harmonic progression, that is, movement from one chord to a succeeding chord or chords, unfolds in this excerpt on several different and perceptible levels. Viewed as a whole, the movement can be understood as an elaboration in time of the chords that begin and close the two principal sections of the piece: the tonic triad of D major in measure 1, the dominant triad that closes the first section, and the tonic triad reasserted at the end of the piece. Defined thus, the work's harmonic movement encompasses the axis-like span of I–V–I.

This prolonged articulation of tonic–dominant–tonic, which clearly maps out the tonality of D major, is roughly analogous to the *melodic* tonality frame in that it provides a simple background, or harmonic frame, for the elaboration and detail of shorter, contrasting musical spans such as sections, phrases, and shorter tonal units as well.

On another level one may observe tonic–dominant relations defining and connecting each of the phrases of the Clementi sonata. The pattern in Example 61b shows the succession of tonic–dominant chords that defines this level of activity.

Ex. 61b. Tonic–dominant progressions at the level of the phrase.

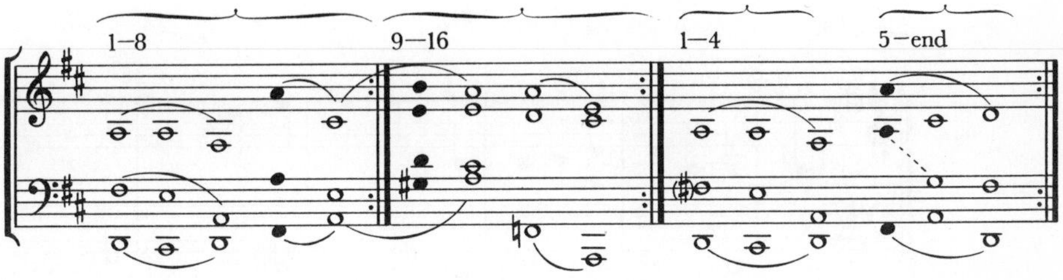

Contrast Example 61b, which includes only tonic- and dominant-rooted activity, with Example 61c, a reduction of the entire progression underlying the sonata in which contrapuntal details in the form of melodic decorative activity have been eliminated.

Ex. 61c.

Ex. 61c continued.

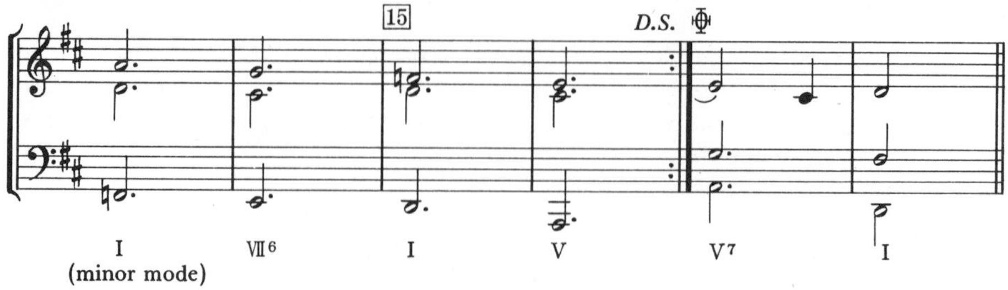

Ex. 61d.

Ex. 61e.

Most tonal music reveals tonic–dominant relations on one level or another of harmonic activity, if not on all levels. In Example 61a, one finds root relations between *d* and *a* operative on various structural levels. For example, measures 1–4 project an immediate tonic–dominant–tonic progression; this represents detail. On the other hand, measures 1–8 are framed by the tonic-to-dominant motion of the opening section of the piece. The same fifth relation may be observed in the hint at a key-change to A major, the dominant key of D, that is introduced in the second section of the piece. This brief emphasis on A via the V^7 of A represents the midpoint of a three-stage cycle of harmonic activity formed by the opening establishment of D, a motion away from D towards A, and a subsequent re-emphasis of D at the *dal segno* (D.S.): I–V–I. In this piece, then, the same type of activity that is present in harmonic detail—that is, a reliance on the tonic and dominant—also occurs at the level of larger structural sections. The use of tonic and dominant at various structural levels is typical of tonal music exhibiting simple, diatonic pitch materials.

Although the music in Example 61a relies to a great extent on tonic and dominant chords, I and V are by no means the only triads present. Both the subdominant and supertonic triads occur, as well as the diminished triad, VII, built on the leading tone. The I, IV, and V triads are sometimes called *primary* chords, and the II, III, VI and VII triads are referred to as *secondary;* these descriptive classifications are applied to a variety of styles.

The details of harmonic progression are far too numerous for any definitive discussion at this point. However, some general observations regarding more or less typical and expected treatments of diatonic chord progressions can be made on the basis of Example 61a, as well as *most* traditional pieces.

The essential function of the dominant triad, or V^7, is to progress to the tonic, for example, in measures 3–4 of the Clementi sonata, or in the final cadence of this piece, an *authentic* cadence. The characteristics of such V-to-I patterns include the 7–8 leading-tone-to-tonic step motion (often exposed in the main voice), the root relation by fifth often evidenced by the bass, the 2–1 motion from the fifth of the dominant triad to the root of the tonic, and the usual resolution by descending step of the seventh of the V^7; these are all apparent in Example 61a, as reduced here:

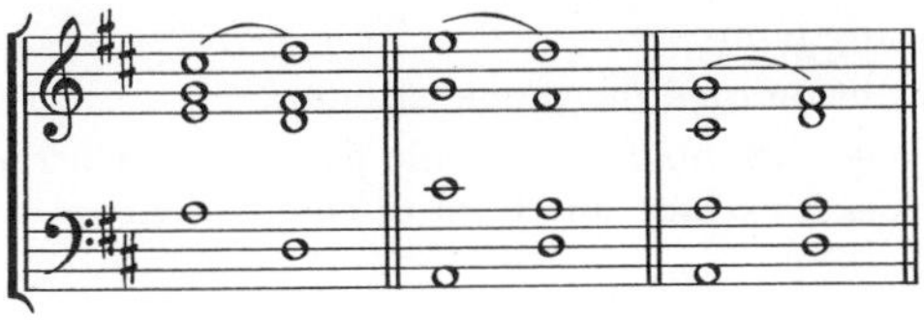

Both the subdominant and supertonic triads appear as links or intermediary chords between tonic and dominant. As such, they are often called pre-dominant, that is, "dominant approach" chords. Their role in the definition of tonal feeling is decidedly secondary.

The leading-tone triad is usually found in first inversion, as seen in Example 61a. Its functional role is decidedly like that of the dominant, and it shares three notes in common with the V^7. It is used most typically to connect, as a passing chord, various positions of the tonic triad, as seen in measure 14 of Example 61a.

The mediant and submediant chords are generally employed to approach the subdominant, in other words, as chords that fill in or elaborate the more essential functions of tonic–subdominant (or supertonic)–dominant: I–IV–ii–$V(V^7)$–I. Note the last four measures of Example 61a, beginning four measures after the D.S.

The chart of typical functional harmonic direction shown in Example 62 will, for our present purposes, give you an adequate reference for harmonic progression in a key. Familiarize yourself with it and restudy Example 61a with it in mind.

Ex. 62. Graph of normal harmonic direction in tonal music.

Stability . . . . *Digression* . . . . *Return* to . . . . Stability

TONIC . . PRE-SUBDOMINANT . . PRE-DOMINANT (subdominant) . . DOMINANT . . TONIC

I, i	vi, VI	IV, iv	V, V7	I, i
	iii, III, III+	ii, ii°	$vii^{\circ 6}$	(vi, VI)
		N6 Aug. Sixths	(iii^6, iii) III)	
		Emb. °7, ø7		
		Secondary Sevenths		
		Secondary Dominants		

N.B. This cycle may begin at any point.

Any step in the cycle may be omitted (harmonic elision).

The above cycle in no way accounts for rhythmic placement or accentuation of any of the chords, nor does it exclude any form of embellishment.

Elaboration of the Tonic–Dominant Relation

If you were to spend a day or two in a music library surveying the existing bibliography on the subject of theories of tonal music, you would come across countless volumes dealing with detailed accounts of chord progression, chord types, rules regarding normative as opposed to exceptional (non-stylistic) harmonic successions, and endless statements regarding acceptable as opposed to incorrect ways of creating voice-leading or harmonic phrases, treating dissonances, and so forth. This book can make no further contribution to such already clouded, contradictory, and often extremely arbitrary issues, and no such attempt is made herein. On the other hand, since most musicians are in agreement that the tonic–dominant relation forms the basis for virtually any analytical approach to tonal music—constituting a framework for the organization of harmonic detail in music as diverse stylistically as that of Mozart and Wagner, or Monteverdi and Brahms—it may benefit us to take stock of some of the essentially simple ways in which composers have utilized the basic tools of counterpoint, voice-leading, and spacing to create music through the elaboration of the tonic–dominant axis. Once such a basis has been established, the details of chord-type and chord progression can be more easily assimilated and placed in perspective. We contend that traditional harmonic practice has been predicated on a few essentially simple and pliable principles, and that we need not endlessly recount rules for this and that situation based on what must necessarily be viewed as a smattering of Western music. Example 61a illustrates, as would most tonal compositions, the relevance of such principles.

Example 61e is a reduction of the two-voice frame of Example 61a to its basic, undecorated activity; this simple skeletal version exhibits a number of rudimentary contrapuntal principles. These consist, among others, of the following:

1. Simple consonances, namely, octaves, fifths, thirds, and sixths form the core of varied harmonic staples.
2. Both parts create acceptable melodic lines, each revealing its own discernible contour, tonality frame, and rhythm.
3. Not only is each part a discrete melodic line, but the harmonic combining of voices reveals considerable variety of intervals with thirds and sixths clearly dominating.
4. The two-voice frame (Ex. 61d) reveals a distinct rhythmic separation of parts involving a combination of third- and fourth-species counterpoint.
5. Rhythmic displacement constitutes the main form of decoration in Example 61a. Step decorations—especially passing tones along with note repetition and leaps within triads, or the V7—also occur.

PROBLEM 22

Familiarize yourself with the layout and details of the piece that follows. In general, it consists of two-voice counterpoint. Make a sketch of the piece's harmonic organization that pinpoints its overall tonal background via main points of definition. Then make a two-voice reduction by eliminating decorative activity and showing basic pitches. Take stock of the various forms of decorative activity that typify and elaborate the basic two-voice frame. To complete the analysis, identify the harmonic roots present in measures 1–16.

Notebook for Anna Magdalena Bach: Minuet in G Minor

Anon.

Optional: Invent your own sixteen-measure piece for piano, or any available two-voice instrumentation, based on the harmonic sketch of measures 1–16 of the above Minuet.

Non-Dominant Seventh Chords

Although triads and the dominant seventh represent the most-used harmonic materials of tonal music, such music is by no means limited in harmonic content to these materials. Most pieces of any length reveal harmonic sounds and progressions involving in one way or another four-note tertian chords (tetrads) other than those rooted on the dominant. *Any* scale degree may act as the root for a seventh chord, and the set of seventh chords so based is commonly called *non-dominant.* A ready illustration of the preceding statement can be found in an excerpt with which we have already dealt; it is shown in Example 63.

Ex. 63. Bach: *Jesu meine Freude* (chorale).

Ex. 63 continued.

The chords shown in Example 64 occur in this chorale; each is a non-dominant seventh chord exhibiting its own special intervallic components and resulting sonority. Familiarize yourself with these sounds and locate them in the context of Example 63. They form some of the chords in the family of non-dominant sevenths.

Ex. 64. Non-dominant seventh chords (from Ex. 63).

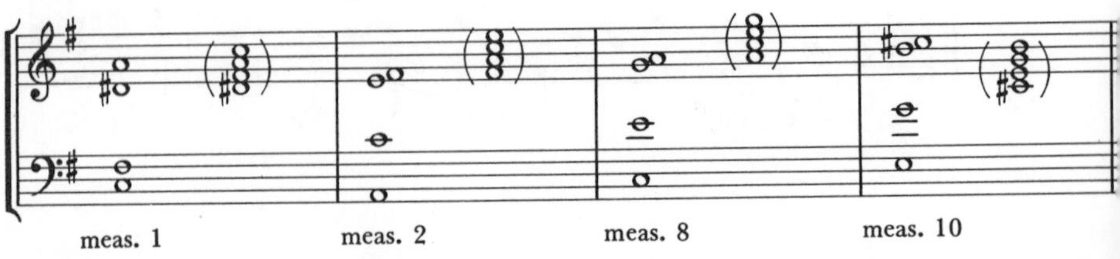

These chords and others of the same family are almost as familiar to our ears as triads; we are perhaps less familiar with the various *treatments* of them that have occurred in the tonal music of the past three hundred years or so. In most tonal music, seventh chords operate within certain limiting constraints, much like the dominant seventh. In some music of this century, especially impressionistic pieces, jazz, and pop music, fewer constraints regarding voice-leading, resolutions, and function occur. The family of non-dominant seventh chords rooted on the various degrees of major and minor scales is charted in Example 65a. The same kinds of sounds are shown again in Example 65b in possible four-part arrangements.

Ex. 65a. Seventh chords in C major and C minor.

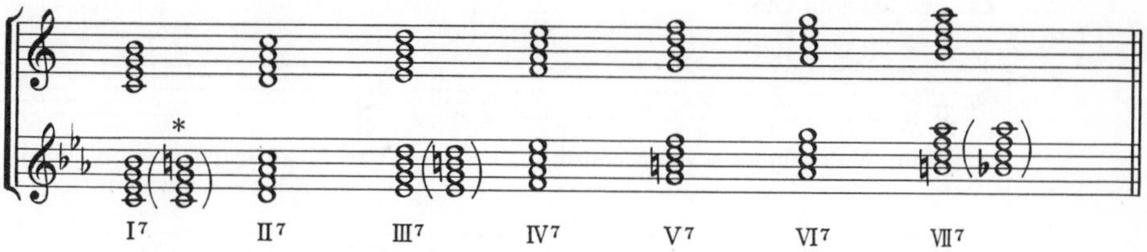

*Occasional chromatic variants are shown parenthetically.

Ex. 65b. Seventh chords voiced for SATB in root position and first inversion.

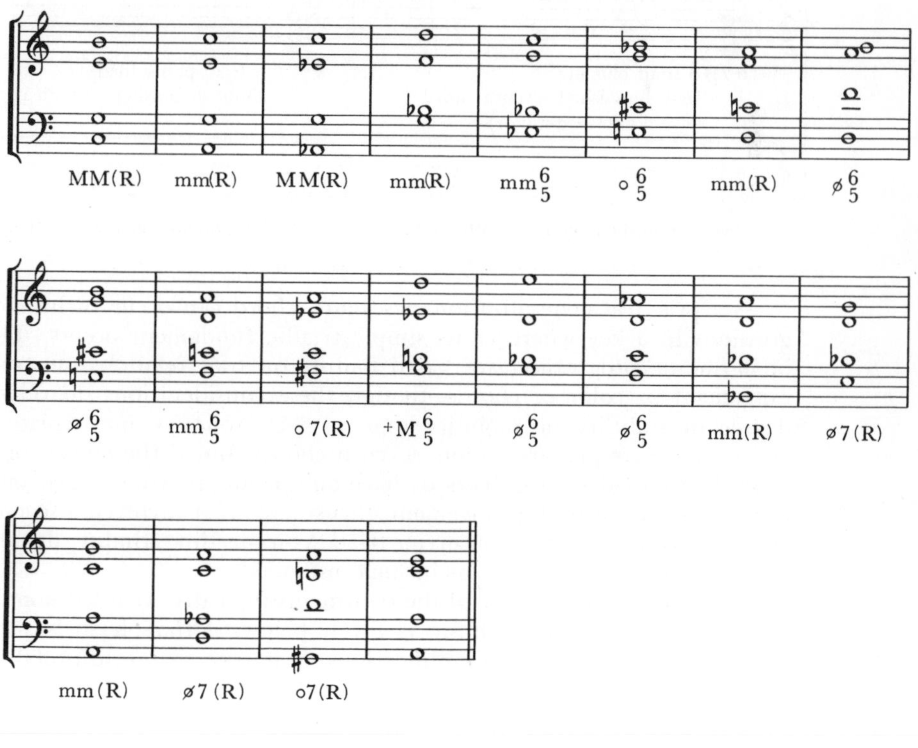

Like all triad-based (tertian) chords, the non-dominant sevenths are described as a rule by their interval makeup, both the fundamental triad as well as the added seventh being included. It has been noted that the dominant seventh consists of the major-minor combination of a major triad plus a minor seventh:  . The family of non-dominant seventh chords comprises the group in Example 66; each chord is shown with a complete description. Some chords have alternate abbreviated descriptions in common usage, and these are also described. The chords marked with asterisks are far *more* common in tonal music than the others.

Ex. 66. Seventh chords.

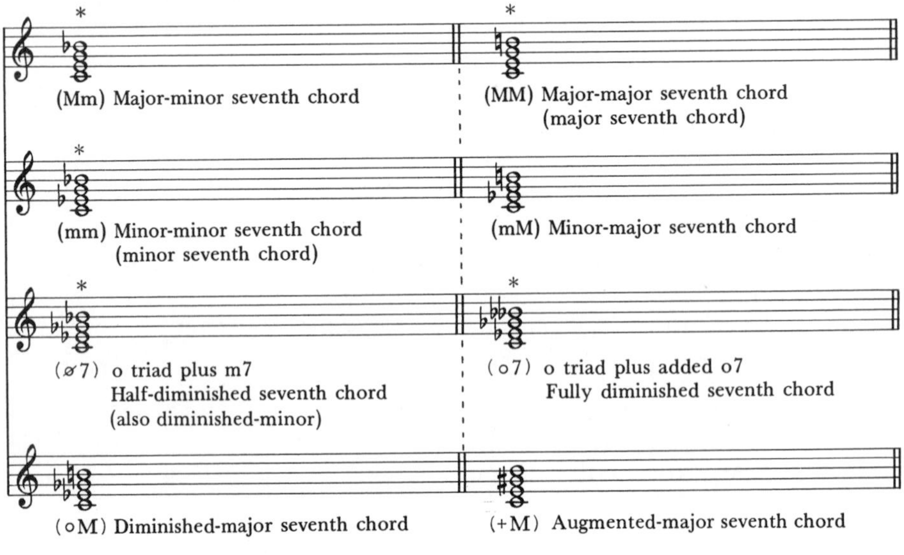

As a practical generalization, a seventh chord can occur in harmonic progressions in a key wherever its simple triadic fundament occurs. The norms of harmonic progression are based mainly on root relations, not on the arrangement or color of chords—though these considerations do relate to the degree of stability or mobility that a given sonority may create. Closing chords, for example, are seldom seventh chords. But if the climax of a phrase were determined on the basis of harmonic color, it would have more effect (tension, expectation for movement, thrust, etc.) if it involved a seventh chord as opposed to a root-position major triad. Voice-leading, timbre, dynamics, and tempo act as mitigating factors in such instances.

A brief summary of some of the treatments typically accorded non-dominant seventh chords in tonal music is given below. Although such summations inevitably risk being oversimplifications, it is true that traditional music almost invariably reveals certain patterned means for dealing with sonority and accommodating its limited repertoire of harmonic materials to a stylistically diverse literature. The simple guides cited below apply in general, except where harmonic effect appears to be paramount.

Some Principles Pertaining to the Use of Non-Dominant Seventh Chords in Tonal Music

1. Seventh chords occur most often within the interior of a phrase rather than at the beginning or close, since stable sonorities such as triads are more often used to begin and end phrases.
2. The *root* is by far the most commonly doubled member of seventh chords, the fifth being omitted frequently. This is especially true in four-part textures containing passages of *successive* seventh chords, parallel fifths being thereby avoided.
3. The most basic melodic tendency observed in the treatment of seventh chords lies in the typical preparation ("presounding" as in a suspension) of the chord seventh followed by a step descent to the third of the following chord.
4. Seventh chords such as II^7 or its first inversion, II^6_5 as well as IV^7, function normally as pre-dominant chords.
5. The $VII^{\circ 7}$, a fully diminished chord in minor, functions as a substitute for the dominant seventh, moving typically to the tonic triad. $VII^{ø7}$ frequently moves to III in major keys.
6. The III^7 is often found as a tonic substitute in major keys.
7. Tonic (I^7) and VI^7 usually precede subdominant or supertonic.
8. In most jazz, seventh chords occur more as a norm than simple triads, providing a basic harmonic ingredient of the style and departing markedly from the constraints of traditional root relations. More than triads, seventh chords are the staples of jazz as well as a great deal of "pop" music.
9. Root position and first inversion $\begin{pmatrix}6\\5\\3\end{pmatrix}$ are by far the most common positions of non-dominant seventh chords. Third inversion $\begin{pmatrix}6\\4\\2\end{pmatrix}$ results commonly from the treatment of the bass as a passing tone or from suspension of the chord seventh.

Several of these principles are illustrated in Example 63.

PROBLEM 19

Construct each of the chords indicated by key and function on the next page; organize them in close position, as shown in Example 65a. Immediately thereafter, show three SATB arrangements of the same sonority and position (or inversion). Try to hear each sonority in your mind's ear without the aid of instrumental reinforcement. Play each sound *after* you have completed the problem; use the chords arrived at for dictation.

Eight varieties of seventh chords were shown in Example 66 for the sake of theoretical completeness. In actual practice, however, only these four seventh chords (besides the major-minor seventh) occur with any frequency in tonal music: the minor seventh chord: 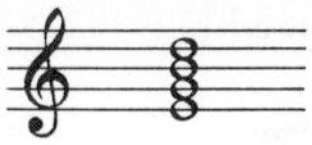 the fully diminished seventh chord: 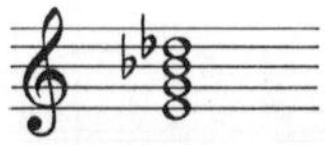, the half-diminished seventh chord: 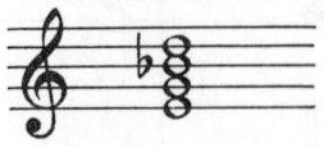, and the major seventh chord: , which is commonly a result in part of the suspended treatment of the seventh:

Harmonic occurrences of the major seventh chord in which there is no contrapuntal treatment of the chord seventh like a suspension or passing tone are relatively rare. Example 67a illustrates such a treatment, quite typical of much twentieth-century music.

Ex. 67a. Bartók: Concerto for Orchestra, III.

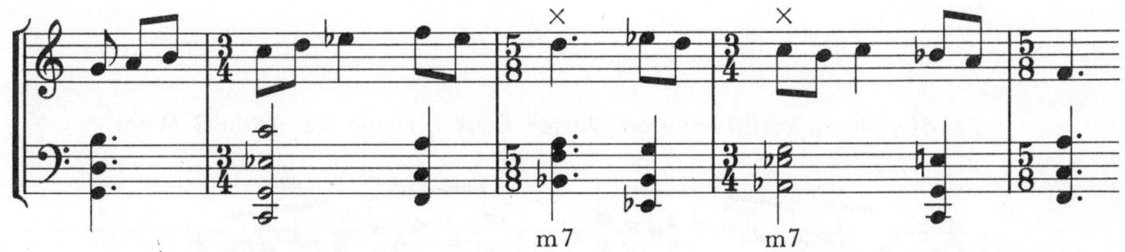

Example 67b, by Corelli, is a more realistic picture of major seventh chords in tonal music; it shows a series of sevenths treated as 7–6 suspensions. In passages such as this, voice-leading and sonority are interdependent and a description of one that does not take the other into account is misleading, if not unmusical.

Ex. 67b. Corelli: Concerto Grosso in C Minor, Op. 6, No. 3, II, mm. 13–23 (reduced to piano sketch).

Ex. 67b continued.

The minor seventh chord and half-diminished seventh chord function similarly in most tonal music, that is, as approaches to the dominant (or tonic $\frac{6}{4}$) at cadences. Preparation and resolution of the chord seventh is so common in tonal music as to be regarded here as virtually axiomatic. Despite other uses of the minor and half-diminished sevenths—generally functioning as supertonic (II) seventh chords (mm in major keys and ø7 in minor)—as passing, neighboring, or cadencing chords, their roles in tonal music are limited, as may be seen in Examples 68a and 68b. Both occur more often in $\frac{6}{5}$ inversion.

Ex. 68a. Bach: *Well-Tempered Clavier,* Book I, Fugue No. 16 in G Minor.

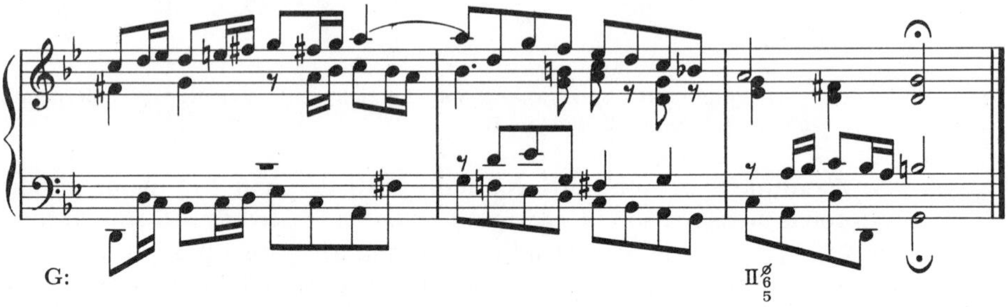

Ex. 68b. Chopin: Mazurka No. 3 in E Major, Op. 6, No. 3.

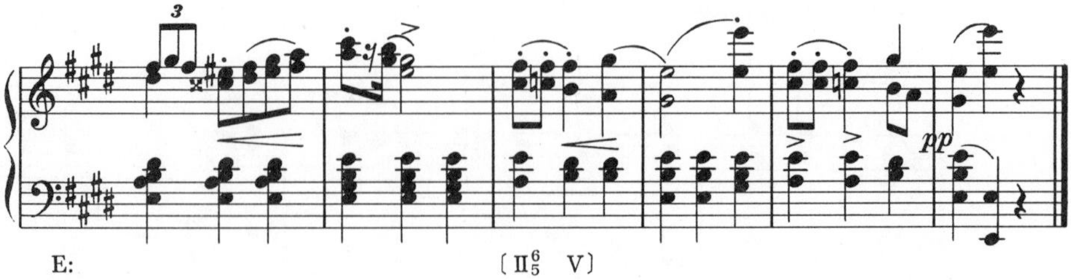

Probably no single chord type has been more exploited for the sake of harmonic color, climax, tonal mobility, musical mood depiction, and other reasons than has the last seventh chord with which we will deal. Whole chapters, indeed (unfortunately) whole books, can and no doubt will be written to do "homage" to the fully diminished seventh chord , the do-it-all chameleon of tonal music. Fortunately, the diminished seventh is truly a relic of the past.

The examples included here show the most basic treatments of the chord in a clearly defined tonality. The homogeneous interval structure of the chord (stacked minor thirds) is such that the very sound seems to invite tonal ambiguity and key change. For that reason the chord is effectively used as an *approach* to or *embellishment* of stable key members, namely, the tonic or dominant, especially in cadences or climactic areas. Prolonged extensions of the fully diminished seventh sound via one or a stream of such chords are common in the work of such late romantic composers as Wagner, Strauss, Liszt, and Franck; and such uses of diminished sevenths are as much a basis for the disintegration of tonality that occurs in general toward the end of the nineteenth century as any other single musical material.

Example 69a shows the use of a diminished seventh chord functioning like the dominant: extending and heightening the resolution-expectation of the dominant triad in measure 5, with which the diminished seventh shares two common tones: *b*♮, the leading tone of the key and the tone that represents a most explicit aspect of the dominant tendency of the chord, resolved here to the tonic $^6_3$; the other being *d*, the chord third.

Ex. 69a. Beethoven: Piano Sonata, Op. 13, III.

Ex. 69a continued.

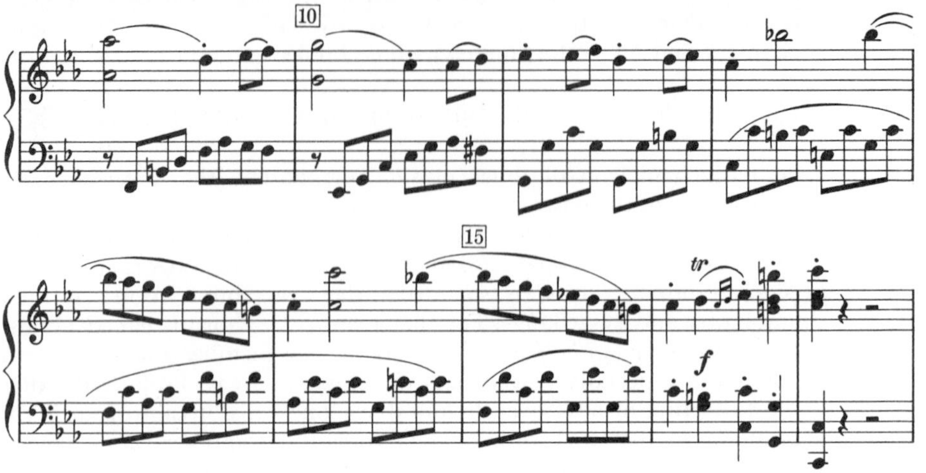

Example 69b contains two occurrences of the diminished seventh built on

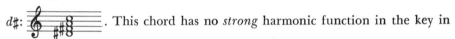

d♯: . This chord has no *strong* harmonic function in the key in which it is used here, C major. Its "function" here, rather than to define tonality like a dominant (see Ex. 69a), is to embellish melodically and harmonically a diatonic chord, namely, the tonic. The melodic aspect of such a role is evinced by the step-neighbor relations of the diminished-seventh-chord tones to the diatonic chord that precedes and follows it: 

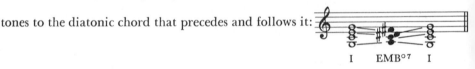

Since the function of the diminished seventh in this capacity is less one of harmony than melody (that is, counterpoint), the sonority is given an appropriate descriptive symbol, Emb, denoting its embellishing rather than harmonic function. Composers frequently spell out such embellishing diminished sevenths as convenience and simplicity in reading dictate, minimizing somewhat the significance of the notation used to encode the diminished seventh sound.

Ex. 69b. Schumann: *Papillons,* No. 10, mm. 1–38.

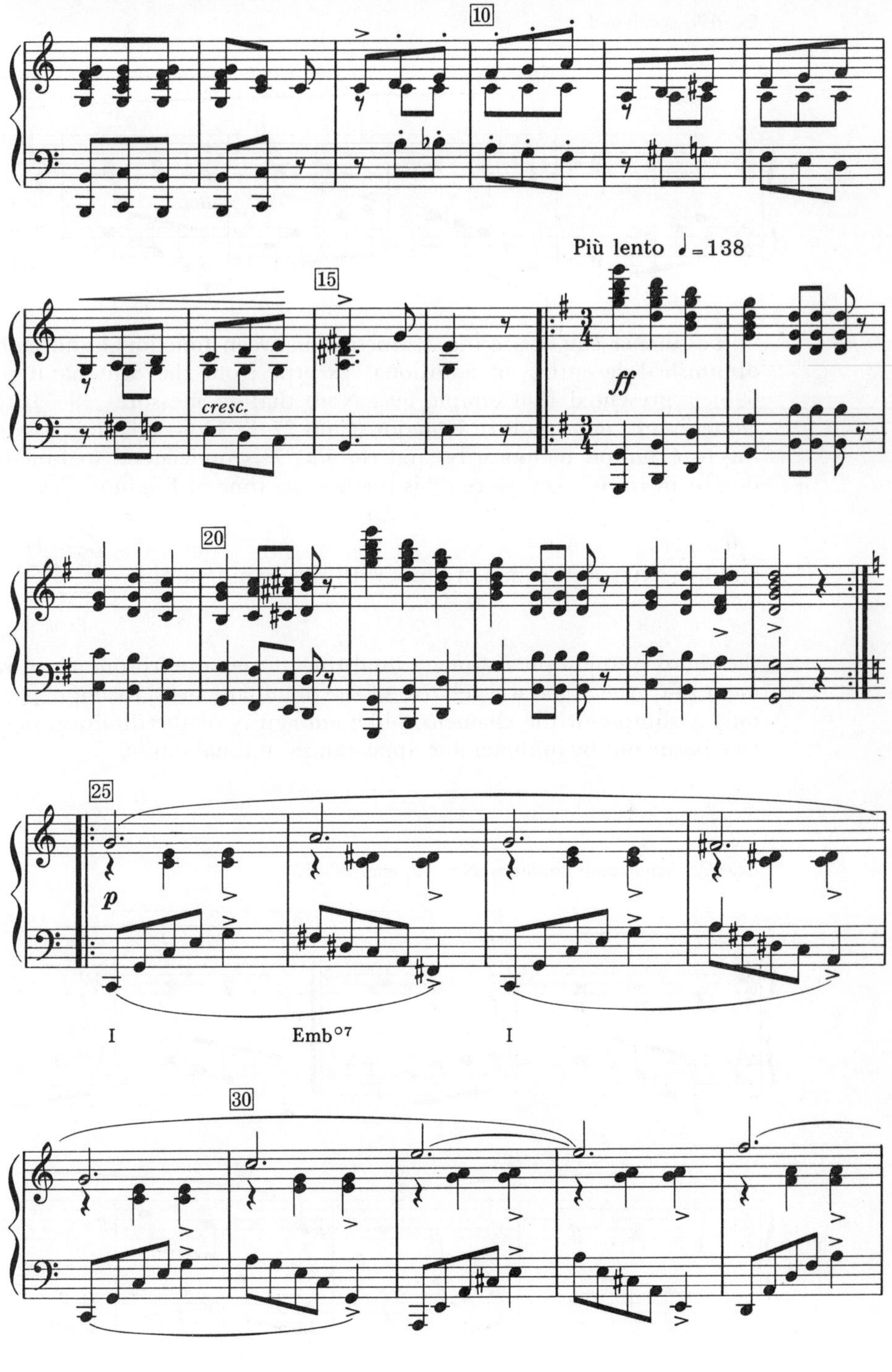
10
15
Più lento ♩=138
cresc.
ff
20
25
p
I
Emb°7
I
30

Ex. 69b continued.

To further emphasize the distinction between functional and embellishing diminished sevenths, an additional excerpt from the Schumann piece (Ex. 69b) is presented in Example 69c. Note that in measures 49–53, the *d*♯ °7 *embellishes* tonic triads in C major (Emb °7–I). However, the passage is moving to *E* minor, temporarily, and the *d*♯ °7 is understood to function like a dominant in that key, since *d*♯ is the leading tone of E minor. For that reason, and by virtue of its common tones with the dominant of E,

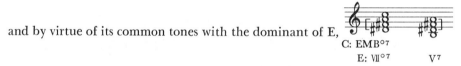

the chord in question assumes a dual role at measure 54, one as an embellishment in C, the other as a relative of the dominant in E. Example 69c provides only a glimpse of the chameleon-like ambiguity of the diminished seventh, a role borne out by innumerable appearances in tonal music.

Ex. 69c. Schumann: *Papillons,* No. 10, mm. 37–65.

PROBLEM 20

The following passage by Bach is an expressive melody supported by an ingeniously fashioned harmonic progression; the latter is enriched by a number of seventh chords. Place a check above every seventh chord (V^7's included) that occurs in this excerpt, and indicate the quality of the chord below the bass.

Mass in B Minor: "Crucifixus,"
mm. 37–49

Bach

45
la - - - - - to pas - - - -
Pon - ti - o Pi - la - - - - to, pas - sus
e - ti - am pro no - bis,
e - ti - am pro no - - - bis,
- - - - - sus et se - pul - tus est, se -
et se - - pul - tus, se - pul - tus est, pas -
pas - sus et se - pul - tus est, se -
pas - sus et se - pul - tus est, se -
p
p
p
p

PROBLEM 21

Complete each of the following short settings, keeping the top voice as is and using the chords indicated; write for the instruments or voices indicated.

(a) Piano

(b) Voices—S.A.T.B.

(c)

Comparative Analytical-Descriptive Systems

There are several useful descriptive systems used by musicians to identify tonal harmonic materials and relationships. Some of these have arisen from the practical needs of composers and performers to code chords; others are a product of theoretical thought, reflecting certain biases about the way chords act in music and proposed means for identifying their activity. Musicians need to be informed about some of the various means that are available to them and that are applied by others in communicating about harmony. Certain analytical techniques or descriptive sets seem to some musicians far more useful and informative than others, but in the final analysis individual musicians will select those descriptive tools that they find most applicable in a given context.

Figured Bass. Figured bass evolved because of the practical needs of musicians to code improvised keyboard accompaniments based on triadic chords. Figured bass accompaniments were in vogue during the Baroque period, and some subsequent composers used figured bass in post-Baroque compositions, especially opera recitative accompaniments. Improvisation based on a figured-bass line became a highly artistic skill during the seventeenth and eighteenth centuries. Bach was a master of figured bass improvisation, as were many of his contemporaries. Both the organ and harpsichord were used for figured bass performance.

In short, figured bass consists of a succession of bass notes denoting the bottom part[10] of a specific chord series. The various chord tones to be sounded above the bass were *not* written. Instead, and as a decided shortcut and time-saver, only numerals denoting certain intervals formed *above* the bass by various chord members were actually written down. Doing so allowed the performer, and frequently the composer, great latitude in voicing, registration, and elaboration. The more exact the figures, the less latitude for improvisational freedom and play. In Example 69d, a short excerpt from a Chopin prelude has been coded via figured bass. This same excerpt will be used to illustrate the other descriptive systems to be described. It is important to note that any one of a number of compositions could be coded with the same figures as are here applied to Chopin. Chopin himself did not, as a rule, utilize figured bass. A fairly complete rundown of the interpretation of figured bass symbols is given here:

FIGURED BASS SYMBOLS

1. Any bass note with no symbol indicates a triad in root position.
2. Any numbers appearing below a bass note refer to *intervals* above the *bass:*

   $\substack{5\\3}$ or 5 root-position triad

   6 or $\substack{6\\3}$ first-inversion triad

   $\substack{6\\4}$ second-inversion triad

   7 or $\substack{7\\3}$ root-position seventh chord

   $\substack{6\\5}$ first-inversion seventh chord

   $\substack{4\\3}$ or $\substack{6\\4\\3}$ second-inversion seventh chord

   $\substack{4\\2}$ or 2 third-inversion seventh chord

---

[10] Not necessarily the root.

Doublings can be indicated by numbers. Here are some examples:

Root-position triads	*First-inversion triads*
$\begin{smallmatrix}3\\3\end{smallmatrix}$ or $\begin{smallmatrix}8\\3\\3\end{smallmatrix}$ doubled third	$\begin{smallmatrix}6\\6\end{smallmatrix}$ doubled root (sixth above bass)
	$\begin{smallmatrix}8\\6\end{smallmatrix}$ doubled third (octave above bass)

3. Numbers appearing under one another refer to intervals which sound *together* above the bass note, as in the inversions of the seventh chords (the largest number is always on top). Numbers appearing alongside one another refer to intervals which sound *successively* above the bass note, as in suspensions and other decorative pitches:

   4 3 4–3 suspension above bass

   8 7 octave moving to seventh above bass (both the octave and the seventh must be in the same voice)

   7 6 7–6 suspension above bass

4. Chromatic alterations or mutations are indicated by various symbols:
   a) An accidental by itself (♯, ♭, ♮, 𝄪) means that the *third* above the bass is to be altered in the way indicated by the accidental.
   b) *Raised notes* are indicated by a line through the figure ($\not 6$, $\not 4$, $\not 2$, $\not 7$) or by a ♯ or ♮ preceding the number (♯6 or ♮6, ♯4 or ♮4, ♯2 or ♮2, ♯7 or ♮7).
   c) *Lowered notes* are indicated by a ♭ in front of the figure (♭7, ♭3, ♭6, ♭2).

5. These symbols can be put together in various ways to show activity above the bass. The following are a few possibilities:

   $\begin{smallmatrix}7\\ \natural\end{smallmatrix}$ seventh chord with a raised (natural) third

   4 ♯ 4–3 suspension in which the 3 is raised (sharp)

   $\begin{smallmatrix}8\ 7\\ \sharp\end{smallmatrix}$ root-position triad with one voice passing to a seventh, with a raised (sharp) third

Ex. 69d. Chopin: Prelude No. 20 in C Minor, mm. 1–13.

Ex. 69d continued.

Jazz-Pop Chord Symbols. Another simple but direct means for coding harmony is associated with, but not confined to use in, jazz and popular music. This system amounts to denoting chords on the basis of a *root* and an abbreviation for the special quality (intervallic structure) of the chord. Chord function is not indicated in either figured bass or jazz symbols. A simple breakdown of three- and four-note tertian chords (triads and seventh chords) is given here. Actually, jazz symbols are applied as well to more complex sounds than these:

Chord tones *	Notated	Jazz symbol
f d b G	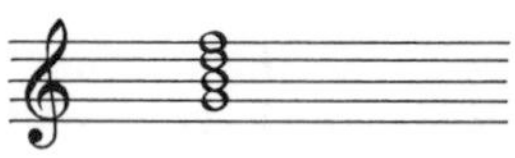	G^{7}
f♯ d b G	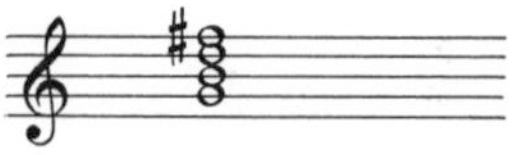	GM^{7}
f d b♭ G	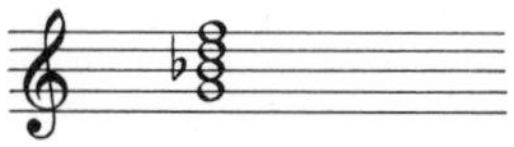	Gmin^{7}
f d♭ b♭ G	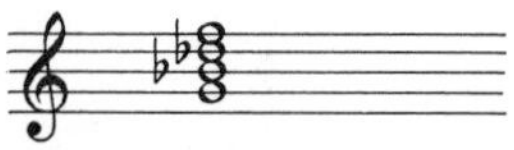	G^{ø7}
f♭ d♭ b♭ G	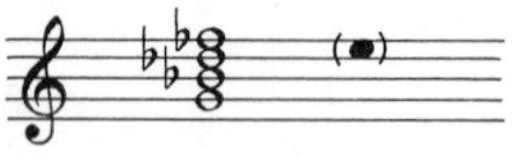	G$^{\circ 7}$
f♯ d♭ b♭ G	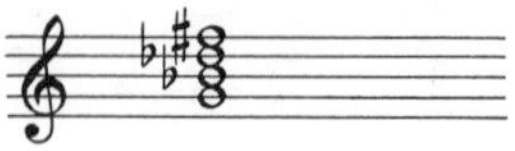	G$^{\circ M}$
f♯ d b♭ G	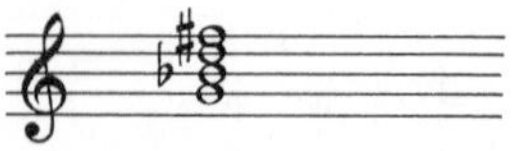	GmM^{7}

*Root in capital letters.

For further differentiation, some use large *M* for major and small *m* for minor. The letter *d,* the abbreviation dim., and the °(circle) all signify *diminished* triads or intervals. Similarly, the letter *A*, the abbreviation Aug., and the + (plus sign) all denote augmented triads or intervals. Jazz-pop chord symbols do not as a rule account for voicing, spacing, or, in particular, *inversion*. All chords are denoted in root position only, though their use in actual practice is by no means so limited. Pianists, guitarists, and other players who must improvise solos are most likely to employ this nomenclature. It goes without saying that composers and arrangers deal with it as a matter of course. Relate the Chopin excerpt to its coding in jazz-pop symbols which appear in the chart on page 234. The symbols for mm, 1–5 appear following the music.

Key of C minor cm fm^7 G^7 cm | A♭ D♭ E♭^{7} A♭ | G^7 C^7 fm C | D^7 G D^7 G | (c) minor

Functional Description Using Roman Numerals. Neither of the two procedures noted above denotes harmonic *function*, that is, the relations of various chords in a key to the tonic. For the past hundred years or so, musicians have employed various nomenclatures using the roman numerals I, II, III, IV, V, VI, and VII to represent chord roots corresponding to the different degrees of diatonic scales. As a result, musicians are able to code harmonic progressions, cadence patterns, sequences, and the like by simply enumerating the succession of chords in terms of their root relation to tonic. This procedure borrows from *figured bass* the numerical symbols for the various chord inversions, seventh chords, and decorative patterns as well. Therefore, I^6 or I^6_3 would denote the tonic triad (I) in first inversion ($^6_3$); V^7 would denote a dominant seventh chord; and so on. Measure 1 of the Chopin Prelude would be coded as: (C minor: I IV^7 V^{8-7}_{6-5}I). Some analysts employ uppercase roman numerals for major sonorities and lowercase for minor. Doing so allows for the immediate coding of both function and chord quality. Recoding the Chopin phrase in accordance with this option results in the following: i iv^7 V^{8-7}_{6-5}i. The entire phrase is analyzed following the music.

Symbols: [C]minor: i iv^7 V^7 i | VI ♭II V^7/VI[11] VI | V^7 V^7/iv iv V/iv | V^7/V V V^7/V V | (i)

---

11 This symbol, V^7, signifies a secondary dominant relation, that is, the use of a chord functioning like a dominant, or V^7, in relation to the chord that it precedes. This

An alternate view presupposes the recognition of brief changes of tonality. In the approach taken immediately above, measure 2 of the Chopin excerpt is related to the principal key of C minor as [VI ♭II V^7/VI]. By the same token but described differently, measure 2 can be heard in the key of A♭ major, and the resulting familiar progression of [I IV V^7 I] would be recognized. Similarly, measure 3 would function in F minor as [V^7/V V^7 i V]. Measure 4 would suggest a change to the key of G major and the progression of [V^7 I V^7 I] in that key. Any choice of terms or analytical decisions, however, should be based on hearing, not on attempts to fit music into conveniently accessible labels.

A more satisfactory description of the Chopin prelude could be arrived at by combining both of the analytical processes involving functional harmonic description noted thus far. This amounts to a kind of *dual-level* or two-stage description of harmonic activity. Level one accounts for chord-to-chord relations by either of the two processes just noted. A second stage reveals harmonic activity on a higher level by showing prolonged emphases or harmonic spans in which various chords in one key are elaborated. The result is harmonic movement over a broader span than that created by the details of chord-to-chord succession. The dual level description via roman numerals that follows attempts to graph such a basic phenomenon of tonal harmony.

C minor: (chord-by-chord movement)

level 1: [i iv^7 V^7 i | A♭ I IV V^7 I | F minor V^7/V V^7 i V | G Major V^7–I–V^7–I] (ci)

level 2: (measure-by-measure harmonic emphases)

i | VI | iv | V | (i)

level 3: [i] (tonic; beginning and ending point)

TONAL VARIETY

Each of the topics to be discussed below—chromatic alteration, secondary dominants, change of mode (mutation), and tonality change (modulation and tonal shift)—has important implications in tonal music and is of sufficient importance to warrant extended study. The aim of this section of the text is to introduce and overview these topics as they relate to tonal variety, without pretending to be comprehensive. We assume that these subjects will recur as you complete subsequent years of theoretical work.

Although tonal variety may occur in music as a result of a number of processes, it is important to establish the fact that regardless of the level at which it occurs—a single pitch, a chord series, or a full-fledged change of key governing an entire section—tonal variety necessitates the introduction

---

is based on the fact that one will in all likelihood *hear* the *E♭*^{7} acting as a dominant of the A♭ chord to which it moves. Chords that relate to others as dominants are commonly called secondary dominants. Any major or minor triad in a key may be preceded or embellished by its own (secondary) dominant. (See the subsequent discussion, pp. 240–245.)

of pitches that lie outside the particular seven-note set, or diatonic key, that prevails. And the processes for creating tonal variety have more in common than their listing under different procedures suggests. This is true because tonal variety and change are often more a matter of degree or emphasis than of process.

Chromatic Alteration

Chromatic alteration occurs whenever the sound (precise pitch) of a given note (there are seven basic notes but twelve pitches in an octave) is changed by one chromatic semitone, such as *c* to *c*♯.[12] Chromatic alteration is frequently observed in monophony, a single strand of melody. See Example 70, for instance. Asterisks mark the chromatically altered notes.

Ex. 70. Schubert: Impromptu, Op. 142, No. 3.

The *b*♮ in measure 4 creates very minimal tonal variety; its role is simply that of a decorative lower neighbor to the c^2 that it embellishes.

In Example 71 chromatic alteration plays a far more extensive role, adding measurably to the variety of patterns and the sheer number of pitches heard. Although the key of the passage, D major, is never in doubt, chromatically inflected melodic and harmonic notes help shape and elaborate an expressive musical statement.

Ex. 71. Beethoven: String Quartet in D Major, Op. 18, No. 3, I.

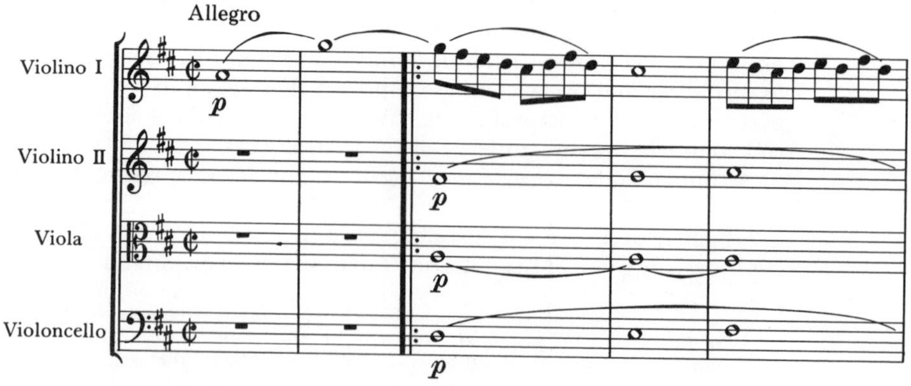

12 Remember that this distinction is to a large extent notational, *c* to *d*♭ being a diatonic semitone and *c* to *c*♯ being chromatic.

p cresc.
p
cresc.
p cresc.
f
p
f
p
f
p
f
p

Ex. 71 continued.

Secondary Dominants

Certain kinds of harmonic progressions involving dominant-functioning chords create considerable tonal latitude and mobility. Because of the greater "weight" of chords as opposed to melodic pitches, harmonic action may emphasize and highlight chords other than the tonic. Such emphases are actually relative and may stress a given triad in one key, or in other instances may establish the tonic of a different key. Consider the two similar progressions in Example 72.

Ex. 72. Two progressions exemplifying different functions.

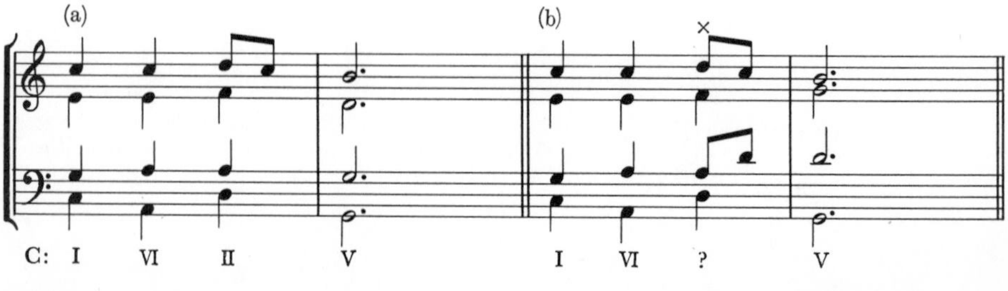

Both progressions span tonic to dominant in C major. The first progression lies entirely in the key of C major, using only pitches of the C-major scale. The second progression, however, differs in one important respect: it contains a note alteration, *f*♯, that both acts as a temporary leading tone to the note g^1 and changes the attendant chord quality from minor to major. As a major chord moving to a stable sonority by fifth-root relation, the chord marked X functions as a dominant in relation to the G major triad to which it moves. As such, it may be interpreted as the *dominant of* V (V / V), in C. This acknowledges the possibility of highlighting and emphasizing tonally any triad in a key by introducing through chromatic alteration the dominant or dominant seventh of that triad.[13] Such temporary dominants are called *secondary dominants* or, when apropos, *secondary dominant seventh chords*, *secondary* because they differ from the primary or principal dominant of the key by virtue of chromatic alteration and root. Example 73 contains a secondary dominant seventh on E. Note that the introduction of the chord V^7/V adds measurably to the tonal variety and interest of the passage without seriously undermining the tonality of the piece, D major, which is reemphasized at the opening of the next phrase.

Ex. 73. Mozart: Piano Sonata in D Major, K. 284, III.

[13] Imagine all the major or minor triads of a given key, say F, as potential tonics; then construct mentally the chord that would normally occur as the V^7 of each were it a tonic triad. Each V^7 thus derived occurs as a secondary V^7 in F.

Ex. 73 continued.

The technique of secondary dominant embellishment is commonly applied to all major or minor triads in major or minor keys. Diminished or augmented triads (those not treated as a rule as tonics) are not preceded by secondary dominants. Several triads in the key of A major are approached by secondary dominant sevenths in Example 74. Like any major-minor seventh chord, secondary dominants can appear in root position or in any of three inversions.

Ex. 74. Bach: *Jesu Leiden, Pein und Tod.*

Both the diminished triad and fully diminished seventh chord can function like secondary dominants; these chords have in common both the leading-tone relation to the chord they precede, as well as the important key-defining tritone found in major-minor sevenths. Compare the three progressions in Example 75.

Ex. 75. Secondary V7, Vii^{6}, and Vii^{o7}/V in F Major.

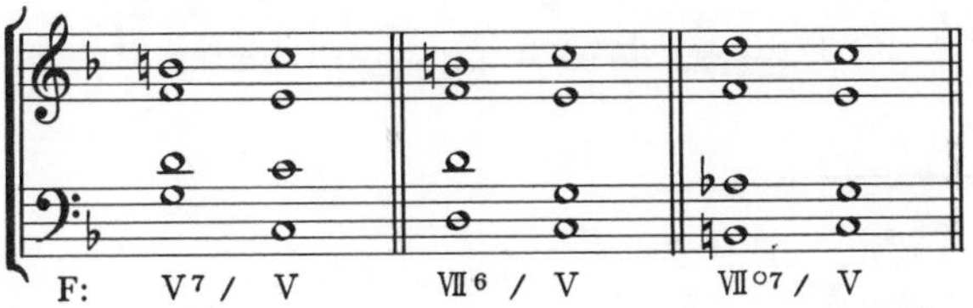

It's easy to hear the similarity of function that these chords have, more similarity than their descriptive labels imply. It is enough to say that all three function like dominants. Example 76 suggests the extent to which such chords can contribute to tonal variety. Here, a number of secondary dominants, as well as secondary diminished triads and diminished seventh chords, broaden the tonal gamut of the D tonality of the passage, which remains intact throughout.

Ex. 76. Mozart: Piano Sonata in D Major, K. 284, III.

Ex. 76 continued.

Secondary dominants are recognized in notation by the presence of altered notes, the most frequent of which form half-step relations with the root of the chord of resolution. Also, secondary dominants reveal the characteristic tritones of all dominant-functioning seventh chords. The tritone generally resolves to the root and third of the chord of resolution. The same characteristics apply to a great extent in inverted arrangements of these chords, which resolve frequently to inverted triads. Short of key-change, secondary dominants provide a degree of variety consisting of temporary focal points that elaborate and expand the tonal scope of passages in which they occur, and they occur in most traditional pieces of any length. Streams of successive secondary dominant seventh chords create a temporary loss of feeling of tonality, relinquishing to sequence or other extensive procesess the stability of key feeling. Such passages are an important aspect of the fluctuating degrees of tonal stability that typify the play of melody and chords and, resultantly, our varying perceptions of them—without which music would be dull and predictable.

PROBLEM 22

Spell each secondary-dominant type chord named, as shown in the sample. Then incorporate the chord into the progression and key given. Write for SATB using as much step motion and singable voice-leading as practical. Employ the chord inversions indicated.

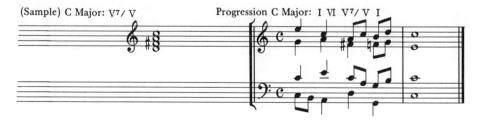

(Sample) C Major: V7/ V   Progression C Major: I VI V7/ V I

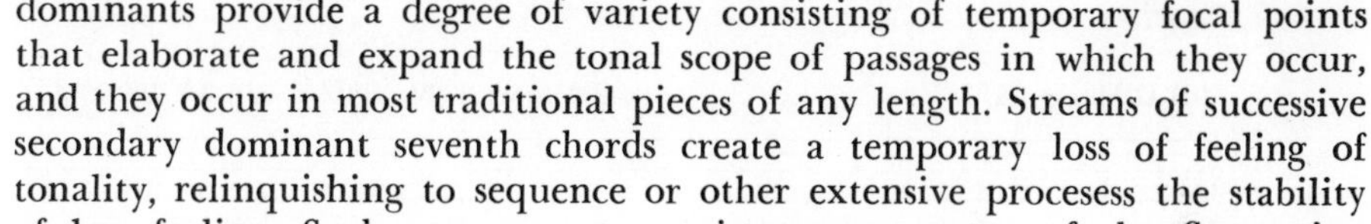

Problem 22 continued.

(a) G Major: V^7 / V   G Major: V VI V^7 / V I

(b) D Minor: VII^6 / III   D Minor: I V^6 I VII^6 / III $VII^{\circ 7}$ I

(c) E♭ Major: V^6_5 / VI   E♭ Major: I V^4_2 I^6 VI V^6_5 / VI II^7 V^7 I

(d) G Minor: $VII^{\circ 7}$/ V   G Minor: I IV $VII^{\circ 7}$/ V V^4_2 I^6 IV^7 I

PROBLEM 23

The following excerpt from a Mozart string quartet (shown here in a piano arrangement) involves considerable use of seventh chords, which contribute to tonal variety and color in this piece. A series of secondary dominant sevenths moving to secondary dominant sevenths begins at measure 12. Scan the passage and attempt to hear it in your mind's ear. Place a check above every seventh chord and indicate its function in A minor, the key of the piece, by placing the appropriate roman numerals below the bass.[14] End your analysis at measure 15, but note the change of key to D minor (the movement's main key) that occurs at that point. (*Hint!* The chords change for the most part at a rate, or harmonic rhythm, of one chord per measure, except for measures 9–11.)

14 Disregard chords with asterisks in your description; they are called *augmented sixth* chords and appear frequently as approaches to the dominant.

String Quartet in D Minor, K.421, Minuet

Mozart

PROBLEM 24

The following excerpt represents some thirty measures from Bach's *Chaconne* for unaccompanied violin. Thoroughly analyze the chords used and their functional relations in D minor. Then make the progressions of the excerpt the basis for a four-part instrumental or vocal piece, keeping the harmonic progression intact, but modifying the chord spacing, voice-leading, and elaboration as desired. The harmonic basis should at all times be clear and essentially unchanged. Invert melodic contours and patterns of rhythm and dynamic usage that add to the satisfactory formal design and elaboration of the piece.

Suite in D Minor: Chaconne for Unaccompanied Violin

Bach

Mutation: Change of Mode

The simple process of shifting from major to minor, or vice versa, is a common agent of tonal variety. Mutation brings into play the contrast between major and minor modes and their respective colors, associations, and qualities. Mutation is a specific kind of alteration involving those scale members (sometimes called *modal* scale degrees), mediant and submediant in particular, that most determine the major or minor mode of a given tonality. Note that scale degrees 1, 4, and 5 (sometimes called tonal degrees) are unaffected by a change from minor to major, or the opposite.

Compare the D major and D minor scales on page 249 and note the pitches common to both, as well as those that differ, mediant and submediant in particular.

Since the mediant and submediant notes are most identified with the major or minor mode of a given tonality, they in turn are the notes most susceptible to and most apt to imply a change of mode, or mutation. Note Example 77. The crux of mutation here is the contrast of major and minor thirds above *c*.

Ex. 77. Beethoven: Piano Sonata in C Minor, Op. 13, III.

Ex. 77 continued.

This excerpt illustrates how the fundamentally simple process of opposing and juxtaposing minor and major while retaining the same tonic can invest new tonal life and variety into an extended passage, without which a certain monotonous re-use of the same pitch set might seem to occur.

Mutation, as noted in Example 77, involves the clear separation and contrast of major and minor, the one following the other in time. In many instances, however, the issue of precise mode is less clear, and elements of both major and minor may appear in what is heard as a mixture that produces a composite (major-minor) mode. Example 78b typifies pieces whose melodies and chords borrow freely from patterns, sonorities, and progressions associated with both major and minor keys. Rather than attempting to label each event that implies a shift from one to the other mode, a laborious task at best, it seems more realistic to acknowledge at the outset the composite mode (mixed-scale basis) and proceed from there.

The chart in Example 78a shows most of the chords with which we have dealt that might occur in a tonal piece based on a composite mode. Many of the chords in the chart occur in Example 78b. Compare the chart with the excerpt.

Ex. 78a. Composite scale as basis for chords in *D*.

Ex. 78b. Beethoven: String Quartet in F Minor (Serioso), Op. 95, II, mm. 35–54.

Ex. 78b continued.

Tonality Change

Tonality provides one of the most important and unique bases for unity in tonal music. By the same token, tonality change, or change of key, provides an essential means by which variety of tonal material is introduced. Key-change makes possible the tonal differentiation of large sections in extended musical forms. The numerous processes and techniques for effecting key-change, often called modulation, reflect to a great extent many of the styles and works of individual composers of Western music. In this brief section two basic processes associated with key-change are discussed, namely, *modulation* by common chord (pivot chord) or chromatic inflection, and *tonal shift,* which is a more direct, if not abrupt, process than modulation. These two techniques are by no means mutually exclusive, though most musicians seem to regard modulating as a more subtle or gradual process than the tonal shift from one key to another.

Modulation

Most modulations are initiated by the introduction of a chord (or series of chords) that is common to both the old and new keys, that is, the key established and the key that is the goal of the modulation. Suppose one were to modulate from C major to its dominant key of G major. An initial step could be to use a chord that occurs in both C and G, say the A minor triad, as a link or connecting chord between the two keys. The A minor triad functions as VI in C and II in G, so a progression might be planned to capitalize on the dual capacity of that chord in providing a common ground or transition between the two keys. In a sense the A minor chord will represent both keys at the point of change. Note the sample progression in Example 79. It shows three steps in effecting the change of key: (1) C major is established; (2) a common or *pivot* chord is introduced so as to be compatible with the functions of the chords that precede and follow it, insofar as the respective keys are concerned; and (3) the new key is defined by its dominant. Changes of key are sometimes marked by the introduction of a new key signature; however, there is no set practice in this respect. Signature changes are sometimes introduced to coincide with sectional divisions rather than at the actual point of key-change.

Ex. 79. Sample modulation.

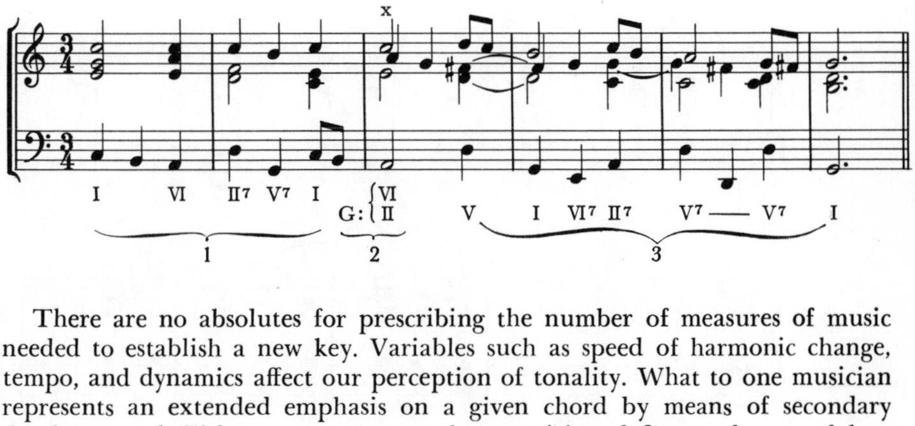

There are no absolutes for prescribing the number of measures of music needed to establish a new key. Variables such as speed of harmonic change, tempo, and dynamics affect our perception of tonality. What to one musician represents an extended emphasis on a given chord by means of secondary dominant embellishment may to another musician define a change of key. Most musicians will agree that at least a phrase or so followed by a confirming cadence, such as V–I, is usually needed to erase one key and establish another. And such confirming cadences are typically followed by the opening of the succeeding phrase in the new tonality rather than the initial one. Compare Examples 80a and 80b.

Ex. 80a. Beethoven: Piano Sonata in D Major, Op. 28, III.

Ex. 80b. Handel: Sonata for Flute and Continuo in A Minor, II.

Ex. 80b continued.

Ex. 80a begins with a thirty-two-measure section composed of four eight-measure phrases. The principal tonality is D major. Phrase 2 (mm. 8–16) forms a sequential answer to phrase I (mm. 1–8). The whole unit, measures 1–16, can be regarded as being in the key of D major, with measures 8–16 creating a brief digression towards A major, the dominant of D–i.e., a short modulation or key-change.[15] The same phrase might also be described as an eight-measure emphasis or prolongation of the dominant of D with the V^7/V occurring; either description seems plausible.

Example 80b, however, presents a far clearer picture of a full-fledged change of key. Here the main key is A minor, defined by the opening ten measures, confirmed by a V–I cadence in measure 10. C major is introduced tentatively via V-to-I patterns in measure 11 and measures 12–13. C major is further elaborated through the embellishment of C: IV, V, and VI by secondary dominants, measures 13–15. A strong V-to-I cadence ends the section at measure 19, and the beginning of a new section in C major follows. Although not all examples of key change are as extended as the one in Example 80b, there are few any more unequivocally clear. The A minor sonority that begins measure 11 can be viewed, in retrospect, as a *pivot* chord linking A minor with C major, the relative major of A. The dual function of the A minor chord can be shown as: $\begin{cases}\text{A minor–I}\\ \text{C major–VI}\end{cases}$

Key changes such as the one just described are relatively "smooth" and subtle. One reason for this is that the two keys share seven common tones. In keys less closely related the effect of key change may be more decisive, have more impact, and even disrupt temporarily one's awareness of tonality. The possibilities for key succession are enormous.

Modulation by Chromatic Inflection (Mutation)

We have noted that mutation can change the quality and function of a chord, especially when the chord assumes the role of a *dominant*. Chromatic inflection, or alteration, is also an important agent of key change. In Example 81, the connection between keys is effected by chromatically altering a note so as to create the leading tone to a new tonic, *g*. No pivot chord as such is actually part of this process.

---

[15] Passages like this are numerous; they seem to be in a kind of tonal limbo, suggesting a short change of key yet failing to erase definitely the prior key. Such brief tonal excursions are sometimes called *phrase modulations*. Theorists also refer to them as *tonal regions*, thereby evading the term modulation, which is more often reserved for passages like the one in Example 80b.

Ex. 81. Mozart: Sonata for Piano in B♭ Major, K. 541, I.

Ex. 81 continued.

Measure 13 contains a reiterated tonic triad in B♭; in the following measure the fifth of the previous tonic chord, F, is inflected—in this case, raised one chromatic semitone to create *f*♯, the leading tone of G minor. The note *f*♯ functions as part of the V^7 of G minor. Although the V^7 is deceptively resolved at this point, delaying the expected movement to the tonic in G minor, there is no doubt that it is here that a transition of keys has been effected. Both the subsequent V-to-I in G minor and the next phrase confirm the change of tonic from B♭ major to its relative minor, G minor.

A somewhat parallel use of chromatic alteration follows at measure 25. Having reached the dominant of G minor—*d, f*♯ and a—the third of V is lowered a semitone, producing a *minor* dominant triad and erasing the expected leading-tone resolution of *f*♯ (to *g*). The *f*♮ prepares the subsequent fifth of the B♭ triad, thus serving as a common tone. The B♭ triad is immediately converted into the V(7) of a new key, E♭, producing an unexpected tonal change. The process is more decisive and perhaps more dramatic than the subtler modulation of Example 80. The procedure here is often called modulation by chromatic inflection—it incorporates mutation (note the change of quality of the D triad from major to minor) as a vehicle for changing key.

Tonal Shift

Key-change is not always brought about by subtle or extended passages devoted to transitions from one key to another. Quite the contrary, key-changes sometimes occur as dramatic turns. Sometimes the keys connected share many of the same notes; in other instances, keys such as C and D♭ or D and A♭ may be involved. Key relations are often described according to the interval separating their tonic notes. For example, keys whose tonics lie a fifth apart (C and G) constitute *fifth relations*; keys spanning a third, major or minor, form *third relations* such as C and E, or D♭ and F. Tonal shifts by third relation are illustrated in Example 82.

Ex. 82. Wolf: "*In der Frühe*" (song).

Ex. 82 continued.

Measures 1–3 are in E major, supported by a pedal fifth in the bass. Without preparation, and emphasized by a sudden shift of register in the voice line, the key shifts from E to G major, a third relation. Only the note *b* creates a pitch-link between the two keys. The subsequent key-changes in the passage, G to B♭ and B♭ to D, are by similar shifts between third-related keys. Note that the tonalities connected in this example are represented more by their tonic triads and pedals than by key-delineating progressions in those tonalities. Each briefly stated key (tonal region) appears as one step in a series of prolonged chords, thereby resulting in a very slow rate of harmonic change, a kind of tonal rhythm. Processes such as this contributed over a span of fifty years or so to the eventual dissolution of tonality and the gradual abandonment by composers of modulatory techniques such as those we have noted here. Composers of our time have yet to solve the problem of structuring large sections of music without recourse to the procedures and techniques of tonal music, among them tonality change.

PROBLEM 25

The extended excerpt by Haydn that follows provides a good example of the various materials and processes that we have dealt with in this unit. Listen to a recording of this movement, two-thirds of which is reproduced here and the final third of which represents in the main a recapitulation or restatement of the materials in measures 1–43. Most of the considerations taken up in this problem have to do with harmony and tonal relations, but you should become familiar with the various motives, melodies, rhythms, and textures embodied in the piece before undertaking the analytical problems. In particular, the thematic materials in measures 1–10, 27–30, and 33–37 should be carefully assimilated. When you are thoroughly acquainted with the piece, answer the questions and perform the analytical tasks below. Compositions along the lines of this movement are in *sonata allegro* form.

Piano Sonata No.52 in E♭ Major, I — Haydn

Problem 25 continued.

30
35
40

Problem 25 continued.

65
70

Problem 25 continued.

1. The first principal section, measures 1–43, is called the *exposition* section. What two keys are established there and what is their relation?

2. In what measure is the second key first in evidence, and what chord function is apparent there?

3. Thematic recurrence coincides with the firm establishment of the new key; where is this found?

4. Secondary dominant embellishment occurs in numerous measures in the exposition of the movement; cite five occurrences of secondary dominants (or dominant sevenths) by measure, and indicate the specific functions involved:

measure(s)	*secondary dominant function*

5. Non-dominant sevenths are obvious in measures 7–14. Place a check on the music above any that occur in measures 7–14, and indicate the chord quality below the bass of each.

6. Changes of mode highlight several passages in the piece. One such example occurs between measures 27 and 37. What key and modes are involved?

   Speculate as to the effect of measures 29–32 on measure 33, insofar as the tonal relations between the two are concerned.

7. Measures 44–78 constitute the development section of the movement, that is, an area for the exploration of materials stated in the exposition. This section is characteristically *unstable* tonally, containing a good deal of tonal variety and frequently innovative key relations. Indicate the keys (or tonal regions) implied at the following points in the section:

measures	*key or region*
46–47	
50–53	
54–57	
58–59 (beat one)	
60–62	
64–67	
68–69	
79	

8. Describe the processes involved in changing keys at measures 44–46:

   and 67–68:

unit

4

TEXTURE

More than any other descriptive musical term, *texture* defines the interacting voices, parts, and layers of activity that constitute the makeup of compositions. It is through the deployment of interacting parts that composers create the depth, span, and illusion of moving and competing parts that contribute to our perception of music as a living and dynamic sound experience. The bases for such qualities lie in the structure and details of musical texture. That no two works are identical is consistent with the fact that no two compositions reveal identical textural components.

QUANTITATIVE AND QUALITATIVE ASPECTS

Texture combines both quantitative and qualitative components. For example, we describe texture by the number of parts or voices that constitute a given piece or section thereof; we also take into account the high or low (registral) placement of such parts, their relative loudness, and the particular tone quality or combination of tone qualities (timbres) that they project.

There are several more or less generally accepted terms used to describe a variety of textural types that occur frequently in music literature. Though describing essentially quantitative aspects of texture, these descriptive terms also imply certain qualitative aspects of part *relations*. These terms allude to general layouts of parts and do not define the details by which *different* pieces of surface similarity are compared and contrasted. *Homophony* is an example of such a general descriptive term.

Homophonic Texture

In essence, homophony is melody (main voice) and accompaniment. Compare Examples 1a and 1b.

Ex. 1a. Beethoven: Op. 59, No. 2, *Finale* (piano sketch).

Ex. 1b. Chopin: Mazurka, Op. 24, No. 1.

Ex. 1b continued.

In Example Ia the main voice, the first violin, is supported by close-voiced chords, mostly triads, repeated so as to maintain rhythmic flow. The supporting chords complement the motion of the main voice while in no way competing with it for melodic interest. The arrangement is clearly one of melody and accompaniment—homophony. Despite the accompanimental character of the lower parts—second violin, viola, and cello—the chord succession is arranged so that a smooth connection is made from chord to chord. This in turn is reflected in the predominance of step motion and repeated notes found in the individual parts, each of which in turn can be seen to have some semblance of linear design as well. This aspect of chord connection is commonly called voice-leading, or counterpoint.

Example 1b also illustrates homophonic texture, in this case for the piano. The waltz-style accompaniment supplied by the left hand consists mainly of a downbeat bass note followed by two weak-beat statements of the other notes of the accompanying chord. Although melodic interest is concentrated in the upper part, there is a feeling as well of smooth progression of voices and logical part movement resulting from the step movement that prevails in the "voices" of the accompaniment. We have previously dealt with examples of two-voice music in which supporting voices created some semblance of melodic as well as harmonic effect. This is the case more often than not. We shall deal with this subject at greater length when we consider in more detail the question of voice-leading.

PROBLEM 1

Study the excerpt from the Schubert song that follows; then complete the following:

Ex. 2.

Die Schöne Müllerin; Op.25, No.7: "Ungeduld"

Schubert

a. The traditional term for the type of texture found here is ________________________.

b. The passage consists mainly of a melody and ________________________.

c. Considered quantitatively, the passage consists of a varying number of parts—from ____ to ____ voices.

d. Describe at least one qualitative aspect of the texture.

e. Attention to effective voice-leading in the accompanying piano part can be noted in this setting. Explain this in a brief statement.

Rhythmic activity and rhythmic continuity are often supplied by breaking up the accompanying chords. In such cases, chord members are often *arpeggiated,* that is, staggered, usually from bottom to top, or in some arrangement wherein the chordal basis is quite clear, allowing for a concentration of melodic activity in the main voice. Example 3 typifies such a texture.

Ex. 3. Brahms: Romanza in F Major.

Many of the more typical kinds of homophonic textures, some of which we have noted, seem particularly well-suited to the keyboard. That this is true reflects the keyboard orientation and training of a great majority of past composers, such as Bach, Mozart, Beethoven, Schumann, Brahms, Tchaikovsky, Chopin, Liszt, Debussy, and countless others. This may explain in part why so many textural arrangements found in instrumental ensemble seem quite compatible with or influenced by the layout of the keyboard. Test this statement by playing Example 4 (a composition for strings) at the keyboard.

Ex. 4. Beethoven: String Quartet, Op. 135, III.

Even though this passage is designed for four strings, its ease of performance at the keyboard is apparent. It is probably not exaggeration to suggest that the influence of the piano is very significant in regard to the variety of homophonic textures and accompanimental patterns appearing in much tonal music. A better grasp of the wide-ranging implications of this statement can be gotten by completing Problem 2, which deals with an extended homophonic passage for the keyboard.

PROBLEM 2

The accompanying excerpt is an extended section of a piano composition by Beethoven. Familiarize yourself with the passage, paying special attention to the various types of textural arrangements that occur in it. Locate, list by measure number, and describe briefly *ten* examples of homophony or monophony found in the excerpt. (We have provided two such examples of textural types in the piece; add eight different ones.)

Sonata Op.31, No.3, I

p
cresc.
p
ten.
ten.
poco stringendo
ten.
ten.
a tempo
p
p
fz
fz
fz
dolce
scherzando
lusingando
cresc.
dimin.

Problem 2 continued.

a. measure 1; melody and supporting sustained chords

b. measure 18; melody and supporting chords above repeated pedal

c.

d.

e.

f.

g.

h.

i.

j.

Homophony dominated musical textures from the latter half of the eighteenth century until the present one. Much contemporary music is also fashioned in essentially homophonic textures. Most folksong settings, pop music, school songs, and hymns, as well as numerous twentieth-century concert pieces, incorporate or rely largely upon homophonic principles and patterns.

Counterpoint

Counterpoint, contrapuntal texture, is the antithesis of homophony; it denotes the interaction and competition of melody against melody, line against line. Simultaneously sounding melodies create counterpoint, or, as it is often called, *polyphony*. Contrast the contrapuntal texture of Example 5 with the homophony of the previous one.

Ex. 5. Bach: Three-Part Inventions, Sinfonia I in C Major.

There are several criteria by which one can assess the textural makeup of a given composition. An obvious feature of the textural layout of Example 5 is that *no* single voice continuously stands out as primary; nor is it possible to speak of an accompaniment and main voice. This is because three more or less equally interesting voices interact and combine in such a way as to distribute melodic activity among them rather than to concentrate it in one.

Each voice forms an effective and acceptable melody. Each voice also reveals a number of characteristics of good melody, such as interesting contour, unity and variety of rhythm, a dominance of step motion, and a clearly defined tonality. The composition's growth and development is mainly a product of melodic activity. Chordal materials and relations are second in importance here, because sonority is far more a product of interacting lines than of clearly stated chords.

The distinction between homophonic and contrapuntal textures is seldom as clearly drawn as in Example 5; in fact, numerous compositions found in different stylistic periods imply that the question of homophony or polyphony (counterpoint) is frequently a moot one, a question that can be answered only by qualification and interpretation. Most music contains elements of both counterpoint and harmony. A realistic interpretation of the textural elements in Example 6 would acknowledge the interaction of both contrapuntal and harmonic materials.

Ex. 6. John Dowland: *"Come again! Sweet love doth now invite."*

This piece is composed of a principal melody for the voice and an attractive accompaniment to be played on the lute. In that the piece consists of a melody and accompaniment, it might be described as homophonic in cast. But there is ample evidence in the details of the accompaniment to militate against such a one-sided description. Melody is by no means limited to the vocal part of this lute song. Both the lute bass line and the upper line of the accompaniment yield satisfactory melodies. Furthermore, both parts move in rhythmic independence of the vocal line (counterpoint), a fact that contributes to their significance as melodies.

Dowland's song is supported by clear triadic harmony, functioning in G major. The chords of the lute part help give tonal meaning and direction to the vocal melody. Clearly, *all* facets of the piece complement one another. The total effect of the composition is a product of both contrapuntal and harmonic elements, and the importance of an appropriate label for the textural synthesis of melody, harmony, counterpoint, text, and lute sound in this piece seems to dwindle as one acknowledges the variety of factors competing for our consideration.

PROBLEM 3

With the preceding discussion in mind, study the following excerpt and pin down the contrapuntal aspects of its texture by answering the questions about it; familiarize yourself carefully with the passage before answering the questions.

Theme for Harpsichord

1. Which of the four voices is the principal one in terms of rhythmic variety, melodic contour, prominence in the dynamic and registral treatment of voices, e.g., ornamentation, and other distinguishing features? ____________

2. Which description best fits the role of the bass voice here?

   a) broken-chord accompaniment

   b) accompanimental melody

   c) succession of harmonic roots lacking linear interest

3. Cite three ways in which the tenor voice is distinguished from or independent of the main voice; consider such things as rhythmic relation to main voice, directional patterns, motion (e.g. conjunct, disjunct, etc.), and types of intervallic motion used.

   a)

   b)

   c)

4. Which term best describes the general texture of the passage?

   a) melody and accompaniment

   b) monophony

   c) melody with accompanimental counterpoint

5. Which two voices create a harmonic melodic framework for the piece's texture?

   a) soprano and tenor

   b) alto and bass

   c) tenor and bass

   d) soprano and bass

Like many musical terms, counterpoint has various meanings, depending on context. In general, the term refers to voice-leading, that is, the techniques by which composers fashion, elaborate, and connect the various parts or voices that constitute the texture. It should be added that the composition of some pieces—for example, pieces for chorus or string quartet—is much more easily discerned in terms of separate voices or parts—and, thus, in terms of voice-leading—than many works for keyboard, or even electronic media, in which separate, discrete strands or lines may be less apparent. Compare Examples 7a and 7b. The former breaks down into four clearly observable voices, but the latter is composed in such a way that separate, discrete lines, except the top one, are hard to perceive.

Ex. 7a. Haydn: String Quartet in G, Op. 76, I.

Ex. 7b. Chopin: Prelude No. 5, in D.

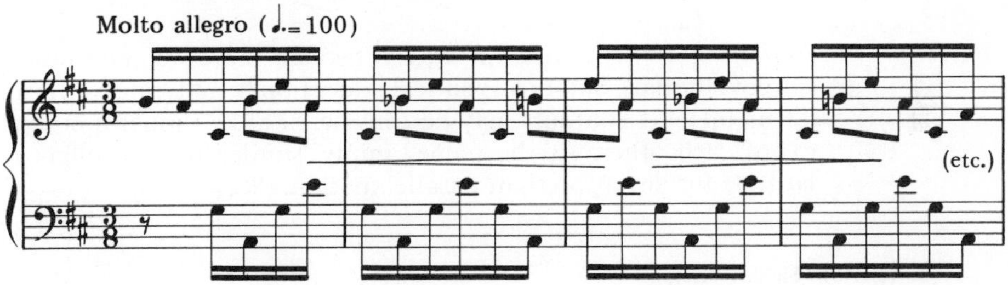

Techniques and principles of voice-leading, as found in various periods of music history and as applied by various composers, constitute important bases for the discrimination of musical style and expression. Although there are certain agreed-upon bases for describing voice-leading, as well as a number of techniques that appear over and again throughout many centuries of musical development, there are few if any absolutes regarding voice-leading, for hard and fast rules regarding this practice are difficult to sustain without considerable qualification. There are, however, a number of voice-leading processes basic enough to a great deal of music of the past four or five hundred years or so to warrant some generalization. These are most easily observed in music composed of two or more separate parts.

Voice-Leading Procedures. Any considerations that apply to a single melodic line can have meaning in describing the activity of any voice or horizontal line in a musical texture. Terms such as step, leap, rise, fall, and others are used for such purposes. They relate to the motion of individual parts. Motion by step is commonly called conjunct motion; motion by leap is known as disjunct motion. Disjunct motion occurs, for instance, in the three upper parts of Example 7a at measure 9, and measures 15–16 in the same passage reveal a predominance of conjunct motion.

Since voice-leading is generally taken to assume motion of combined voices, a number of terms defining composite or combined motion, that is, patterns of *combined* intervallic movement, are useful in assessing voice-leading. These patterns of combined motion consist of the following:

1. *Parallel motion,* motion in which two or more voices employ simultaneously the same directional and intervallic relations (Ex. 8a).

Ex. 8a. Parallel motion.

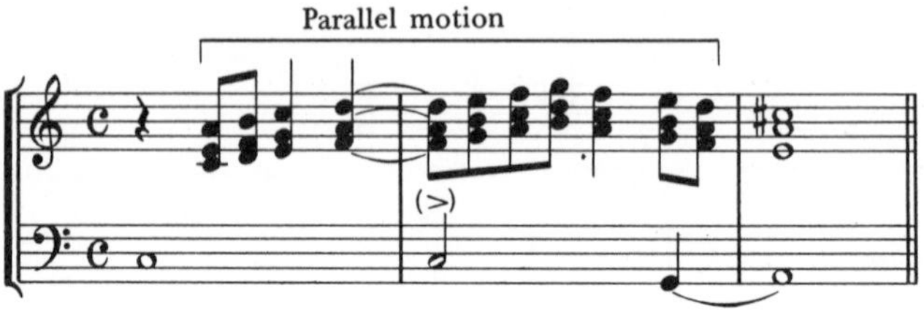

2. *Similar motion,* motion in which two or more voices simultaneously employ similar, but not identical, directional and intervallic relations. Their melodic contours may be considered alike though not exact replicas of each other. As the names imply, similar motion offers far more latitude for deviation than parallel motion. (See Ex. 8b).

Ex. 8b. Similar motion.

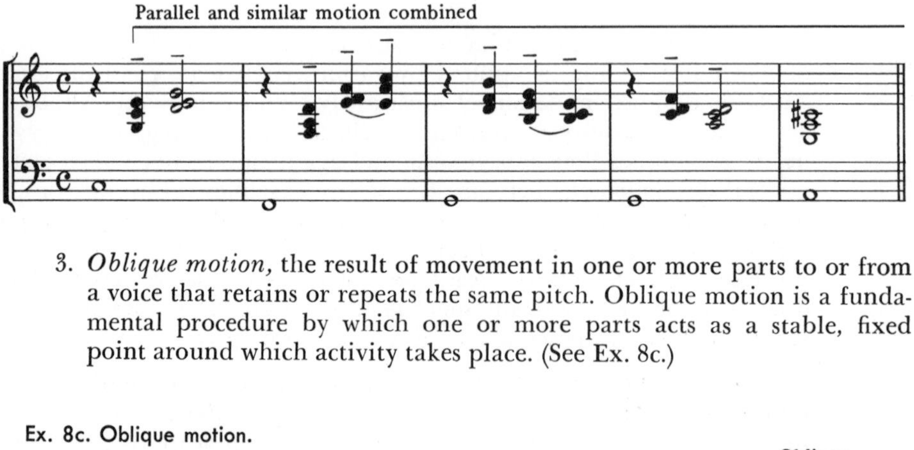

3. *Oblique motion,* the result of movement in one or more parts to or from a voice that retains or repeats the same pitch. Oblique motion is a fundamental procedure by which one or more parts acts as a stable, fixed point around which activity takes place. (See Ex. 8c.)

Ex. 8c. Oblique motion.

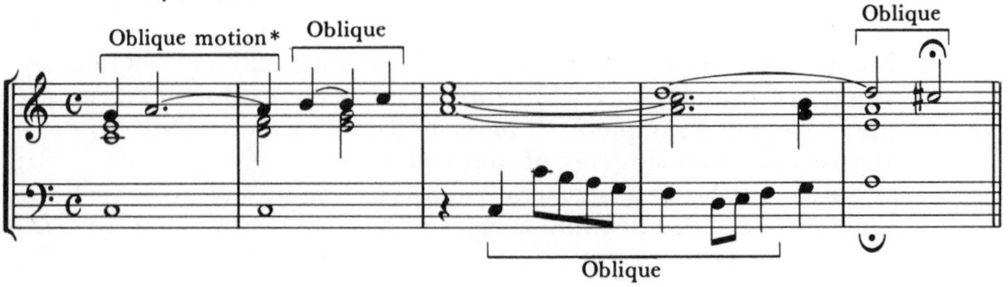

* Oblique relation applies where one voice (or more) moves while other(s) are inactive.

4. *Contrary motion* (counter-direction), any movement by voices that diverge or converge. Contrary motion may be created by steps, leaps, or combinations of both. (See Ex. 8d.)

Ex. 8d. Contrary motion.

Contrary motion (between outer voices)

p
mf
f

PROBLEM 4

Circle the descriptive term that best describes the prevailing type of combined intervallic motion in each of these following excerpts.

a. Twelfth-century polyphony

Excerpt from MIRA LEGE, MIRO MODO

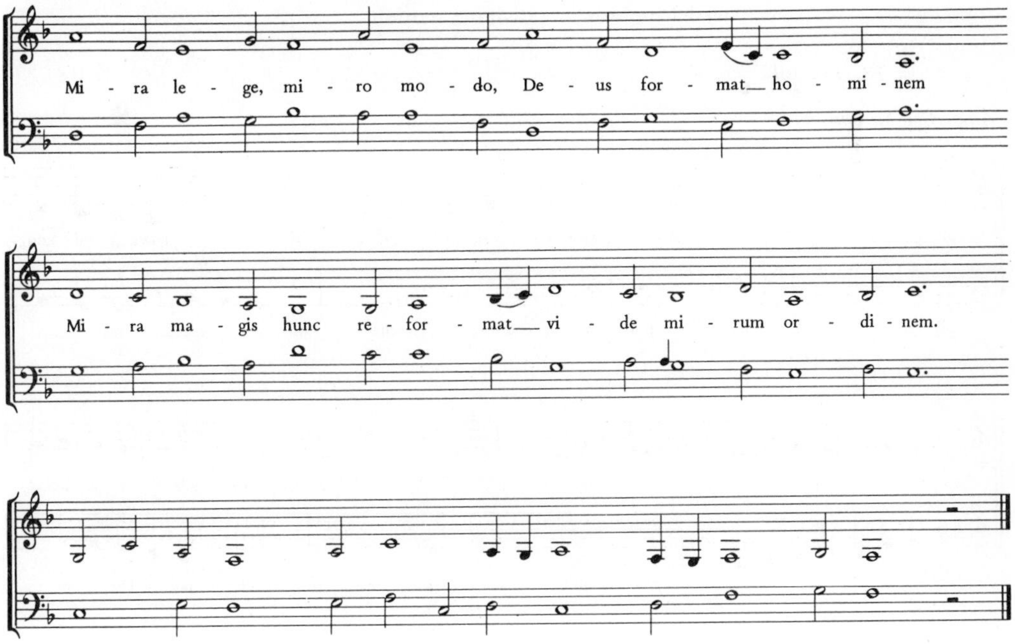
Mi - ra le - ge, mi - ro mo - do, De - us for - mat__ ho - mi - nem
Mi - ra ma - gis hunc re - for - mat__ vi - de mi - rum or - di - nem.

conjunct motion oblique motion contrary motion
parallel motion disjunct motion

b. Organum

Cunctipotens Genitor

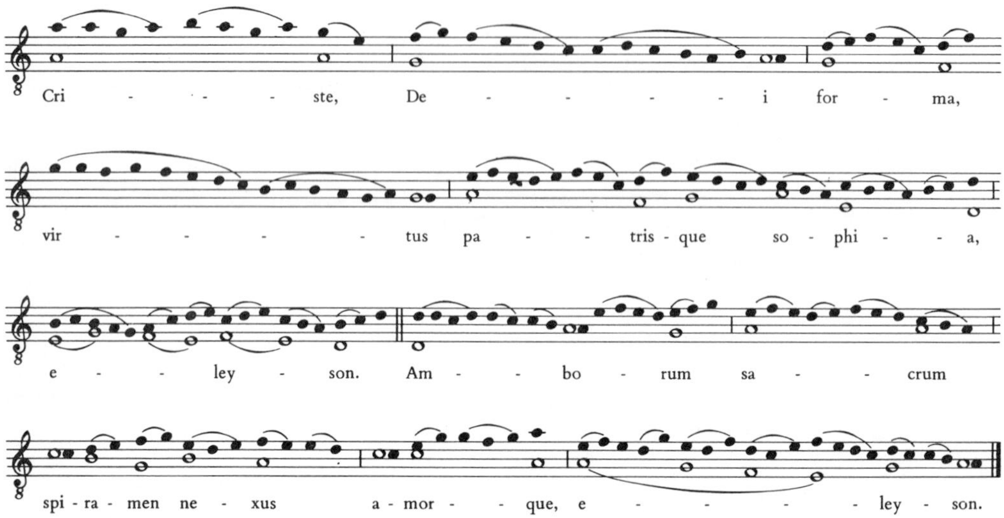

contrary motion oblique motion similar motion
parallel motion disjunct motion

c. Frottola

Amor Che Mi Consigli

Festa

contrary motion   oblique motion   similar motion

parallel motion   disjunct motion

PROBLEM 5

Write the measure numbers of three occurrences of each type of combined motion found in the passage that follows. Be prepared to indicate the precise locations of each example cited.

Bicinium from *Cantio sacra: Warum betrübst du dich, mein Herz*

Scheidt

Parallel: ______________________

Oblique: ______________________

Similar: ______________________

Contrary: ______________________

The voice-leading (or part-writing) found in most vocal or choral compositions typically (but not always) reveals a predominance of step motion. There are several other generalizations about voice-leading that hold for a great deal of vocal and instrumental music. However, as generalizations or as rules of thumb, they are subject to numerous exceptions, as one might suppose. Bach's vocal part-writing and typical approaches to voice-leading are still upheld as model solutions to the problem, especially insofar as tonal music is concerned. Teachers have probably placed too much emphasis on the rule rather than the exception, however, in the reiteration of these part-writing principles over the past two hundred years or so. Several of these guiding principles are well illustrated in Example 9.

Ex. 9. Bach: Chorale No. 14, *O Herre Gott, dein göttlich Wort.*

Check the music as a means of verifying the principles of voice-leading listed below, which are exemplified in this passage.

1. Most of the intervallic motion in the three upper parts is by step; the bass often reveals the most leaps. Measures 6 and 7 illustrate this statement effectively.
2. Contrary motion by step, or leap, is often introduced to create linear independence, especially between the soprano and bass voices. See measures 6–9.
3. Notes common to successive chords are often retained or resounded in the same voice, as in measure 2, beats 2–3, in the tenor, thus creating a binding and balancing effect against the movement in the surrounding parts.

4. Passing and neighboring tones, together with suspensions, add effectively to the polyphonic-rhythmic interest of the voice movement. Dissonant tones, that is, pitches creating varying degrees of harmonic tension and unrest, are almost invariably resolved by succeeding step movement to more stable tones. A passing tone connects c^1 to e^1 in the alto part, measure 1. Similarly, a passing *f* resolves to *e* in the tenor, moving from measure 4 to 5. Note the continuous step activity in the bass, measure 8. Each successively dissonant tone—*f, d,* and *c*—is a passing tone. Suspensions may be noted in measure 2, alto voice (a^1 to g#^{1}); measure 3, beat 4 to measure 5, alto (d^1 to c^1); measure 4, alto (d^1 to c^1); and in measure 7, beats 1–2, tenor (*a* to *g#*).
5. Triads form the core of the harmonic staples used in the piece. Major (measure 1, beat 1) and minor (measure 2, beat 1) prevail, though first inversions of major and minor triads also occur often, as in measure 3, beats 2 and 3. Note that root-position sonorities generally begin and close phrases, and that inversions are used more to create a variety of sonority and to accommodate step activity in the bass within the phrase. The chord fifth is often omitted, the chord third is not.
6. Care is taken by the composer to heighten the independence of the voices, especially the soprano and bass, by avoiding repetition of the same vertical interval. This is exemplified by the variety of intervals formed by these outer parts, as seen, for example, in measures 1–5. The successive accented verticals formed by these two parts reveal the following: P5, M3, P8, m3, m3, P8, P5, M3, m6, m6, M3, m6, M3, M6, P5, P8. Parallel motion between these outer voices, or any pair of voices, resulting in successive perfect fifths, octaves or unisons is, as a rule, not found in Bach's part-writing. Most tonal music written prior to this century reveals the influence, if not absolute loyalty to, this principle.
7. Each voice is generally restricted to a range of a twelfth or less. Sopranos lie within c^1–g^2, altos within f–c^2, tenors within c–g^1, and basses within f–c^1. Note the following chart:

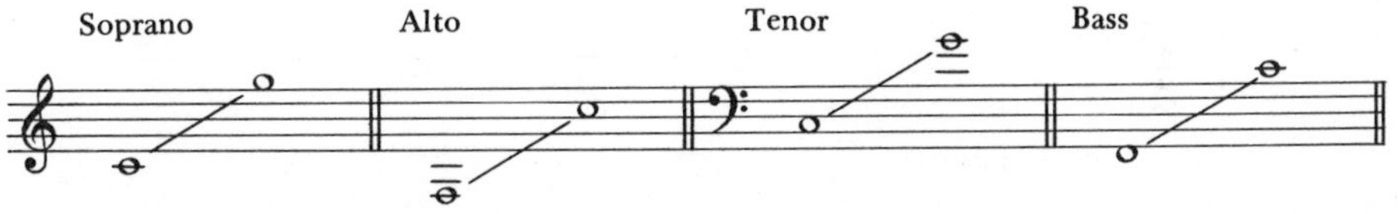

Adjacent voices, tenors and basses excepted, generally lie within an octave of each other. Part-crossing—altos above sopranos, for instance—though often quite effective, is rarely found in Bach's chorale settings.

8. Some, if not all, of these principles may be found to apply in varying degrees to instrumental and keyboard compositions of the same and subsequent historical periods and to the present day.

It's easy to misconstrue the meaning and relevance to today's musicians of principles of part-writing that evolved over hundreds of years and that were already mastered by composers such as Bach over two hundred years ago. If, on the other hand, one regards such procedures as part of a far-ranging tradition of part music, that is, music for any medium in which each of a discernible number of parts or voices retains individuality, then he has a reasonable basis for applying them to contemporary music, which is to some degree an extension of tradition.

PROBLEM 6

The music in the following passage lacks coherence. This is due primarily to the unmusical and awkward manner in which the voice-leading has been handled. Refer as often as necessary to the principles cited in regard to Example 9, as a basis for locating at least *five* errors or improvable details of the voice-leading in the passage below. Begin by circling questionable procedures, as shown below, labeling from one to five the errors found. Identify the errors in the space provided below the music; then rewrite the passage, correcting as imaginatively and musically as you can, the errors that you found. Be careful not to create new problems in correcting the original ones.

Music for Problem 6 (contrived):

Based on "My Country 'Tis of Thee"

Errors:

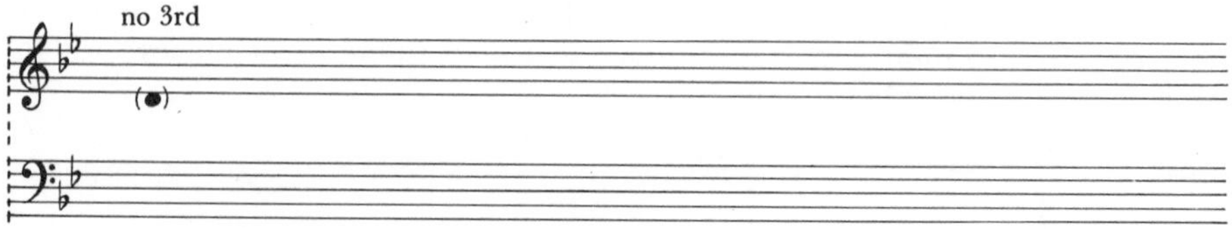

Corrected Version:

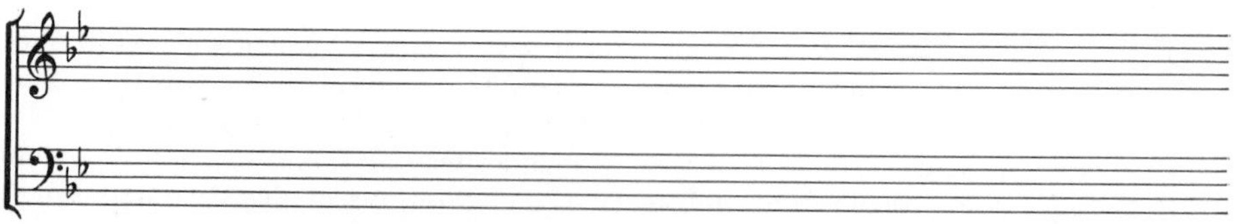

In music in which a specific number of parts is maintained throughout, it is easy to understand the various voice-leading techniques utilized in the texture. Music written idiomatically for the keyboard, however, is often organized in such a way as to make any identification of strictly maintained voices very difficult, if not altogether impossible. In such cases, musical textures often *imply* voices—and as a result, voice-leading—rather than explicitly revealing them. Although not an SATB composition, Example 10a subtly reflects many of the traditions of effective voice-leading cited above. Example 10a is reduced to a contrapuntal framework in Example 10b. This framework reveals the outer-voice motion that serves implicitly as the linear-harmonic foundation of the piece, that is, as a linear support for the elaboration of the piece into an idiomatic piano style.

Ex. 10a. Chopin: Mazurka No. 43 in G Minor, Op. posth. 67, No. 2.

Ex. 10b. Two-voice framework of Ex. 10a.

Ex. 10b continued.

Ex. 10c. Adaptation of Ex. 10a to chordal style, showing implied part-writing procedures of the original.

Example 10a is homophonic; it consists of accompanied melody, presented in such a way as to exploit the medium of the keyboard. We have also shown, however, that even a simple homophonic setting such as this incorporates elements of linear design. This can be better understood by playing the bass of Example 10b, which forms an acceptable, if rudimentary, melodic voice. Each voice of Example 10c, furthermore, reveals characteristics of melody such as a predominance of step motion, leaps followed by steps, and some degree of contoural interest. A variety of simple voice-leading procedures such as contrary motion, retention of common tones, and balanced spacing, can also be seen. In other words, principles of effective voice-leading are almost always operative in any texture, regardless of the particular emphases created by the relative independence of the parts.

PROBLEM 7

The following passage for the piano by Beethoven is basically homophonic. By the same token, it reveals a number of voice-leading and melodic procedures that are of essentially contrapuntal origin. Familiarize yourself with the passage, and then cite by measure number at least five examples of effective voice-leading that occur in it.

Piano Sonata in D Major, Op.28, II

Contrapuntal Texture; Rhythmic Combinations. Counterpoint was described earlier as a product of combined melodies, that is, competing and interacting lines. The essence of counterpoint is rhythm, more particularly, rhythmic combinations. Although questions of melodic contour, pitch variety, motion details, and the like must be taken into account, rhythm provides a basis for contrapuntal activity in virtually any musical style or medium. The rhythmic relations of two or more parts frequently create more or less systematically exploited combinations of activity, that is, clearly observable patterns of combined movement.

Note-Against-Note Movement. The simplest of rhythmic combinations occurs when two or more voices move in identical or similar durations. Such tandem movement minimizes their contrapuntal impression. In such examples, pitch relations such as directional patterns and intervallic movement must be taken into account before any assessment of contrapuntal individuality can be made. Compare the note-against-note rhythms of Examples 11a and 11b. In the former, little if any individuality results, because the voices lack directional or contoural contrast. In the latter, however, a more pronounced contrapuntal effect results from the individuality of motion and direction formed by the two lines.

Ex. 11a. Beethoven: Piano Sonata in G Major, Op. 14, No. 2, III.

Ex. 11b. Beethoven: Shring Quartet in C Major, Op. 59, No. 3, III.

Two, then three strings move in note-against-note rhythm in Example 11b. Part individuality results from the fact that the outer voices are consistently moving in contrary motion, primarily by step.

The essence of counterpoint lies in rhythmic independence, that is, movement that allows the voices to be distinguished through their own rhythmic motion. There are several ways in which this can be achieved. One of the simplest occurs when two or more parts divide interest on an equal basis through a staggering of activity. In Example 12, two voices state in turn a rhythm consisting of  ; the result is a contrapuntal texture based on an imitative division of activity shared equally by two voices.

Ex. 12. Bach: Partita No. 6 in E Minor, Gigue, mm. 3—6.

The same principle occurs in Example 13, for four strings. Here, two rhythms, 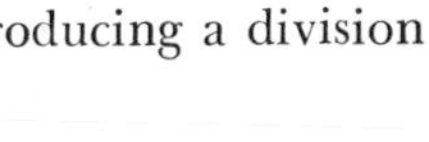 and 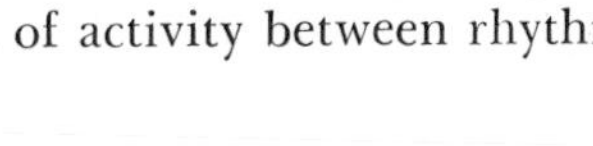, are combined and staggered, producing a division of activity between rhythmically contrasted parts.

Ex. 13. Mozart: String Quartet in A Major, K. 464, IV.

The three-part texture of Example 14 is defined primarily by three distinct rhythms; they occur for the most part as the rhythms of the main voice, the top, and the accompaniment. The top line emerges by virtue of its concentration of activity and varied patterns; the lower parts recede into the background because they are both less active and less varied. Note, furthermore, that both of the lower lines lack the significant melodic characteristic of a predominance of steps. Their role is limited more to establishing a harmonic background for the elaboration of the main voice. The effectiveness of the main voice is in part due to the fact that it moves independently of the supporting counterpoint.

Ex. 14. Bach: *St. Matthew Passion,* No. 61.

Ex. 14 continued.

Three different rhythmic combinations appear in the changing arrangements of texture that open the Mozart rondo in Example 15. This excerpt begins with an imitative dialogue staggered between two rhythmic parts; it continues with two measures of sixteenth-note activity in the main voice, accompanied by a less active supporting line. At measure 8, both voices compete on an equal rhythmic basis; however, the lower part assumes the role of accompaniment by reason of its chord-outlining[1] and its absence of linear interest. As we noted above, passages such as this appear to present a texture of two equally important voices if viewed only in terms of their rhythm. The relation of melody and accompaniment is clearly a product of the relative *contours.*

---

[1] This type of broken-chord figure is commonly called Alberti bass.

Ex. 15. Mozart: Piano Sonata in C Major, K. 545, III, mm. 1–13.

Contrapuntal interest is maximal when two or more equally interesting voices compete simultaneously. Such textures are the result of several factors, such as rhythm, contour, timbre, and dynamics; the primary one, however, is rhythm. This can be observed in Example 16, in which the rhythmic independence of two woodwind voices is maintained, beginning at measure 8. The voices are in canon, a strictly carried out imitative relation. Textures in which two or more voices compete on an equal footing for extended periods are relatively rare. Fugues[2] are good examples of such works.

---

[2] See Christ et al., *Materials and Structure of Music,* Vol. II, 2nd ed.

Ex. 16. Carter: *Eight Etudes and a Fantasy for Woodwind Quartet*, Fantasy, mm. 1–12.

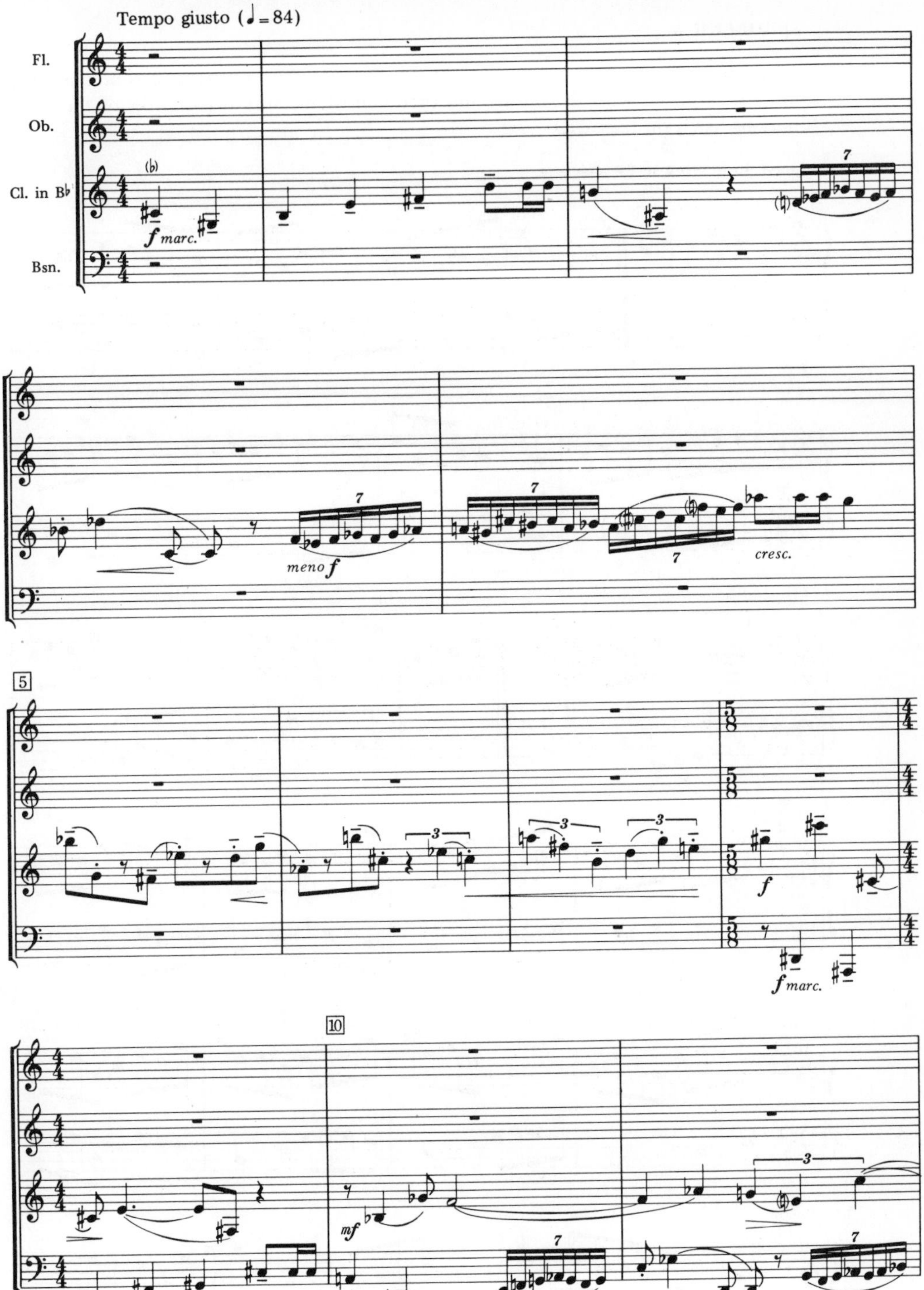

PROBLEM 8

The following passage contains examples of a variety of rhythmic combinations; familiarize yourself with the music, and then cite by measure occurrences of the combinations listed on page 303.

French Suite No.4 in E♭, Gavotte

Bach

a. Note-against-note rhythm:

b. Imitative sharing of eight-note activity on a staggered basis:

c. Main voice and accompanimental counterpoint:

PROBLEM 9

Invent eight to twelve measures of two-voice rhythm in $\frac{3}{4}$ meter, *allegro,* in which each of the rhythmic combinations that we have dealt with is exploited.

PROBLEM 10

Complete the elaboration of the two-voice framework that follows, in the manner in which it has been begun. Use neighbor and passing tones as well as occasional leaps within the prevailing triad as a basis for doing so. Exploit each of the rhythmic combinations noted previously.

Sketch:

from Beethoven

Elaboration:

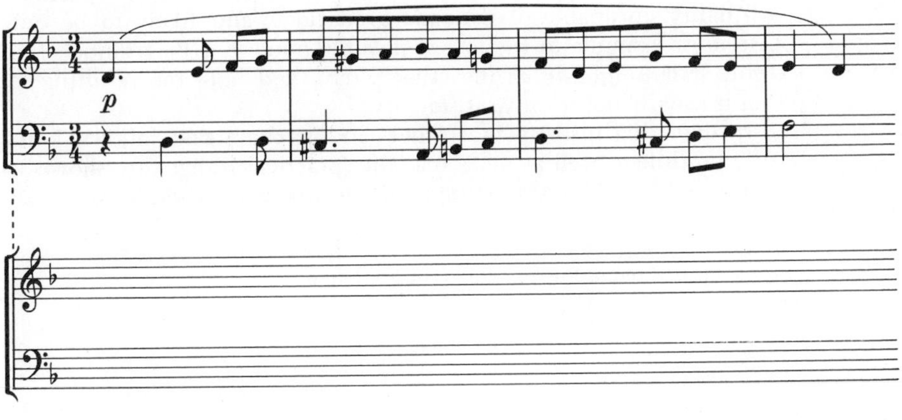

INSTRUMENTATION

Texture and timbre are closely related. This is true because the planning or understanding of a given texture must take into account the particular instrumental, vocal, or keyboard medium by which it is to be realized. Many of the principles with which we have dealt are more or less valid in the context of a specific instrumentation or medium of performance. The brief discussion that follows is intended to provide a frame of reference for music-reading, composing, and conducting. In any of these capacities musicians must be acquainted with basic information regarding problems of score format, instrumentation, ranges, transpositions, and the potential variety of timbral effects associated with different instruments or with instrumental groups such as strings, woodwinds, brass, and percussion.

The fundamental information with which we are concerned here is presented in chart form on pages 314–316. The chart is broken down into five units, each dealing with a separate instrumental family. The instruments are those associated in the main with the standard orchestra, band, and jazz group. The questions itemized are those of range, transposition, and characteristic effects. The following brief explanation will help you interpret the chart. Realize that the information provided here is rudimentary and by no means thorough or detailed.

Range

In the case of some instruments, such as the piano, harp, or celeste, range is entirely fixed. In the case of all string instruments, such as the violin or violoncello, the bottom notes of the instrument's range are fixed, that is, virtually unalterable,[3] whereas the upper playing limits are quite flexible, depending on the skill and training of individual players. This, of course, is true of all brasses; we are well aware that a trumpet virtuoso such as Doc Severenson can play "miles" above a less experienced or a beginning player. The same is axiomatic in the case of most winds, especially clarinets and saxophones. With certain exceptions, however, brasses and woodwinds are limited to a fixed bottom note, just as strings are, unless retuned. Oboes, for example, cannot play below *b*♭ below the treble staff, and violins cannot play below *g* below the treble staff. It should be pointed out that the bottom notes on some instruments are especially satisfactory and in tune. This is true for all strings. The lowest possible notes on most winds, however, are sometimes poor in quality, incapable of dynamic gradations, and likely to be out of tune. Listen for example to the lowest possible note on a B♭ trumpet, *f*♯ below the treble staff (*sounding e*♮ in actual pitch), and note the resulting sound, one that is usually not wholly satisfactory.

In depicting instrumental ranges in the chart that follows, both theoretically possible as well as more realistic (practical) ranges are shown where it is useful to do so. This applies especially to woodwinds and brass.

---

[3] Unless retuned by the process of *scordatura*.

Transposition

You have probably noticed that some instruments, winds in particular, are indicated on a score or individual part in association with a specific note designation such as B♭, E♭, F, or others, as in Example 17. Trumpet parts are usually indicated as Trumpet in B♭ (or B♭ Trumpet), or Trumpet in C, or A, etc. Similarly, French horn parts are notated as French Horn in F, or Horn in E♭, or B♭, or D, etc. This indicates that the instrument in question is a transposing one, that is, so constructed that the note read by the player differs by one interval or another from the actual sound heard in concert pitch. Concert pitch is that of the piano, or any other non-transposing instrument such as the oboe, flute, or violin.

Ex. 17. Beethoven: Symphony No. 9, III.

Though musicians not familiar with transposing instruments are often perplexed by the principle of transposing instruments, and frequently question the need for it, there is no reason to avoid the question. As is the case with most serviceable and traditional facets of practical musicianship, understanding the principle underlying transposition, not necessarily the historical and acoustical implications of it, is quite simple. It consists, for practical purposes, of the following simple axiom: the note-name associated with a particular instrument, such as B♭ Clarinet, F Horn, etc., defines the actual pitch heard when the performer plays *his notated c*. For example, when a B♭ trumpet sounds *his* c^2, we *hear* $b\flat^2$. This is another way of saying that a B♭ instrument transposes, that is, actually sounds a major second below what is written. Conversely, when writing a part for the B♭ trumpet, the composer must notate the trumpet one whole step *above* the desired sounding pitch. The actual interval distance involved in some transpositions having the same note-name differs by an octave with some instruments. For example, B♭ trumpets sound a major second below what is written, and B♭ tenor saxophones sound a major ninth (a major second plus an octave) below what is notated. Although the actual pitch distance of the transposition may vary among some instruments of the same transposing family—that is, instruments carrying the same note-name, such as E♭ horn or E♭ clarinet—the general relation between the written note and actual sound always applies: namely, the note-name of the instrument designates the note heard (not the precise octave) when the player reads his notated *c*. A French horn in F then sounds *f* when *c* is read, and a clarinet in A sounds *a* when *c* is read. That is the same as saying that an A clarinet sounds a minor third below what is written. The interval of transposition is, as a rule, the same as the distance between *c* and the note-name of the instrument.

On the transposition segment of the chart on pages 314–316, the note-name of the transposing instrument, the note it sounds in concert pitch, and the precise interval of the transposition are shown. Test your grasp of the preceding explanation by completing the various exercises in Problem 11. Doing so will help you interpret the chart that follows.

PROBLEM 11

Transpose to concert pitch the transposed parts in the score page that follows. Note the interval of transposition implied in the listing of instruments on the score. Use the same clef that appears in the score.

Symphony No.4 in B Major, Op.60, III

The practicality of knowing transposition becomes immediately clear if you attempt to follow an orchestral or band score. For that matter, a piano accompanist is at a disadvantage in attempting to play ensemble pieces or sonatas for winds or brass and piano unless he has a command of transposing parts. A glance at Example 18, the opening pages of a Beethoven symphony, suggests the necessity for knowledgeable musicians to have a ready ability to read transposing instrumental parts. Note the number and variety of transposing parts on the page.

Ex. 18. Beethoven: Symphony No. 7 in A Major, I.

1.
Fl.
Hb.
Kl.
Fg.
Hrn.
Vl.
Br.
Vc.
u.Kb.
dimin.
pp
dolce
cresc.
ff
p cresc.
Tr.
Pk.
sf

Ex. 18 continued.

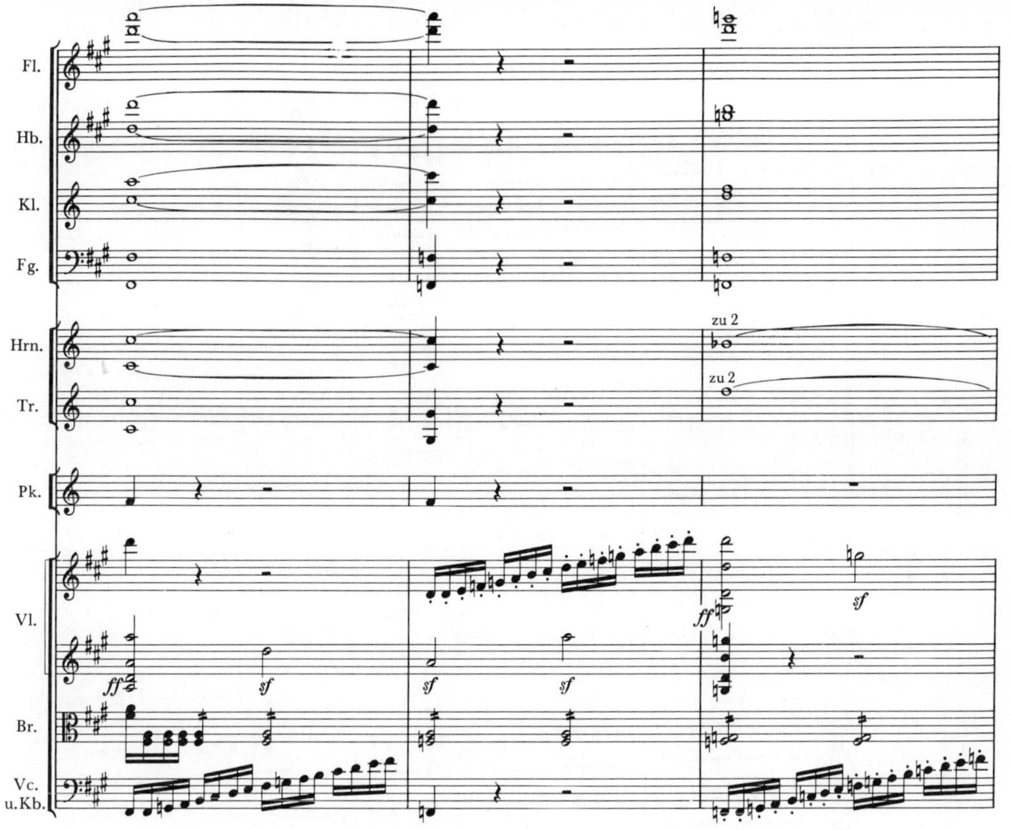

PROBLEM 12

Make a transposed version of the following excerpt from Copland's *Appalachian Spring* by rewriting each transposing part as it sounds. Recopy the non-transposing parts as an exercise in making a score. Examine your work for neatness as well as accuracy.

Appalachian Spring Copland

Transcription:

The chart that follows is meant to be a ready reference for beginning attempts to write for instruments, a source for reviewing transpositions, and a simple overview of common instrumental ranges. Obviously, detailed study of the kinds of information noted here demands intensive work and application as well as considerably more time than is involved in merely studying the chart.

INSTRUMENTATION CHART

Woodwinds	*Written Range*	*Sounds*
Piccolo		Octave higher
Flute		As written
Oboe	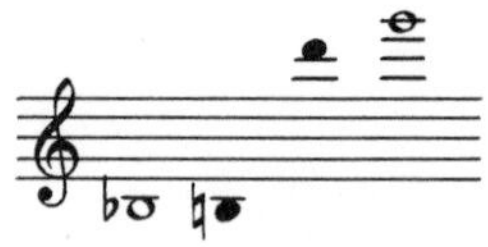	As written
English Horn	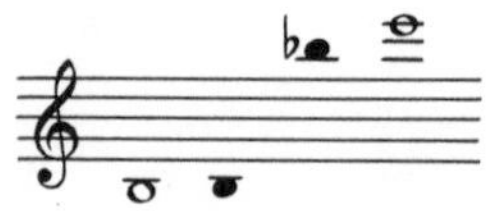	P5 lower
Clarinet		In B♭: M2 lower In A: m3 lower
Bass Clarinet		In treble clef: M9 lower In bass clef: M2 lower

Woodwinds (cont.)	*Written Range*	*Sounds*
Bassoon	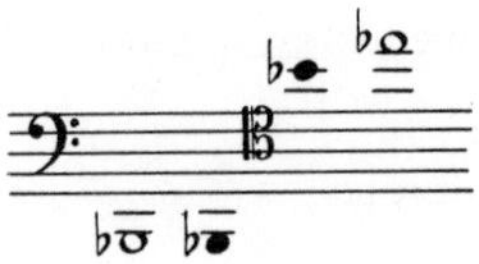	As written (uses bass and tenor clefs)
Contrabassoon	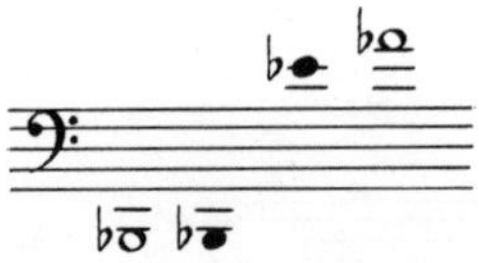	Octave lower

Brass	*Written Range*	*Sounds*
Horn		In F: P5 lower
Trumpet	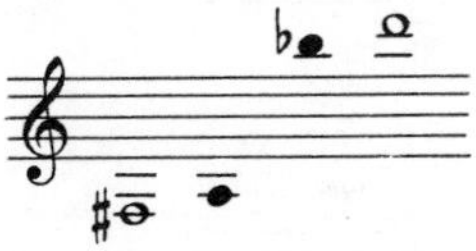	In B♭: M2 lower In C: as written In D: M2 higher
Tenor Trombone		As written (uses bass and tenor clefs, occasionally alto)
Bass Trombone		As written
Tuba	 *8va lower*	As written

Percussion

Timpani, range from *F* to *f*, sound as written
Other nonpitched instruments: xylophone, bells, celeste, harp, piano, etc., sound as written

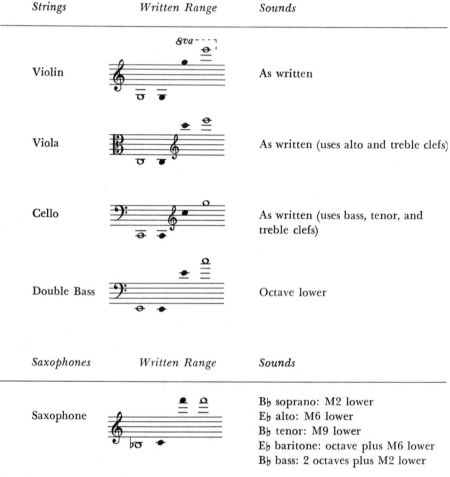

Strings	*Written Range*	*Sounds*
Violin		As written
Viola		As written (uses alto and treble clefs)
Cello		As written (uses bass, tenor, and treble clefs)
Double Bass		Octave lower

Saxophones	*Written Range*	*Sounds*
Saxophone		B♭ soprano: M2 lower E♭ alto: M6 lower B♭ tenor: M9 lower E♭ baritone: octave plus M6 lower B♭ bass: 2 octaves plus M2 lower

Score Arrangements and Preparations

Over the years, composers, arrangers, and publishers have developed a number of formats for various instrumental and vocal ensembles. We have already cited the open and closed vocal scores, the former (Ex. 19) allowing a separate staff to each voice (or group of like voices, such as sopranos, altos, tenors, and basses), and the latter (Ex. 20) placing sopranos and altos on the upper of two staves (with stems always taking opposite positions) and tenors and basses on the lower (bass) staff.

Ex. 19. Bach: Chorale No. 17, *Freu' dich sehr, o meine Seele.*

Ex. 20. Praetorius: *Ich dank dir, Lieber Herre.*

Open-score formats are also used for small instrumental ensembles such as the string trio, string quartet and quintet, brass quintet, and woodwind quintet. Such an arrangement facilitates score-reading and seems particularly appropriate where each part may assume a soloistic or dominant role at any time. The passage from a string quartet shown in Example 21 typifies this format.

Ex. 21. Beethoven: String Quartet No. 13 in C-Sharp Minor, I.

Ex. 21 continued.

The piano-vocal score combines open- and closed-score forms. The excerpt shown in Example 22 is very common. Each voice is given a separate line (open score), and the piano accompaniment, in this case a keyboard arrangement (adaptation) of the orchestral accompaniment for which the work was composed, is notated in the traditional keyboard format.

Ex. 22. Bach: *St. Matthew Passion,* No. 1.

Although the format and deployment of instruments and staves found in orchestral scores may vary somewhat, particularly as regards notation for winds and brasses, the same general layout of instruments on the score page exists throughout most literature of the past two hundred years or so. It is important for any knowledgeable musician to know the order of instruments that is standard in orchestral scoring. This order is illustrated in the music for Problem 12; however, an even larger orchestra might contain the following:

Piccolo
Flute I
Flute II
Oboe I
Oboe II
English Horn in F
Clarinet I in B♭ (or A)
Clarinet II in B♭ (or A)
(Saxophone family notated here when called for.)
Bass Clarinet in B♭ (or A)
Bassoon I
Bassoon II
Contrabassoon

French Horns in F:
I and III
II and IV
Trumpet I in B♭ or C
Trumpets II and III in B♭ or C
Trombone I
Trombones II and III
Bass Trombone
Tuba

Timpani and Percussion (3)
Harp (1)

Violins I	(18)
Violins II	(16)
Violas	(12)
Celli	(10)
Basses	(8)

Although there may be various additions to or deletions from the number of instruments demanded for each section of a particular score,[4] the general order in which they are listed on the score page is virtually unaltered:

Woodwinds
Brasses
Percussion
Voices or Solo Instrument(s)
Strings

Most scores contain transposed notation for instruments not pitched in C, rather than notation of actual pitches to be sounded. Many recent composers, though, have initiated a trend in which all voices are notated as they sound—transposed—even though the player must then transpose from his part. Parts for transposing instruments have always had to be transposed; however, only in rare exceptions (some trumpet and French horn parts that are written for historical instruments such as the E♭ trumpet or the D horn) has the player actually had to transpose his part.

Reduced Scores

For purposes of greater accessibility and readability, full scores frequently appear as piano scores, adaptations playable on the piano. As such, they are not unlike the yet-to-be-orchestrated working drafts of many composers. The piano score, in relation to the full orchestra score, is perhaps best described as a piano reduction. In condensing the score to a playable keyboard reduction, one must preserve all essential linear or harmonic elements while eliminating octave duplication, unplayable figurations or embellishments, and parts that are judged not to be essential elements of the piece. Piano scores eliminate the element of timbre from a consideration of the piece's texture, presenting the reader with a relatively colorless abstraction of the fabric of a composition, roughly analogous to a black-and-white television view of a colorful landscape. Obviously, the value of a particular piano reduction is in inverse proportion to the investment of instrumental color in a specific piece. Compare the orchestral excerpt in Example 23a with the piano reduction of it in Example 23b.

---

[4] Many eighteenth-century symphonies call for only one flute, or no clarinets. Not until the close of the nineteenth century were three or four trumpets, three trombones and tuba, and four or more French horns called for. There is no absolute norm for the entire repertoire of symphonic music, only periodic norms. The complement of players listed above are on the payroll of most major symphony orchestras.

Ex. 23a. Mussorgsky-Ravel: *Promenade* (from *Pictures from an Exhibition*).

Ex. 23b. Piano reduction of Ex. 23a.

PROBLEM 13

Make a playable piano arrangement of Example 18.

unit

5

ANALYSIS AND PERFORMANCE

Analysis is not, as a rule, an end unto itself. One of the main functions of analysis should be to provide bases for interpretive decisions in performance. Analysis should result in an understanding of the materials and the shaping processes whereby such materials are organized into the coherent succession of related musical events that constitute a piece. The purpose of this brief unit is to establish a working relation between analysis and performance.

As a focal point for discussion in this unit, as well as for dealing with questions of musical style, we have devised the outline that appears below. Such an outline is general enough to act as a kind of cue sheet for virtually any form or type of music. On the other hand, such outlines fail to remind us sufficiently of the interrelatedness of virtually all components of music—musical experience being far *more than* the result of the sum of occurrences of a number of separable elements such as pitch, rhythm, timbre, and intensity.

ANALYTICAL CHECK LIST

Texture and Timbre

Medium of performance:	instrumentation, voices, variety of timbre and potential timbral contrasts
Deployment and Use:	number of parts (instrumental or vocal), range explored, characteristic versus unusual (special) effects, dynamic range and articulation, part-individuality

Texture:	organization (monophonic, homophonic, polyphonic), textural variety
Melody: (linear pitch succession)	Primary or secondary melodies or counterlines, range and contour (curve) motion by step or leap, note repetition, variety and balance, direction change pitch complement—scale basis, key or mode, serial chromaticism, modulation or mutation, decorative patterns, ornamentation rhythm-meter-pulse; levels-patterns-displacement, unity and growth (melodic), repetition and restatement of motives, phrases, sections; variational treatments, sequence, change of mode, inversion, etc.
Harmony (simultaneous pitch occurrences)	sonority types, intervallic makeup, tertian or non-tertian (quartal, quintal) mixture tonal or atonal, diatonic or chromatic modulation, mutation root relations and characteristic patterns cadence harmonic rhythm, dissonance treatment, contrapuntal aspects, key-defining, coloristic, percussive, relative degrees of stability-instability (tension-relaxation)
Form	
Gross sectionalization	large formal dimensions
Unifying factors	repetition, return, tonality
Contrast	thematic, tonal, textural, rhythmic
Processes creating growth and development	motivic restatement, variational procedures, rhythmic recurrence, textural change, tonality change opposition of stable versus unstable areas instrumental contrast, dynamic change
Extramusical considerations	
Predication of music on text, painting, myth, allusion to particular emotional association or ideal	specific loyalty to form suggested by text accompaniment for dance or narration ideal

Two movements by Mozart are shown in Examples 1 and 2. Familiarize yourself with the pieces. The discussion that follows these examples relates several of the topics cited in the analytical checklist to the preparation of these works for performance.

Ex. 1a. Mozart: Piano Sonata No. 7 in F Major, K. 331, II.

Ex. 1a continued.

S.T.SS.
30
35
cresc.
Close.
(SchlS.)
40
Coda.
Anh.

TEXTURE AND TIMBRE

The movement in Example 1a is characterized by the melody and broken-chord homophony found at the opening. The limited range and minimal timbral and dynamic contrasts of the movement are such that the player should devote considerable attention to details of voice-leading in the accompaniment, which add measurably to the piece's textural interest. Note the secondary line implied in the unaccented sixteenths of measures 3–4, renotated in Example 1b to emphasize the implied middle voice of the accompaniment.

Ex. 1b.

Subtly woven counterpoints such as this occur frequently in the movement. The player is challenged by the problem of projecting the primary thematic material of the upper voice while simultaneously allowing lower voices to emerge wherever their motion creates melodic interest.

Contrast *within* the two main sections of the piece (mm. 1–20 and 21–end) is heightened in part by the contrasting accompanimental figures used. Part one is supported by a broken-chord figure (Alberti bass), and the accompaniment introduced at measure 8 incorporates a pedal-like note repetition. These figures have steady sixteenth-note rhythm in common. This similarity is diminished somewhat by the contrasting articulations given these two figures: legato, 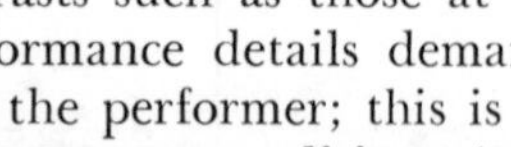 , and legato-staccato, 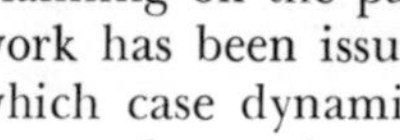 . Such details enhance a texture that may appear at first reading to be less interesting and varied than is actually the case.

The mood of the movement is unified by the overall low dynamic level of the piece. Occasional indications of *sforzando-piano* and *forte-piano* help emphasize textural contrasts such as those at measures 10, 30, and 35. The realization of such performance details demands considerable thought and planning on the part of the performer; this is especially true if a composer's work has been issued in numerous editions (as is true of Mozart's work), in which case dynamic indications are not necessarily those of the composer, but perhaps of an editor who assumes the responsibility for clarifying or, hopefully, improving upon the performance instructions of the composer.

MELODY

The artistic performance of melodies such as those found in Ex. 1a is a lifelong study for many outstanding musicians, let alone those of less accomplishment. Questions regarding phrasing, accent, ornamentation and other performance techniques demand faithful consideration and evaluation. One simple illustration from this movement may suggest the importance of knowledgeable performance preparation. The rhythmic details of measures 1–8 are such that one may become so absorbed in each figure that continuity may suffer. In this case, continuity and a sense of direction toward a goal is provided by the step progression of measures 3 and 4 (shown in Ex. 1c), which clearly contrasts with the staggered triadic outlines of the first two measures. Since both phrase-segments contain a predominance of conjunct motion, the delayed, structural steps of measures 2–4, which lead to the tonic, B♭, seem all the more important. In all likelihood, such a progression should be clearly articulated, if not somewhat emphasized, in performance.

Ex. 1c.

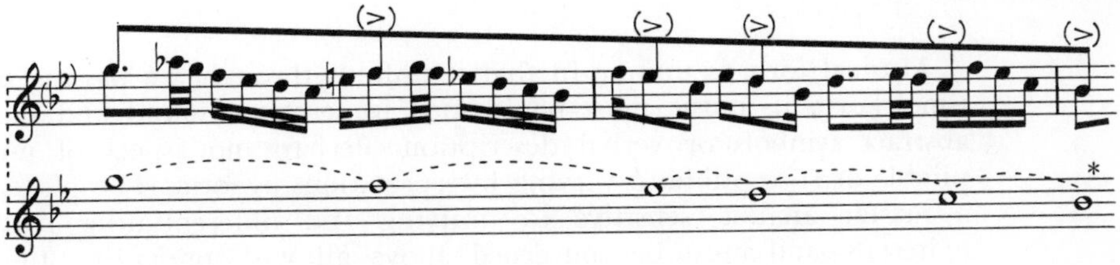

* - - - - - - means implied connection.

HARMONY

An effective rendition of this movement demands an understanding of the various harmonic materials and the several ways in which harmony interacts with other materials in the piece to help delineate form, create color, and define tonality. The feeling of stability, as opposed to heightened expectation or restlessness, that is elicited by different phrases or sections of the movement is in part a result of harmony.

The feeling of tonal digression, quickened motion, and direction toward an anticipated point of arrival (tonic?) that must be projected in measures 3–4 contrasts markedly with the stability and tonal repose of measures 1–2. It can be seen that measures 1–2 derive their relative repose and stability from a decided emphasis on the tonic, B♭. Measures 3–4, on the contrary, fill in motion from the subdominant to a half-cadence on the dominant, providing a digression *from* tonic and creating an anticipation for a re-emphasis of it. The movement reveals a series of cycles of varying lengths based on similar harmonic contrasts.

The player must note the deployment of harmony in the movement's second section, measures 9–20. In this passage complete chords, usually major or minor and occasionally dominant sevenths, are, as a rule, stated on the beat. This mode of presentation of chords varies considerably with the broken-chord (two-voice) deployment in measures 1–8. Obviously, the recognition of such contrasts by the listener hinges on a clear and sympathetic playing. Carefully prepared articulations, dynamic shading, and even rhythmic emphases are at the disposal of the player who is attentive to such contrasts among harmonic materials. Note furthermore that the rate of harmonic change in the latter section is more rapid than that of the piece's opening eight measures, adding to its distinctive character and effect.

Lastly, the player should note the care with which the composer has limited unadorned occurrences of triads that have their root in both the bass and the top voices. Such sonorities occur only at important junctures (or at the closure) in the movement.—note measure 1, 8 (beat 3), 21, 28, and the final cadence. By skillfully avoiding the terminating effect of root-position tonic (major) and dominant chords, the composer helps insure an easier connection of ideas. This presents the player with the task of linking sections and phrases, while at the same time allowing breathing room for them.

FORM

Musical form is unique in that it unfolds through the passing of musical time. Form in music must be grasped in terms of sound and motion, not abstract symbols or verbal description. Perhaps no aspect of music is as pliable or susceptible to varying interpretations as form. The player must be a master analyst, sensitive to unifying and differentiating patterns and materials—and must be concerned above all with presenting the piece as clearly as possible. His playing capacity must be geared to present the music in its best possible light; the music should never be a mere vehicle for technical display.

Though by no means a complex piece, the composition in Example 2a raises a number of questions that should be examined by a performer wishing to present a thoughtful and knowledgeable reading of the piece. The movement's form is shown in outline in Example 2b.

Two questions are paramount to the consideration of form in this or any composition: how is the piece unified into a coherent and continuous whole, and how are the various sections of the piece contrasted? Unity and contrast, or variety, are present to different degrees in virtually any piece. It is the task of the performer to present in performance a clear profile of the piece insofar as he perceives the unity and contrast in it. Unity in this movement is a product of several factors. Perhaps the most obvious unifying element in this movement and many like it lies in its tonality. Both the presentation section (exposition) and the return section (recapitulation) define the piece's tonic key (F minor). Since the return at measure 37 coincides with the tonal return of F minor, the performer may logically emphasize this through some interpretive nuance or gesture, such as a special accent or slight ritard in approaching it. Note the crescendo that heightens the approach to measure 37. Such emphasis is perhaps all the more suggested by the fact that the four measures immediately preceding the return (mm. 33–36) clearly preview the A theme. This type of previewing or anticipating the recapitulation in a key other than the principal one is called a false reprise.

Ex. 2a. Mozart: Sonata in F, K. 280, II.

Close
Coda
Ped.
25
D.
D.
30
P.T.
T.P.
35
P.T.
T.P.
40
S.T.
T.S.
poco espress.

Ex. 2b. Schematic diagram of the form of Ex. 2a.

Presentation of Material			Digression and Development	Return		
Theme A	Theme B♭	Close (C)	Keys: B♭ and C minor	Theme A	Theme B (modified) and extended	Close (C)
mm. 1–8	mm. 9–21	mm. 21–24	Thematic material derived			
Key: f minor	A♭	A♭	from A (♩. ♬ ♩ ♪) and	F Minor ________		
			accompaniment of B (♬♬♬)			

It is a kind of formal deception in that the material of the expected return is heard, but is cast in a key other than tonic—in this case, C minor—thus postponing temporarily the psychological impact of the true return of the same material in its "proper" tonality. Although the listener may at first regard the false return as the actual return, in all likelihood he grasps intuitively the formal deception of this little compositional game when the true return arrives. The player must be sympathetic to the procedure and make interpretive decisions regarding dynamic level, rhythmic accents, ritards, and other changes of pace that make the form clear but not obvious. An oblivious reading at such a formal juncture may yield an unmusical result.

One further observation about this piece may add some importance to the proposition that good performances demand prior analysis and decisions regarding formal design. Note that the A theme is characterized by an overall *descent* following the arrival of f^2 in measure 2. We can graph this by showing the basic contour of the melody of measures 1–8.

Ex. 2c. Basic pitches of the melody of mm. 1–8.

Theme B, however, reveals a marked *ascent* over its first eight measures (mm. 9–16), and thus contrasts in contour with theme A. One would assume that a similar contrast would occur at the recapitulation of these themes; such is not entirely the case. Note that Mozart does not simply restate the B theme's melodic line in the return section. On the contrary, although the key, rhythm, and accompaniment of the theme recurs, the same pitch contour does not. One may speculate about this. Surely the performer must be aware of it: he must take care to show in performance the elements of the theme's initial presentation that are intact in the return section, while at the same time bringing out carefully its *new* contour. It is entirely possible that the composer was seeking to relate through a common descending line two initially contrasting themes, themes that were contrasted initially through adherence to different keys, one minor, one major, but were related in the return through their common employment of the same F minor key. At any rate, the study of most music that projects the depth and range of emotion of this piece will frequently reveal formal relations and processes that require equally if not more demanding analyses and interpretations. When such is the case, analysis of form is a practical if not essential expedient to performance, and a procedure that should precede and accompany serious practice and resulting authoritative interpretation.

EXAMPLES FOR ANALYSIS

The complete pieces or selected excerpts that appear here are intended for use in aural analysis. Though no strict format is recommended for their use, several suggestions are provided. In each case, we recommend that one or more playings of the entire piece or excerpt selected for discussion be heard. The analytical checklist that appeared at the beginning of this unit should provide a uniform basis for general discussion and description of the pieces. Shorter segments should be explored aurally in more detail. The following pertain to one or more of the examples:

1. identification of repeated or recurring rhythms
2. identification of repeated or recurring motives or figures
3. recognition of points of climax and tension and the processes by which they are achieved
4. organizing procedures such as imitation, canon, sequence, or variational treatments that seem most indicative of the organic growth of the piece
5. the degree to which the piece is marked by either periodic cadences, or by more or less continuous activity that lacks periodic cadential punctuation
6. vertical relations that most typify the piece as a whole or any of its various parts

The following excerpts are included for analysis. They may also be used for practice in music-reading and dictation. Wherever possible, these excerpts should be performed by members of the class.

Ex. 3. Machaut: *Chanson balladée.*

Ex. 3 continued.

Ex. 4. J. S. Bach: Chorale (with English translation).

Ex. 5. J. S. Bach: *French* Suite in D Minor Menuet II.

Ex. 6. Haydn: String Quartet No. 68 in E♭, Op. 64, No. 6, I.

10
f
3
20
mf

Ex. 6 continued.

f
60
tr
70
dim.
p

Ex. 6 continued.

110
120

Ex. 6 continued.

Ex. 7. Beethoven: Piano Sonata in B♭, Op. 22, II.

Ex. 8. Schubert: *Moment Musical,* Op. 90, Scherzo (trio).

Ex. 9. Bartók: *Mikrokosmos,* Vol. III, Chromatic Invention.

Several sources for additional aural training and music-reading are listed below.

DeLone and Winold, *Music Reading, An Ensemble Approach* (Addison-Wesley).
Hindemith, *Elementary Training for Musicians* (Associated).
Kliewer, *Music Reading, A Comprehensive Approach,* 2 vols. (Prentice-Hall).
Ottman, *Music for Sight Singing* (Prentice-Hall).
Thomson, *Introduction to Music Reading,* 2 vols. (Wadsworth).
Thomson and DeLone, *Introduction to Ear Training* (Wadsworth).
Winold and Rehm, *Introduction to Music Theory* (Prentice-Hall).

unit

6

STYLE AND PERSPECTIVE

One of the most important capacities that a knowledgeable musician can have is style discrimination. Study of works or compositional proccesses of different composers and periods is greatly colored by prior association with some of their general characteristics. Depending on our previous experience and musical literacy, we approach different composers or styles with certain expectations. Subsequent study or performance of a given work confirms or negates our expectations about it. Courses in music literature and history are intended to provide a systematic basis for such study. Theoretical study provides the analytical and aural equipment for the assimilation and articulation of information about past and present musical literature and practice. Unfortunately, such a learning procedure has sometimes proven less than adequate. This is true in part because there is little vocabulary or general theoretical information that has meaning without *some* association with actual music.

The purpose of this brief unit is to establish familiarity with some of the stylistic norms or practices that have shaped and influenced traditional Western music, as we find it today. This unit is not meant to preclude further detailed study of music literature and history, but merely to provide a frame of reference with which we can apply our theoretical training to our knowledge of prior musical practice. Such application involves and relates cognition, aural understanding, and performance.

For the sake of brevity and easy reference, we will use the analytical checklist introduced in Unit 5 as the basis for surveying various aspects of style in the periods dealt with here. A number of references that may be useful in a more detailed study of style are cited at the end of this unit.

BAROQUE MUSIC

The Baroque period encompassed about one hundred and fifty years—from about 1600 to the year of Bach's death, 1750. No period of musical development except the present one has exhibited the diversification of musical-expressive means and forms that occupied musicians during those years. Musical activity centered in Italy and Germany; France and England offered nominal competition in the development of innovative forms and modes of expression. The instrumental and vocal forms that took hold during this period are still represented on concert programs today, and are still influencing, to varying degrees, the forms and expressions of many current composers. The most innovative musicians of the Baroque epoch included such gifted Italians and Germans as Monteverdi, D. Scarlatti, Corelli, Froberger, Buxtehude, J. S. Bach, and Handel. Among the numerous musical fields in which they worked were opera, oratorio, cantata, trio sonata, concerto (several types), and a vast array of keyboard forms—toccata, fugue, suite, and sonata, to name only a few.

Generalization about Baroque style is difficult because of the great diversity of the music. Of prime importance is the fact that the tonal procedures of key organization and modulation were established gradually during the period, replacing to a great extent the modality of the Renaissance. Melody, rhythm, and harmony were shaped by the observance of metered pulse, which, in turn, reflected the influence of fashionable dances such as the allemande, courante, sarabande, and gigue, which formed the core of the dance suite. The development of keyboard, wind, and, in particular, string instruments and related performance techniques and traditions, some of which continue to the present, took place. Italy led the field in this regard. Music assumed expressive capabilities associated with a range of human emotions seldom found in the church-centered musical activity and expression of previous centuries. Music became an art of the populace rather than a trapping of religious services or court festivities.

Checklist for Baroque Music

I. *Texture and Timbre*

Contrasts of large against small (or solo) sound bodies, such as solo violin and string orchestra, or flute and continuo or voice and small orchestra of winds, strings, and continuo.

Dynamic contrasts more a product of weight (number of parts) than of nuance and articulation.

Outer voices (soprano and bass) create two-voice outer-part polarity in which supportive bass melody (line) pins down harmonic changes.

Polyphonic textures elaborated by contrapuntal lines and varying degrees of rhythmic independence typify much Baroque music.

II. *Melody*

Often contains strung-out, continuously unfolding rhythmic activity in which several figures predominate; such activity often involves divisions and sub-divisions of the beat as well as frequent rhythmic displacement. Dance rhythms abound.

Most Baroque melodies, instrumental or vocal, are expressly vocal (singable) in their conception. As such they vary from simple step successions to intricate patterns emphasizing the chordal outlines on which they are commonly based. Melody and harmony frequently act as one.

Major and minor *key* organization prevails; many Baroque melodies reveal a high degree of key change, usually emphasizing motion to closely related keys such as the dominant, relative major, or relative minor.

Step progression is found in most Baroque melodies.

A rich filigree of melodic ornamentation colors many Baroque melodic lines, especially cadence approaches.

Phrase-endings are often irregularly spaced.

III. *Harmony*

Triads and dominant seventh chords and their respective inversions form the staples of Baroque harmony.

Secondary (non-dominant) seventh chords as well as a variety of altered (mutated) chords play a subsidiary limited role in Baroque harmony. Altered chords occur most predictably as approaches to the dominant, heightening cadences.

Harmonic ambiguity (uncertainty) often results from the contrapuntal complexity and elaboration.

Harmonic sequence, particularly involving sequential movement in the cycle of fifths, is very prominent.

Harmonic cadences generally involve motion to the tonic (V–I), dominant (I–V), or submediant degrees (V–Vi, deceptive).

IV. *Form*

Among the many form types serving as the basis for Baroque music are binary (two-part) and ternary (ABA) forms; variations forms based on both harmonic and melodic ostinati; *cantus firmus* works for the organ (usually based on Lutheran chorale melodies); fugues; recitatives (usually through-composed); and many others.

Unifying processes such as the alternating of a recurring tonal-thematic passage with sections marked by disgression and contrast (episodes) are common.

Repetitive devices such as imitation, sequence, and elaborated restatement are typical.

Musical unfolding is often the product of a kind of motivic rhythmic reiteration that spins out thematic material; the spinning process often results in long, continuous phrases and sections unmarked by periodic, even-spaced cadences.

V. With the exception of works such as operas or oratorios, which are based on texts, most Baroque music lacks any direct association with extramusical allusions or meanings. Its impact is for the most part a result of the interaction of purely musical materials.

Several of the style elements noted above appear in Example 1. Familiarize yourself with this piece, and test the validity of the preceding outline by applying it to the piece.

Ex. 1. Bach: Partita in B Minor, *Sarabande.*

VIENNESE CLASSICISM

Most musicologists date the Classical period from 1750, the death of Bach, to 1827, the death of Beethoven. This short span embraces the development and perfection of a number of stylistic and formal principles that have since had an inestimable impact and influence on the course of music, its composition, and performance. Viennese classicism relates specifically to the works of Haydn, Mozart, and Beethoven. Beethoven forms a direct link with the beginnings of the Romantic period in that many of his works not only reveal characteristics that stem from the prior practices and traditions of Haydn and Mozart, but also open new paths and reflect changing attitudes about music, as well as ways of organizing it. Beethoven's innovations were to be identified with music for several generations after his death.

Checklist for Viennese Classicism

I. *Texture and Timbre*

Textures in the Classical period were characteristically homophonic; the continuo was abandoned in favor of a bass whose main role was essentially to afford harmonic support. Accompanimental figures such as the Alberti bass replaced the more contrapuntally fashioned accompaniments of the Baroque era.

The advent of the piano as well as the standardization of the orchestra contributed to an expanded pitch range. The timbral resources of Classical composers were augmented by the introduction of a number of relative newcomers, such as the clarinet.

Dynamic nuance and contrast became a much more significant element of compositional design and stylistic individuality; this was especially true with Beethoven.

II. *Melody*

Melodies characteristically reflected the medium for which they were composed. Keyboard melodic style often involved figures that spanned a wide range or introduced considerable chord outlining.

The tonal basis for most melodies was established through beginning and ending elaboration of tonic–dominant relations.

Most melodic structure was clearly fashioned from simple major or minor keys, elaborated by decorative or passing chromaticism.

Four-measure phrases became the norm. Melodic cadences occurred at periodic intervals. Symmetrical phrases and larger units created formal balance and clarity.

Ornamentation, like counterpoint, was treated with more reservation, often signaling certain kinds of events, such as closure or climax, or heightening modified repetition. Cadenzas were formal areas of display in which excessive ornamentation, often improvised, occurred frequently.

III. *Harmony*

Triads, dominant seventh chords, and inversions of these are the staples of Classical music.

Non-dominant sevenths and altered chords occur essentially as pre-dominants.

Sequences involving the cycle of fifths are typically found in exploratory or developmental sections.

Changes of key to closely related areas such as the dominant and relative minor are common.

The cadential vocabulary of the Classical period is for the most part inherited from the Baroque era.

Classical music is in general characterized harmonically by a slower rate or pace of harmonic change than that of the Baroque period.

IV. *Form*

Classical music is embodied in the works of Haydn, Mozart, and Beethoven, three composers who possessed an almost impeccable sense of musical design; in their music, all parameters frequently interact to delineate sections and create patterns of unifomity and contrast.

Realization of such recurring formal patterns as sonata allegro, rondo, ternary, and variations forms is usually a result of the coordination of such basic structural materials as key, theme, rhythm, texture, and dynamics.

Contrast of thematic material is an essential component of musical form in Classical movements; this is in contrast with the principle of *alternation* of keys, textures, and forces—more a part of form creation in Baroque music.

V. *Extramusical Considerations*

Mozart and Haydn composed instrumental and keyboard works that have, in general, no intended extramusical meanings; they are abstract music. Their operas, songs, and choral works are based in part on extramusical ideas.

Much of Beethoven's best work is so emotionally stirring as to suggest for many listeners that its appeal is in part due to musical imagery or attempts by the composer to picture or suggest in music ideas, ideals, or even specific events that are not in themselves musical. In some works, such as his *Pastoral* Symphony or *Emperor* Concerto, such extramusical connotations are justified. In most of his works they are not.

Ex. 2a. Mozart: Piano Sonata in C Major, K. 545, II.

Ex 2a continued.

P.T.
H.S.
cresc.
cresc.
p
cresc.
mf
cresc.
mf
p
pp
cresc.
cresc.
dimin.
p
pp
cresc.
cresc.
f
f

Ex. 2b. Beethoven: Piano Sonata Op. 109, II (theme and first variation).

THE ROMANTIC PERIOD

Whereas composers of the Classical period concentrated on the creation of sound and form for the sheer delight that they found in shaping musical materials within the framework of a tradition of musical patterns and ideals, Romantic composers such as Schubert, Chopin, Schumann, and Wagner placed a high priority on individuality of expression, originality, exploration of new means of musical expression, and extramusical influences. Some of these influences included mythology, poetry, nationalism, pre-existing art-works, plays, and fictional and legendary characters. Musicians seem to agree that nineteenth-century Romantic music reveals far more about the personalities, ideals, and feelings of its composers than had previously been the case.

Checklist for Romantic Music

I. *Texture and Timbre*

Full, rich sonority is explored insofar as the resources of any medium permit.

Sudden and dramatic shifts from one texture or timbre to another reflect the array of contrasts frequently found.

Fundamentally homophonic writing is often elaborated and colored in such a way as to produce an illusion of polyphonic complexity.

The potential for dynamic nuance and contrast are explored to the utmost.

Musical values and economy are sometimes sacrificed for the sake of overpowering effects and pictorialism.

Performance demands by composers and the fascination of audiences for performance virtuosity led to new feats of solo playing as well as unprecedented technical demands on ensemble performers.

II. *Melody*

Romantic melodies are often lyrical or dramatic in character; they frequently attract attention more because of their expressiveness and self-conscious subjectivity (Berlioz, Wagner, Liszt, Tchaikovsky, and Strauss) than because of their economic use of materials or their unified development.

Romantic melodies are typically rich in chromaticism and often highly modulatory.

The heightened expression of these melodies is often exemplified by an expanded range and by wide leaps such as tritones, sixths, and sevenths.

The four-measure phrase remains the basic unit of melodic phrase construction.

Patterns and melodic figures implying modal-scale bases occur often in the works of composers such as Brahms, Chopin, and Mussorgsky.

Mixed meters (alternating metric schemes such as $\frac{2}{4} - \frac{3}{4}$ or $\frac{4}{8} - \frac{5}{8}$ etc.) appear, especially in vocal music (operas, songs, etc.).

Repetitive devices, especially sequence, often extend melodic phrases to the point of monotony.

III. *Harmony*

Romantic harmony extended the use of triadic sonority to include a rich palette of seventh and ninth chords, used at times on virtually every scale degree in major or minor keys. The fully diminished seventh chord  °7 the half-diminished seventh chord 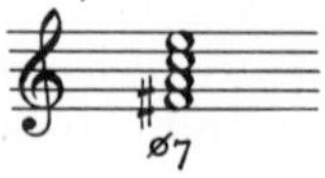 ø7 the Neapolitan sixth chord (♭II6), the family of augmented sixth chords

C: Tonic N6

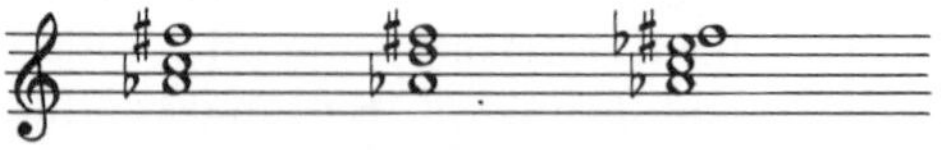

C: Italian +6 French +6 German +6

and chords containing chromatic alteration in numerous other forms occupy such a position in harmonic progression as to weaken beyond the point of repair the stability of key and tonic that made possible the structuring of music in keys. Tonality as a form-creating element in music was seriously undermined.

The distinction between major and minor keys became irrelevant; twelve tones replaced seven, and the *chromatic* scale became the basis for pitch organization.

IV. *Form*

Numerous nineteenth-century composers, such as Brahms, Bruckner, Mahler, and others, created instrumental works within the formal framework of the sonata and symphony. More progressive composers such as Berlioz, Liszt, Strauss, and many composers associated with nationalistic musical portrayal worked within the framework of the tone poem, or symphonic poem, an instrumental work whose formal unfolding was based more on extramusical dictates than on musical abstraction.

Numerous short forms such as the intermezzo, mazurka, waltz, romance, and prelude provided a simple basis for the presentation of brief, frequently highly contrasted musical images or ideas. These pieces utilized thematic materials not suitable for extended musical development. Their impact was essentially lyrical, expressive, simple, and direct. Many of these short works, associated mainly with the piano, were depictive or meant to evoke a single mood or character.

No form better served the expressive and artistic needs of the nineteenth century than did the art song, a typically short form that was the vocal counterpart of the instrumental forms mentioned above. Many composers concentrated in their songs the same harmonic and textural materials that led to the dissolution of tonality and form in everextended symphonic works (tone poems especially) of the same period. These harmonic materials seemed most effectively deployed in association with short songs.

V. *Extramusical Considerations*

The nineteenth century was a period in which music and extramusical allusion or depiction interacted to an unprecedented degree. The character and appeal of the music of such nineteenth-century exponents of explicit musical expression as Wagner, Liszt, and Strauss is so tied to attempts to reflect in their compositions a wide range of nonmusical experience that it is often difficult to deal with their music objectively. In no other period did composers so condition and at the same time so limit the potential appeal of their music to matters not explicitly musical. It is unfortunate that a great deal of nineteenth-century music suffers from guilt by association (in the minds of many listeners) with extramusical matters not at all intended by the composers. Such associations continue to be made by many of today's listeners, if not by musicians themselves. Compare the two examples of musical Romanticism that follow.

Ex. 3a. Chopin: Mazurka, Op. 41, No. 2.

Ex. 3a continued.

Ex. 3b. Wolf: *Silent Love* (Eichendorff-Lieder No. 3).

Sanfte Bewegung und immer sehr zart
(With a gentle motion and very delicately)

ausdrucksvoll und weich
(with expression and soft touch)

Ex. 3b continued.

THE TWENTIETH CENTURY

The tempo of musical change in our century has been so quick that few, if any, of us have been able to assess the host of developments and counter-developments, forms and techniques, that have permeated twentieth-century music to date. Like the Baroque era, ours is the logical consequence of events of the prior century, most notably the trend precipitated by Debussy in the early twentieth century that involved in part the abandonment of the musical emotionalism and pictorialism of Wagner and Strauss. Looking back over some seventy years of music in this era, the following trends appear most telling:

1. Major-minor key organization has been replaced by other bases of tonal organization, such as serial technique.
2. Rhythm in much current music has assumed new dimensions in time; traditional metered pulse and periodic bar-line accentuation has given way in the works of many composers to more subtle, more complex, and more innovative principles of organization: ameter (absence of meter), rhythmic serialization, and chance procedures are a few of them.
3. Melody has assumed meanings and shapes not typical of previous music. Any linear configuration or any series of pitch-time events may constitute melody.
4. Numerous new sound sources, of both traditional and electro-acoustic means, have been introduced.
5. Almost every conceivable means of organizing simultaneous sounds—harmony, in the broadest sense of the word—have been utilized. Chords constructed of any and all available intervals, such as fourths, sevenths, seconds (clusters), quarter tones, and other microtonal combinations, appear in various contexts. Serialization, chance, improvisation, probability theory, and computer programming have been used as bases for inventing vertical sonority. The one constant feature of most twentieth-century harmony has amounted to the absence of traditional function in a key.
6. Though many traditional formal patterns or procedures have continued to be employed by current composers, many novel formal principles or approaches to musical organization have also been employed. Among these, perhaps the most conspicuous is the absence in some works of perceptible return or repetition, large or small. Much recent music lacks the recognizable unity and clear differentiation of large-scale divisions traditionally created by tonality and key-change.
7. Unlike many nineteenth-century composers, composers of this era have shown an interest in manipulating musical sound without the constraints and dictates of self-conscious emotionalism, pictorialism, and imagery. Unlike composers of previous times, twentieth-century composers have found virtually no common stylistic ground—no basis for a common practice such as that provided by tonal harmony in the past. Perhaps the only really common ground relating most (but by no means all) music of this century has been the absence of tonality—atonality.

See to what extent the preceding assertions are borne out in Example 4, by the twentieth-century Austrian composer, Arnold Schoenberg.

Ex. 4. Schoenberg: Op. 19, No. 6 (from *Six Pieces for Piano*).

REFERENCES FOR ADDITIONAL READING

Apel and Davison, *Historical Anthology of Music,* 2 vols.
Christ *et al., Materials and Structure of Music,* 2 vols., 2nd ed.
Crocker, *A History of Musical Style.*
DeLone, *Music: Patterns and Style.*
La Rue, *Guidelines for Style Analysis.*
Salop, *Studies on the History of Musical Style.*

INDEX OF SELECTED MUSICAL EXAMPLES

GENERAL INDEX